C000087999

ORGANIZATIONAL RULES

A framework for understanding
organizational action

Albert J. Mills
and
Stephen J. Murgatroyd

Open University Press
Milton Keynes · Philadelphia

Open University Press
Celtic Court
22 Ballmoor
Buckingham
MK18 1XW

and

1900 Frost Road, Suite 101
Bristol, PA 19007, USA

First Published 1991

Copyright © Albert J. Mills and Stephen J. Murgatroyd 1991

All rights reserved. No part of this publication may be
reproduced, stored in a retrieval system or transmitted,
in any form or by any means, without written permission
from the publisher.

British Library Cataloguing in Publication Data

Mills, Albert J.
    Organizational rules: a framework for understanding organizational action.
    1. Organizational behaviour
    I. Title Murgatroyd, Stephen, 1950–
    302.35
    ISBN 0-335-09908-4
    ISBN 0-335-09907-6 (pbk)

Library of Congress Cataloging-in-Publication Data

Mills, Albert J., 1945–
    Organizational rules: a framework for understanding organizational
    action/Albert J. Mills & Stephen J. Murgatroyd.
        p. cm.
    Includes bibliographical references and index.
    ISBN 0-335-09907-6 (paper). ISBN 0-335-09908-4 (cased)
    1. Organizational behaviour. 2. Employee rules. I. Murgatroyd,
    Stephen J. II. Title.
    HD58.7.M543 1990
    302.3′5--dc20   90-7340 CIP

Typeset by Burns and Smith Ltd., Derby
Printed in Great Britain by St Edmundsbury Press Ltd, Bury St Edmunds, Suffolk

10
/95

£8-99

(S) £8-99

Organizational rules

This book is dedicated

by Albert J. Mills:
to my 'unruly' children Josh, Mags, Nathan and Zac who fill my life with wonderment and joy.

by Stephen J. Murgatroyd:
to my mother Denise and father Horace, without whom none of this would be possible. Take care.

Contents

About the authors

Albert J. Mills, PhD is Associate Professor of Organizational Behaviour and former Associate Dean of Administrative Studies at Athabasca University, Alberta, Canada. His research activities centre on the impact of the organization upon people – focusing on organizational change and human liberation. This is reflected in his writings which, to date, have dealt with the development of sit-in strikes in the UK, educational barriers confronting adults, organizational culture and its impact upon employment equality, the law and discriminatory practices, and sexuality and power in organizations. He holds degrees from the Universities of Durham, Sheffield and Southern California. With qualifications in the field of sociology, occupational psychology, industrial relations and education, Albert has taught at institutions of higher learning in the UK, the USA and Canada. He is currently working on two major book projects on *Gender and Organizations* (with Peta Tancred-Sheriff) and on *Wardair* (with Peter Chiaramonte and Michael Owen).

Stephen J. Murgatroyd, PhD, FBPsS is Professor of Applied Psychology and Dean of Administrative Studies at Athabasca University, Alberta, Canada. Author of several books in the field of counselling and psychotherapy and a frequent contributor to the literature on school organization, consulting practices and organizational change and development, Stephen has acted as a consultant for major corporations, public organizations, international development agencies and small firms. He has taught in universities in Canada, the UK, Holland, Belgium, Norway, India, Nepal and the USA. He is a Fellow of the British Psychological Society and holds his doctorate from The Open University.

Acknowledgements

In developing this text we have been aided by many colleagues and friends in both formal and informal ways. It is not possible to recognize all of the contributions made by others. We would however, wish to acknowledge the contributions of Dr Peter Chiaramonte (University of Western Ontario), Dr Michael J. Apter (Purdue University) and Marco Adria (Athabasca University) whose assistance and support has been more than casual. In addition, the Open University Press have again been both tolerant and supportive of our endeavours.

Our family and friends, as authors will know, have also made sacrifices in supporting the development of this text. We acknowledge and appreciate these, especially during a cold winter with some days at $-41°C$. In particular, we acknowledge the contributions of James Glyn and Lynne Murgatroyd to the tasks of proof reading and indexing.

Albert J. Mills and Stephen J. Murgatroyd
Athabasca, Alberta, Canada

__ 1 __

Rules as dimensions of organizational life

Introduction

> [A] concern with the production of what passes for 'true' knowledge should focus not only on the 'reality' of these objects, but on the ways of seeing which provide for such a reality. . . . [C]onsensual ways of seeing are maintained through shared paradigms of rules and standards for correct scientific practice. Collectively . . . we would call these rules the 'grammar' of theorizing, because they underlie and are constitutive of whatever passes for adequate theorizing. . . . These consensually shared rules thus exercise a 'theorizing power' over the theorist, in that he has first to submit to the collectively recognized grammar before whatever he produces can be 'warranted' in the ordinary course of affairs. (Clegg, 1975, p. 10)

This book is about *organizational* rules, but our explanation and exploration of the subject is inevitably bound up in a set of understandings or 'rules of knowing'. In many ways those rules will be uncovered by the reader as he or she accepts or rejects the things we have to say – a process that conforms with the 'rules of exposition' that we have set ourselves; namely, to provide a readable guide to the significance of rules for making sense of organizations. None the less, we feel obliged to make the reader aware up front of some of the outline features of our approach.

A primary feature underlying our approach is a dissatisfaction with many of the existing ways of viewing organizations, and in particular the way various levels of analysis and concerns have been fragmented within paradigms. For instance, it makes sense to us that organizations can appear to confront people as an objective entity, as something external to them. It also makes sense to us that organizations are human creations, moulded out of the interactions of people. It does not make sense to us to focus, as so many studies of organization have done, exclusively on one or the other of these two features. Nor does it make sense to us to view the construction of organizational reality as a genderless process. It makes sense to us that organizations can appear to be given, self-contained entities that set them apart from other organizations. It also makes sense to us that organizations cannot be fully understood apart from the broader social relations within which they are a part. It does not make sense to us to approach an understanding of organizations as if only one or the other statement were true. It makes sense to us that problems of order, stability and efficiency should be central concerns of organizational analysis. And, it makes sense to us that problems of identity, psyche, conflict and change should be essential concerns of organizational analysis. It does not make sense to us to completely divorce one set of concerns from the other.

Through our brief exploration below of the development of organizational analysis we have attempted to indicate some of the major ways in which issues, concern and foci have become separated into fragments within fragmented theories of organization. Organizational paradigms have developed and are maintained through a complex series of rules and standards which give legitimacy and an air of authenticity to those studies that are in compliance with the rules. As Burrell and Morgan (1979) point out, for many years the dominant functionalist paradigm within organizational analysis operated in such a way as to deny legitimacy to any but those studies that were informed by functionalist theory.

Unlike Burrell and Morgan (1979), who argue that the rules underlying the major organizational paradigms prevent those paradigms from 'talking to each other', we contend that a synthesis is possible and clearly desirable – rules were meant to be broken! We share the concern of Chua *et al.* (1982) that there is no need to integrate what they call empirical, interpretive and critical theory. Viewing organizational paradigms from a Jungian perspective – seeing each as somehow reflective of a different style of thought processes, Chua *et al.* (1982, p. 11) go on to make the point that:

In Jungian terms, all inquirers play their own unique and important part in the problem formation and solution design, but without any one of the stages the end result becomes the poorer. For a Conceptual Theorist or Conceptual Humanist looking at the problem situation would only see the conceptual issues, missing all aspects of modelling detail and implementation issues. Likewise an Analytical Scientist would miss the conceptual and implementation stages in the problem formulation and solution design in his blind desire to see the world in a technical way. In a similar fashion a Particular Humanist would omit the conceptual and modelling stages in his great desire to smooth out the emotional difficulties obviously present in the problem situation. All these insights are necessary but individually they are not sufficient to bring about truly rich solutions to or discover the complex problems which face social scientists.

Astley and Van de Ven (1983) offer a useful way of approaching synthesis. Drawing upon the work of Benson (1977), they attempted to overcome 'the problems associated with excessive theoretical compartmentalization by focusing on the interplay between divergent theortical perspectives while attempting to preserve the authenticity of distinctive viewpoints'. In short:

to properly study organizations across levels of analysis is to understand the dialectical relations between forces of conflict, coercion, and disruption at one level of organization, and forces of consensus, unity, and integration at another level – forces that are prerequisites and reciprocals of each other. (Astley and Van de Ven, 1983, p. 269)

This approach, quite simply, contends that by granting legitimacy to competing paradigms at one level we are able to use them all as valuable resources at another level through analysis of the tensions and contradictions that they reveal.

A third approach to synthesis that we find useful is the work of Gareth Morgan (1980, 1986). Morgan's work focuses upon the notion of *metaphor* and its value for exploring and understanding organizational reality, arguing that:

> our theories and explanations of organizational life are based on metaphors that lead us to see and understand organizations in distinctive yet partial ways. Metaphor is often just regarded as a device for embellishing discourse, but its significance is much greater than this. For the use of metaphor implies *a way of thinking* and *a way of seeing* that pervade how we understand our world generally. (Morgan, 1986, p.12)

Morgan argues, in the spirit of 'theoretical and methodological pluralism' (1980, p. 605), that each of the major metaphors that has been generated within organizational analysis offers valuable insights into organizational life. However, given that metaphor is based upon partial truth that requires of its user a one-sided abstraction in which certain features are emphasized and others supressed, the value to be gained rests in subjecting a given organizational reality to a series of metaphorical insights. For example:

> Any realistic approach to organizational analysis must start from the premise that organizations can be many things at one and the same time. A machinelike organization designed to achieve specific goals can simultaneously be: a species of organization that is able to survive in certain environments but not others; an information processing system that is skilled in certain kinds of learning but not in others; a cultural milieu characterized by distinctive values, beliefs, and social practices; a political system where people jostle to further their own ends; an arena where various subconscious or ideological struggles take place; an artifact or manifestation of a deeper process of social change; an instrument used by one group of people to exploit and dominate others; and so on. (Morgan, 1986, pp. 321-2).

Hence, Morgan goes on to argue that a useful way of understanding an organization is to first 'produce a *diagnostic reading* of the situation being investigated, using different metaphors to identify or highlight key aspects of the situation' (1980, p.322) and secondly, to 'make a *critical evaluation* of the significance of the different interpretations thus produced' (ibid.)

We are very much attracted to the notion of *rules* as a root metaphor for integrating many of the concerns raised by Chua *et al.*, Astley and Van de Ven, and Morgan. Rules are an essential focus of each competing paradigm, metaphor and range of puzzle-solving activities within organizational analysis. Better yet, a thoroughgoing analysis of rules allows us to explore issues within organizational life in a way that is immediate and relevant: while the metaphor of, say 'machine' or 'organism' is somewhat abstracted from common experience, 'rules' are an everyday part of our organizational existence. As we discuss in greater depth below, we are concerned that the concept of rules be sufficiently broad in definition to accommodate different levels of analysis. Thus, we view rules as phenomena whose basic characteristic is that of generally controlling, constraining, guiding and defining social action. They exist in both written and unwritten forms; in formal and informal statements; in legalistic and moralistic pronouncements; and yet they do not wholly rely for their efficacy on being known or understood by each and every member of a given situation into which they are applied.

Ways of viewing organization

The very inception of *management* and *organizational* fields of analysis shaped their character as managerial, functionalist accounts. Beginning with the work of Frederick Taylor, organizational analysts have viewed organizations from the perspective of management-derived problem solving. Taylor, for instance, was concerned with management issues of productivity and control – how to control the activities of workers more efficiently so as to achieve greater productivity. The results are well known (cf. Bendix, 1974). Taylor advocated the development of a 'scientific' approach to management in which jobs are efficiently designed in a way that workers can be trained to follow a series of logical steps that require very few thought processes (cf. Taylor, 1911). It has been argued that Taylor's image of organization drew upon the metaphor of the machine (Morgan, 1986). In the words of one of his harsher critics:

> He regarded the worker as an appendage to the machine who ought blindly to carry out a specific set of purely mechanical operations that have become completely automatic. (Bogomolova, 1973, p. 11)

We can only speculate that Taylor's training as an engineer and his location in 'the machine age' of American industrialization helped to shape his image of the organization!

The organizational paradigm set by Taylor – and his counterparts in France (Henri Fayol), England (Lyndall Urwick) and the USA (F.W. Mooney) – has remained the predominant one in organizational analysis through to the current day. None the less, developments within that framework have been many and varied, generating a rich debate on the character of organizations. The next major steps in the development of the field, from the *Hawthorne Studies* of the late 1920s/early 1930s through to the work of Maslow, Herzberg and Argyris in the mid-1940s to the 1960s, owe much to the work of humanistic psychologists. These psychologists, with some initial impetus from anthropologists*, turned attention to the 'human factor' of production, viewing the organization more like an organic entity than one with machine-like qualities. This general phase in the development of organizational analysis continued Taylor's focus upon the internal *environment* of organizations but shifted attention to 'human needs' and their relationship to organizational effectiveness. The 'human needs' focus has concerned itself with

---

* An important stage in the progress of the Hawthorne Studies was undertaken by a small team of anthropologists led by Lloyd Warner.

such issues as the importance, for employees, of social relations at work (see Roethlisberger and Dickson, 1939), the impact of 'democratic' and 'participative' climates (cf. Lewin *et al.*, 1939) and, for supervisory and managerial employees, the relationship between 'higher-order' psychological needs and work-related patterns of motivation (cf. Maslow, 1943).

A third broad stage of development within organizational analysis involved the development of structural analysis. This carried on that part of the scientific management tradition which focused upon the structural context of organizational effectiveness. This aspect of organizational development can be traced through the work of the Tavistock researchers of the early 1950s (in particular, the work of Trist and Bamforth, 1951), the work of Joan Woodward and her colleagues in the late 1950s (see Woodward 1958), to the work of Burns and Stalker (1961) in the early 1960s and culminating in the *Aston Studies* of the early to late 1960s (cf. Pugh and Hickson, 1976). Within this tradition, the focus has been on such issues as the impact of technological structure upon work groups (Trist and Bamforth, 1951), the effect of technology upon organizational structure (Woodward 1958) and the impact of environmental (i.e. market: Burns and Stalker, 1961) and contextual factors (i.e. origin and history, size, ownership and control, technology, location, charter, and interdependence in relation to other organizations: Pugh and Hickson, 1976).

By the late 1960s, a dominant paradigm was well established within organizational analysis that was, despite the richness of debate and research that had been generated, 'objectivist' (Burrell and Morgan, 1979) and 'deterministic' (Astley and Van de Ven, 1983). From the psychologistic perspective, human actors are viewed as variables to be manipulated – however kindly – in the service of organizational outcomes, whereas from the structural perspective the focus is:

> not on individuals, but on the structural properties of the context within which action unfolds, and individual behaviour is seen as determined by and reacting to structural constraints that provide organizational life with an overall stability and control. (Astley and Van de Ven, 1983, p. 247)

Within the paradigmatic constraints of organizational analysis, research into the relationship between structure and action has been further hindered by the parallel nature of the psychologistic and structuralist developments and their division, particularly in North America, into separate areas of study, viz. Organization Theory and Organizational Behaviour. The overriding problem, however, has been the inability and, at times, unwillingness to absorb into organizational analysis approaches and methods of study not deemed compatible with the dominant paradigmatic ways of viewing organization (Burrell and Morgan, 1979). The work of Ervin Goffman (1959), Alvin Gouldner (1954, 1965) and John Goldthorpe and his colleagues (1968), for example, were not considered by organizational theorists to be central to the discipline of Organizational Theory. Yet these were approaches that told us something about how actors view organization, about how their broader social understandings shape the way they view events within the organization.

With the onset of the 1970s, two major challenges to the existing organizational wisdom made some impact on the field. An article by John Child (1972), albeit by way of a sociological journal, substantially challenged the way the Aston Studies were shaping the notion of organizational structure. A book by David Silverman (1970) challenged the field head on, proposing a 'social action framework' as a 'clear-cut' alternative. He proposed that any understanding of organizational reality needed to take into account the understandings that actors bring to bear on a situation. Child challenged the notion that organizational members are determined in their action by a number of structural and contextual factors, arguing instead that the design of organizational structures are 'an essentially political process in which constraints and opportunities are functions of the power exercised by decision makers' (Child, 1972, quoted in Buchanan and Huczynski, 1985, p. 369).

It is organizational decision makers who decide in the first place whether an organization should operate in a certain market, whether it should expand its operations and whether it should diversify. Child also pointed to the fact that the existence and character of organizational uncertainty and complexity will, in large part, depend upon the *perceptions* of decision makers: the decision to pull out of, or expand into, a certain market may well depend upon the way higher management perceive a particular situation.

Silverman (1970, p. 127) also baulks at the notion that 'action is determined by external and constraining social or non-social forces'. Action, he argues, 'arises out of meanings which define social reality', meanings which, through interaction, can be modified, changed and transformed. From this – social action – perspective, any understanding of organizational reality must start with the meanings attributed to a given situation by the actors involved.

The work of Child and Silverman served to open up debate on the relationship between structure and action but within the limitations of functionalist analysis (Burrell and Morgan, 1979). The action frame approach, while shifting attention from objectivist to more subjectivist ways of viewing organizations, does so in a way that substitutes one at the expense of the other. As Michael Rose (1978, p. 240) has noted, the action frame approach tends to 'suspend analysis at the factory *entrance* just as systems orthodoxy had done at its exit: action is as divorced from structure in this approach as structure is divorced from action in the dominant systems approach'. The structure/action problematic had to wait almost another decade before being addressed within organizational analysis, and then within the framework of alternative paradigms. The major development within functionalist analysis over this period was in a broadening of the level of analysis, shifting attention from organization as a unit of study to consideration of populations of organizations.

In the mid- to late 1970s, the work of Howard Aldrich (1979) and of Michael Hannan and John Freeman (1977) confronted existing organizational wisdom in the form of a *population ecology* model of analysis. From this perspective, organizations are viewed against a foreground of the environment. It is the environment, not strategic management or organizational adaptation, that determines the survival of an organization: 'environmental resources are structured in the form of "niches" whose existence and distribution across society are relatively intractable to manipulation by single organizations' (Astley and Van de Ven, 1983, p. 249). Drawing upon the language of Darwin, the environment is depicted as allowing an organization to 'fit' in or be 'selected out'. It is an approach which takes determinism to new extremes.

Allied developments in this way of thinking about organizations included the work of Williamson (1975) and Chandler (1962), who added to the notion that environmental forces contribute to the development of organizational structures and form in determinant ways. Alongside the development of this 'natural selection' (Astley and Van de Ven, 1983, Morgan, 1986) perspective, there arose a 'collective-action' view (Astley and Van de Ven, 1983), which while contributing to the focus upon organizations as populations or communities, strengthened the voluntarist way of understanding organizations. Through the work of such people as Emery and Trist (1973), Ackoff (1974), Schon (1971) and Warren et al. (1974), there developed a view of organizations which places emphasis upon their collective character, arguing that in fact organizational survival is ensured through 'the construction of a regulated and controlled social environment that mediates the effects of the natural environment' (Astley and Van de Ven, 1983). From the development of this school of thought has come the concept of the *inter-organizational network* – a coherent system of inter-organizational relationships that are negotiated and maintained with the aim of effecting control over the respective environments of those involved.

As the 1980s approached, the dominant paradigm within organizational analysis could be characterized into four major views of organization and management (see Fig.1.1); rich and varied, reflecting competing levels of analysis and ways of conceptualizing structure and action but ultimately fractured in a way that inhibited any kind of synthesis between the viewpoints.

Astley and Van de Ven's (1983) characterization of the debates within organizational analysis is interesting in that while they include reference to approaches from alternative paradigms, they fail to convey the impact of those alternatives upon organizational analysis; their schematic representation of schools of thought all but exclude non-functionalist accounts. Yet alternative perspectives, from the late 1970s on, were and are making an impact. Interpretive accounts (cf. Bittner, 1974, Emerson, 1970; Jelineck et al., 1983; Smircich, 1983; Sudnow, 1978; Zimmerman, 1971) have enriched our understanding of the contribution of actors' interpretations to the *creation* of organizational reality. Linda Smircich (1983), for example, in applying this perspective to the notion of organizational culture, views organizations as:

> expressive forms, manifestations of human consciousness. Organizations are understood and analysed not mainly in economic or material terms, but in terms of their expressive, ideational, and symbolic aspects. Characterized very broadly, the research agenda stemming from this perspective is to explore the phenomenon of organization as subjective experience and to investigate the patterns that make organized action possible. (Smircich, 1983, pp. 347–8)

Macro level
(Populations
and communities
of organizations)

Micro level
(Individual
organizations)

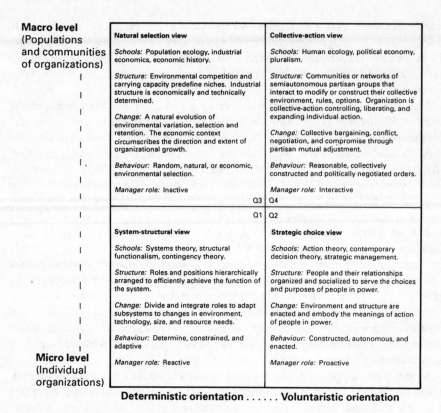

Natural selection view	Collective-action view
Schools: Population ecology, industrial economics, economic history.	*Schools:* Human ecology, political economy, pluralism.
Structure: Environmental competition and carrying capacity predefine niches. Industrial structure is economically and technically determined.	*Structure:* Communities or networks of semiautonomous partisan groups that interact to modify or construct their collective environment, rules, options. Organization is collective-action controlling, liberating, and expanding individual action.
Change: A natural evolution of environmental variation, selection and retention. The economic context circumscribes the direction and extent of organizational growth.	*Change:* Collective bargaining, conflict, negotiation, and compromise through partisan mutual adjustment.
Behaviour: Random, natural, or economic, environmental selection.	*Behaviour:* Reasonable, collectively constructed and politically negotiated orders.
Manager role: Inactive Q3	Q4 *Manager role:* Interactive
Q1	Q2
System-structural view	**Strategic choice view**
Schools: Systems theory, structural functionalism, contingency theory.	*Schools:* Action theory, contemporary decision theory, strategic management.
Structure: Roles and positions hierarchically arranged to efficiently achieve the function of the system.	*Structure:* People and their relationships organized and socialized to serve the choices and purposes of people in power.
Change: Divide and integrate roles to adapt subsystems to changes in environment, technology, size, and resource needs.	*Change:* Environment and structure are enacted and embody the meanings of action of people in power.
Behaviour: Determine, constrained, and adaptive	*Behaviour:* Constructed, autonomous, and enacted.
Manager role: Reactive	*Manager role:* Proactive

Deterministic orientation . . . . . . Voluntaristic orientation

Fig. 1.1 Four views of organization and management (adapted from Astley and Van de Ven, 1983, p. 247).

The major contribution of interpretive accounts is their focus upon the role of 'understanding' and 'meaning' in the comprehension of any given organizational situation. The focus is on how, through interaction, 'a sense of organization is created and maintained and how common interpretations of situations are achieved so that co-ordinated action is possible.

Interpretive accounts differ from the action frame in placing a fundamental emphasis on the role of human comprehension in the creation of organizations and organizational situations. Whereas in the action frame the actor's understandings are *received* through a process of socialization, in the interpretive approach actors' sense of meaning is constantly part of a process of creativity in which understandings are *negotiated*. Interpretive accounts have pushed the notion of voluntarist action to new frontiers but, in so doing, they clearly divorce action from structure. Interpretive accounts have also strengthened the focus upon the internal aspects of organizational sense-making, 'rather than to look to the external, societal, cultural context within which organizations are located' (Jelineck *et al.*, 1983, p. 338). In short, interpretive accounts fail to locate human ideas in material practice.

Radical accounts (Beynon, 1973; Illich, 1973; Dickson, 1974; Braverman, 1974; Allen 1975) of organizational reality have served to challenge the managerial bias and problem of order foci of existing functionalist and interpretive accounts, viewing organizations as spheres of domination. Developing in prominence towards the turn of the 1980s, radical studies of organization have been concerned with issues of power, control, ideology, class, resistance and struggle. The focusing of these issues, however, initially seemed to reflect a growing philosophical schism within the radical, left as a whole (Anderson, 1980), with some theorists (e.g. Beynon, 1973; Illich, 1973; Dickson, 1974) focusing upon the processes of *ideological* domination, and others (e.g. Braverman, 1974; Allen, 1975) focusing upon domination as a *mode of production* or class system. Burrell and Morgan (1979) have characterized this schism as a division between 'radical humanism' and 'radical structuralism'. The following is a theme developed by Morgan (1980):

> When organizations are approached from the perspective of the radical humanist paradigm, all the concepts and modes of symbolic action that sustain organizational life are scrutinized for their alienating properties. The guiding metaphor here is that of the psychic, prison, an image which focuses upon the way human beings may be led to enact organizational realities experienced as confining and dominating . . .
>
> The radical structuralist paradigm generates a radical organization theory based upon metaphors such as the instrument of domination, schismatic systems and catastrophe. [It is an approach] . . . informed by the image of organizations as powerful instruments of domination to be understood as an integral part of a wider process of domination within society as a whole. Although such analyses often utilize insights deriving from the machine metaphor, organizations as machines are studied from their oppressive qualities. (Morgan, 1980, pp. 617–18).

The major strength of the radical perspective has been a methodological concern with integrating various levels of analysis – linking internal with external organizational concerns and balancing a focus on the organization as a unit of analysis with that of the collective character and interrelationship of organizations. Hydebrand (1977), for example, in analysing US law courts explains specific incidents within those organizations through a relationship to broad social 'contradictions'. He argues that changing 'forces of production (productivity measures, new technologies, rationalization of procedures)' impact upon key organizational members within the law courts and lead to tensions and contradictions within the system as they encounter 'the increasing resistance of the relations of production (i.e. the accumulated legal approaches and status systems of the judiciary)' (Hydebrand, 1977, p. 98).

Radical approaches, at least by 1980, had been less successful in dealing with the structure–agency problematic. Burrell and Morgan's (1979) ground-breaking analysis of the field provided a schematic representation of the field as it entered the 1980s (Fig. 1.2). The division of radical theory into a reflexive humanism and a systems structuralism was designed, by Burrell and Morgan, as both a statement of historic fact and as a challenge to be overcome (Mills, 1988c), but it is likely that it

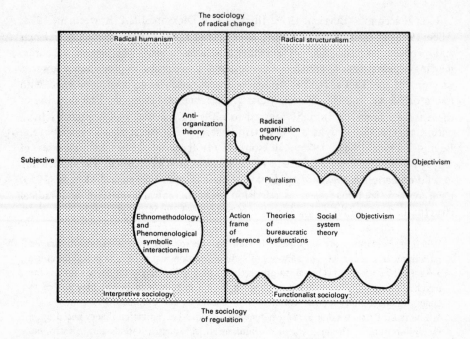

Fig. 1.2   1980: Four paradigms of organizational analysis (adapted from Burrell and Morgan, (1979, pp. 29–30).

has also served to solidify those divisions: Morgan has gone on to develop his radical humanism, while Burrell continues in the vein of radical structuralism!

Recent developments within organizational analysis have gone in two key directions:

1 The development of a body of work that deals with the structure–agency divide.
2 The development of women-centred analysis.

In developing an analysis of organizations that adequately takes into account the structural context of action and the understanding of the actors that contributes to that context, the work of J. Kenneth Benson, Stewart Clegg, Anthony Giddens and Peter Leonard have been of particular significance.

In the mid-1970s, Clegg, through an analysis of power relations on a construction site, introduced the notion of *rules*, arguing that power relations within organizations can only be understood as part of the rules of the game laid down within the context of a wider 'form of life' (Clegg, 1975). For Clegg, organizational members act within a framework of rules, a framework that provides a ready-made sense of reality as a guide to action within the organization. Rules, none the less, have to be interpreted and enacted, and it is through that process that actors may decide to ignore, change, challenge or reject the rules; organizational power struggles often result. The rules, according to Clegg, retain some validity because of their links with and reflection of the wider context of capitalist relations, but come to be challenged due to the contradictory relationships of organizational members in regard to the rules. Clegg's development of the notion of rules is taken up in the next section.

Benson (1977, p. 1) proposes a 'dialectical approach [which] . . . places at the center of analysis the process through which organizational arrangements are produced and maintained'. Analysis, Benson continues:

> is guided by four basic principles – social construction, totality, contradiction, and praxis. The organization is seen as a concrete, multileveled phenomenon beset by contradictions which continuously undermine its existing features. Its directions depend upon the interests and ideas of people and upon their power to produce and maintain a social formation (Benson, 1977, p. 1)

It is Benson's contention that 'people are continually constructing the social world' but that, as a result, they 'produce a social world which stands over them, constraining their actions'. In regard to organizations, this process needs to be understood as occurring within a social context but in ways that are none the less 'partially autonomous' – the linkages between components with a social system not being complete nor wholly coherent. Hence:

> Because social construction is an emergent, partially autonomous process, the realities accepted by participants at any given time may be continually undermined by ongoing acts of social construction. Even powerful actors may be unable to maintain an orderly, rationalized system of social relations in the face of this ongoing process. The totality, conceived dialectically then, includes newly emerging social arrangements as well as those already in place. (Benson, 1977, p. 4)

While the processes of structural constraints are developed and maintained, in part, by the actions of powerful organization members (i.e. owners, managers), processes of contradiction and praxis constantly threaten and undermine existing institutional arrangements:

> The social order produced in the process of social construction contains contradictions, ruptures, inconsistencies, and incompatibilities in the fabric of social life. Radical breaks with the present order are possible because of *contradictions*. (Benson, 1977, p. 4)

In the face of contradictions – at both the societal and the organizational level – organizational members, individually and collectively, may reject currently held notions and commitments and, hence, recreate their versions of organizational reality. Benson concludes that 'an organization as part of the social world is always in a state of becoming.'

Benson's approach to organizations provides us with a model that combines stable with unstable features; constant with changing factors; actors who are shaped by the structural arrangements that they enter into but who *reflect* upon and reshape those arrangements; and relationships of power in which powerful organization members have a more determinant say over definitions of organizational reality. The notion of reflexive actors is an essential argument in Gareth Morgan's (1980, 1986) radical humanist approach, i.e. that we need to educate organizational members to constantly examine the realities that they take for granted. Benson puts this notion in the context of structural contradictions with constantly challenge and change existing realities and, thus, constantly challenge people to rethink how they view any given situation. Both these arguments are coherent: clearly it may take significant structural changes to challenge people to think about the realities they are confronted with, but a number of people do actually rethink and confront existing versions of reality without any requisite structural contradictions or education.

The notion that organizations are in a constant state of becoming very much echoes Giddens' (1982) concept of *structuration*. The work of Giddens provides a highly useful framework for the analysis of organizations. A central point in the theory of structuration is that 'social structures are both constituted by human agency, and yet at the same time are the very *medium* of this constitution' (1982, p. 121). This provides us with a particularly simple yet subtle way of understanding organizations – not as mechanical outcomes of human interaction nor the structural determinants of human action, but as situations which reflect dual context and processes of human action:

> Structures must not be conceptualized as simply placing constraints upon human agency, but as enabling. This is what I call the *duality of structure*. Structures can always in principle be examined in terms of their *structuration* as a series of reproduced practices. To enquire into the structuration of social practices is to seek how it comes about the structures are constituted through action, and reciprocally how action is constituted structurally (1982, p. 161)

In focusing upon interaction, Giddens makes a number of crucial points. Simply put, at the root of human action is a basic need to make sense of the world; interaction provides the medium through which understandings of reality are explored and maintained; within given interactions actors draw upon 'a stock of knowledge' to help them make sense of what is going on; but interactions are relations of power in which the ability to effect outcomes affects the sense-making process. In terms of organizations, Giddens helps us to see that the production and reproduction of organizational reality is 'the accomplished outcome of human agency' – not necessarily a painless outcome!

In the concept of *ontological security*, Giddens may well have provided us with one of the most significant factors of explanation of organizational behaviour. He argues that an essential element of the socialization process of human beings involves 'the development of the capacity for "tension management" on the part of the infant', i.e. we are born with a set of organic needs which make us dependent upon others and serve to mediate our experience and involvement in social life. Human wants, as a result, develop a core 'basic security system' that impel human beings to constantly concern themselves with 'the maintenance of a framework of "ontological security"'. We have a need to make sense if what is going on and we have a need to make it seem that we have a sense of what is going on! Hence, certain ascepts of the success of organizational interaction might be attributable to human desire to appear to know what they are doing and in the process convincing others and themselves. In short, Giddens convinces us that organizational behaviour can be attributed to something other than rational motives.

Peter Leonard's (1984) work draws attention to the relationship between organizational life and personality. In dealing with the structure–agency divide, Leonard attempts to fuse together *historical materialism* with *symbolic interactionism*: the work of Marx with that of Mead. Briefly, Leonard accepts the symbolic interactionist argument about the importance of social interaction to the construction of self and of social reality but he seeks to root that focus within an historical analysis of the actual processes of power-based relationships that serve as the context for those interactions. In this way, argues Leonard, we can see that the *self* comes to reflect – in considerable part – the extent to which certain social interactions more or less allow the development of human potentiality. In organizational terms this could mean, for example, that where working conditions are arduous, where rules are highly bureaucratic and constraining, where pay (and status within the organization) are low, where the work is routine and boring, those involved may develop a sense of self that is burdened with notions of low esteem, limited creativity and a lack of imagination. Such conditions may

> have the effect of reducing the motivation to continue one's capacities and so the personality will become 'stagnant and ossified'. Psychological progress falls as the acquisition of new capacities loses its appeal because of the domination of abstract activity and its limitations of self-expression. (Leonard, 1984, p. 98)

For Leonard, personality development does not end, nor is it largely restricted to the period of childhood; it is a continuous process that lasts throughout most of a person's life; it too is a process of becoming:

> Entering the social order is a long process of preparation for adult roles: direct material experiences combined with what has been internalised from diverse and conflicting ideologies constitute the base of the psychological resources which the young person brings to the socially defined tasks and relationships of adulthood. But childhood, although it is influential, does not finally *determine* the personality characteristics of the adult individuals. (Leonard, 1984, p. 153).

Unlike more orthodox Marxian approaches (e.g. Allen, 1975), Leonard does not see the process of the development of self as being a simple reflection of the structure and relationships of production, but rather than an essential element of symbolic interaction is the relative autonomy of the individual and the ability of people to reflect upon and question the realities they confront. Contending that there is a 'dialectical relationship between consciousness and existence', Leonard states that contradictions in social life encourage people to rethink the reality they have constructed:

> As an adult, the individual enters into relationships, especially those involved with wage

and domestic labour, which are profoundly influential in the construction of self. But this is not simply a matter of further determinants reinforcing, overlapping or contradicting the derminants of childhood. Central to our thesis has been the conception of the individual as not simply the passive recipient of external determinants, but as actively, dialectically involved in constituting herself within her given social relations. Experiences subsequent to childhood can counteract the ideological penetration of the early years and the individual may construct a self on the basis of alternative ideologies related to alternative material experiences. (Leonard, 1984, pp. 153–4).

Leonard goes on to argue that human personality growth can be achieved through process of resistance, particularly collective resistance.

Leonard provides us with a dimension of organizational analysis that suggests that our focus upon organizational interactions take into account not only the processes of sense making but upon how those processes relate to the psychological development of the individuals involved. Leonard also provides us with a way of understanding resistance and its relationship to psychological growth.

Throughout traditional, and indeed most radical, accounts of organizations, the question of gender has been 'neglected' (Hearn and Parkin, 1983); it is as if researchers failed to notice that organizations consisted of men *and* women and that this had implications for understanding organizational dynamics. Since the later 1970s, a number of studies have attempted to analyse and rectify that neglect (e.g. Mills and Tancred-Sheriff, in press).

In terms of the actor's perception of organizational reality, Clegg and Dunkerley (1980), for instance, argue that while the action frame of reference explains 'the ways in which social, economic and technical aspects of a worker's market and work situations are mediated by his definition of their significance', this can also be applied to:

> *her* definitions, *her* actions, *her* perception of the various options open to *her*, and *her* priorities. In doing this . . . the notion of 'orientation to work' may be usefully seen as the outcome of processes over time. These processes are those of the female's socialization, her choice in the labour market, her life cycle, and her adaptation and reaction to work experiences. (Clegg and Dunkerley, 1980, p. 405)

However, as Clegg (1981) and Morgan (1986) indicate, females adapt and react in the context of male-oriented organizational value systems. Organizations reflect 'extra-organizational rules' about the respective social worth of women (and of non-whites) in ways that reproduce and maintain those values. This acts in a number of ways:

> [Organizations] often segment opportunity structures and job markets in ways that enable men to achieve positions of prestige and power more easily than women, and often operate in ways that produce gender-related biases in the way organizational reality is created and sustained on a day-to-day basis. This is most obvious in situations of open discrimination and various forms of sexual harassment, but often pervades the culture of an organization in a way that is much less visible. (Morgan, 1986, p. 178)

The way organizational realities come to be structured and maintained also has profound implications for the way we come to view ourselves, for our identity, for our sense of self. Leonard (1984, p.109) argues that 'The individual's life experience and personality structure is detemined ... by a unique biography situated within a specific set of class, gender and ethnic relations.' In other words, the sense of self is mediated through a set of master rules (Mills, 1988a) that differs not just individually but according to what class of person you have been designated:

> The individual connects to the social world through two kinds of interrelated experiences: of *material relations* and of *ideology*. The individual's *material activities and exchanges* at work, in the family, in community interactions, with state officials and in many other contexts are penetrated by *meanings, definitions, and 'common sense' assumptions* which reflect the ideologies through which a class, gender, ethnic group or other collectivity maintains its internal coherence, makes sense of the world, and either legitmates its dominant position in the social order or validates its resistance to domination. (Leonard, 1985, p. 109)

The work of Clegg, Leonard, Mills and many others make it clear that any consideration of organizational life must centrally come to terms with the dynamics of gender. (Figure 1.3 provides an updated representation of the field of organizational analysis to take account of feminist analysis.)

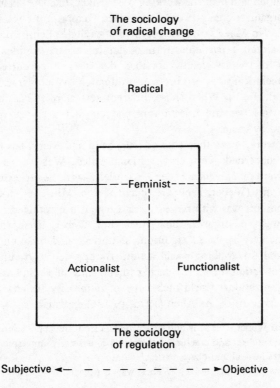

Fig. 1.3   Four faces of organizational analysis (from Mills, 1989b).

Ways of viewing rules

The concept of *rules* has long been afforded importance within social and organizational analyses. Durkheim's (1966, 1968) concept of *anomie*, for instance, pertains to a condition of individual and social breakdown in which those affected are no longer able to comprehend or are confused about the social and normative rules that make their lives understandable. Durkheim provides an organizational resolve to what he sees as a growing problem of anomic breakdown. He argues that the decline of the old normative rules generated through community and religion can be replaced by organizationally based rules generated by the integrative effect of economic interdependence. Three decades later, Elton Mayo (1933) drew upon Durkheim's work to argue that companies such as General Electric and their Chicago Hawthorne Works provided formal and informal networks of rules that served to socially integrate the large numbers of diverse immigrants that were streaming into the USA in the 1920s.

In the work of Marx, the explicit concern with rules is focused more upon mechanisms of physical and ideological control – as explored through his respective analyses of the state (Marx, 1966, 1973) and of ideology (Marx and Engels, 1969, 1976) – as key ways in which the dominant capitalist class imposes/maintains its rule (and rules) upon and over the working class. Marx, like Durkheim, foresaw the importance of organizationally (workplace) based factors in the resolve of a wider social concern (i.e. in Marx's case the problem of capitalist domination). For Marx, the rules that maintain a particular form of dominance are complex and reside in different levels of reality (e.g. capitalist development occurred through a concurrence of technical rules or 'forces of production' with organizational rules or 'relations of production'). When those different sets of rules become unalligned, they contribute to a general questioning and conflict over the rules by those previously bound by them.

Max Weber's work, more than that of Durkheim and Marx, has been centrally and explicitly concerned with organizational rules. Weber's classic, and oft misunderstood work on *bureaucracy* deals essentially with the processes of rules and organizational reality (Weber, 1969; Gerth and Wright Mills, 1974). Briefly, one of Weber's main concerns was with *rationality* and how it is constituted and maintained by the development of organizational rules. For Weber, in the modern world *rationality* has largely replaced tradition, sentiment and emotion as a way of understanding and undertaking social action. As opposed to traditional societies where the rules of action reflect the deeper (meta) rules of sentiment and belief, in the modern, organizational world meta-rules of rationality are enacted through a series of bureaucratic rules. As Allen (1975, p. 124) explains:

> A rational act, in Weber's view, is one which results from the application of reason, is controlled by the intellect and is achieved through a consistently impersonal motivation. It is devoid of traditional and charismatic elements.
>
> In his discussion of bureaucracy Weber was concerned with acts motivated by

economic interests and therefore rational acts were those which were determined solely by the pursuit of these interests.

An important part of the reason why bureaucratic rules have been so successful in engaging the obedience of organizational members has been their congruence – in spirit if not always in detail – with the dominant *weltanschauung*, or view of reality, rooted in rationality.

As will be evident, definitions and the use of the concept of rules have, not unexpectedly, followed the same epistemological divides seen within the analyses of organizations:

> [Different] sociological perspectives on organizations give rise to different conceptions of organizational rules. While some consider rules as the means whereby organizational orderliness is directly achieved, others consider the origins and consequences of organizational rules with an emphasis on the political implications of rule design, enforcement and application. Such a view too, sees rules as concerned with organizational structure, but in this case as a result of the negotiations, interpretations and modifications that produce a constantly changing orderliness. (Salaman, 1983, pp. 150–51)

So, how are organizational rules to be viewed? What is the value in exploring organizational rules?

In the section above we suggested criteria for the exploration of organizational rules. Each criterion provides us with a number of ways to understand the character of rules. Firstly, and of central importance, we argued that any adequate approach to organizations must attempt to take account of both structure and agency. This generates the following rules: (1) rules are the creation of actors and (2) rules stand over and above actors. Let us begin by examining these two propositions as uncovered by respective interactionist and structuralist approaches to rule.

1 *Rules as the creation of human actors*. The law provides a first-rate example of rule use. On the surface our common perception is of a legal system central to which are a series of rules for judging and dealing with offenders – rule breakers in fact! In the movie *The Accused*, we are given a glimpse of how this works *in practice*. The movie deals with the subject of multiple rape and shows how, through a context of plea bargaining, the charge against the actual perpetrators is reduced to *reckless endangerment*. The prosecution and the defence negotiate to arrive at an agreed-upon rule to handle the situation. The common assault charge satisfies the prosecution in that it carries an imprisonment term, and it suits the defence because their clients, while facing a jail term, are not 'tainted' with a 'sex crime'. The central actors in the situation – the prosecution and the defence – have managed to *create* a particular view of reality to fit an actual situation. The situation depicted in the movie mirrors very much the sociological study of David Sudnow (1978) into what he calls 'normal crimes'. Sudnow, in studying sociological features of the penal code in a public defenders office, documented the various ways in which plea bargaining, rather than the penal code itself, determines how any given 'crime' is to be viewed.

In a similar vein, Egon Bittner's (1974) study of the police on skid-row details how a particular group of patrolmen come to define the reality of the skid-row life that they have to monitor, arguing that 'on skid-row, patrolmen often make decisions based on reasons that the law probably does not recognize as valid; decisions in which considerations of momentary expediency are seen as having unqualified priority as maxims of conduct'.

2 *Rules as structures standing over and above actors.* In Sudnow's (1978) study of 'normal crimes', while demonstrating that legal rules cannot be treated as hard 'social facts', he fails to come to terms with the rule context in which decisions are negotiated. He fails to deal with the 'more concrete' form of social organization' – the penal code – that he alludes to as background features (Burrell and Morgan, 1979, p. 272). And yet both the public defender and the prosecution can be seen as adapting broader rules to fit a particular situation.

The work of Max Weber is a classic statement of the power of rules to influence and organize the potentially multiple behaviours of organization members. For Weber, bureaucracy works (i.e. it is a more efficient form of organization than traditional forms) because of its ability to co-ordinate the activities of organization members through a series of rational-legal rules. 'It is through this rule-bound quality of organizational activity and the consequent dominance of a spirit of formalistic impersonality that organizations achieve their distinguishing feature of calculability' (Salaman, 1983, p. 142). Anyone who had read real* or fictional† accounts of life within the confines of total institutions will readily concede the fact that rules can be felt as existing over and above the actors whose behaviour they seek to control.

In exampling the first two rules above, a number of further rules are suggested: (3) rules are negotiated, but (4) rules may involve powerful actors.

3 *Rules as negotiated order.* In the Sudnow case (quoted above) we saw that rules can be arrived at through a process of negotiation. Negotiation can imply various levels. At one level, viz. face-to-face, actors directly negotiated with each other to arrive at a decision. At another level, not examined by Sudnow, the actors were in fact negotiating through a set of existing rules (the penal code). The work of Strauss *et al.* (1978) has developed the theme of *negotiated order*. In a study of a psychiatric hospital, Strauss and his colleagues detail how the process of maintaining a sense of order is achieved through a continual process of negotiation that involves various hospital groups, including the patients. As they argue, 'order is something at which members of any society, any organization must work':

> For the shared agreements, the binding contracts – which constitute the grounds for an expectable, non-surprising, taken-for-granted, even ruled orderliness – are not binding and shared for all time. Contracts, understandings, agreements, rules – all have appended to them a temporal clause. That clause may or may not be explicitly discussed

---

* For example. *One Day in the Life of Ivan Denisovich, The Gulag Archipelago or Cancer Ward.*
† In particular Franz Kafka's *The Trial.*

by the contracting parties, and the terminal date of the agreement may or may not be made specific, but none can be binding forever – even if the parties believe it so renewal or revision or what not. In short, the bases of concerted action (social order) must be reconstituted continually; or . . . 'worked at'. (Strauss *et al.*, 1978, p. 304)

The concept of *negotiated* order recognizes that various parties contribute to the outcome. Hence, in the hospital setting:

> The patients are also engaged in bargaining. . . . Most visably they can be seen bargaining, with the nurses and with psychiatrists, for more extensive privileges (such as more freedom to roam the grounds); but they may also seek to affect the course and kind of treatment – including placement on given wards, amounts of drugs, and even choice of psychiatrist, along with the length of stay in the hospital itself. (Strauss *et al.*, 1978, p. 313)

4 *Rules as the dictates of powerful actors.* Looking at the various rule studies that we have discussed above, it should be clear that not all actors stand in the same relationship to the rules. In Sudnows' study, for example, it was the lawyers above all who decided the outcome of a given situation. This can have serious consequences for the less powerful actors. In the movie *The Accused*, the decision to charge the rapists with common assault has the impact of creating a reality in which the victim is viewed as some kind of 'tramp' who just happened to get injured during a series of sex acts in which she participated. She is no longer a woman who has been brutally attacked: by the definition of the crime she is reduced to sex object.

In the skid-row case, it is the police and not the inhabitants of skid-row who make up the rules. In Strauss *et al.*'s hospital, the patients can be seen 'negotiating' with more powerful hospital staff. And, in regard to bureaucracy, Alvin Gouldner (1954) has pointed out that 'bureaucracy is man-made, and more powerful men had a greater hand in making it'.

From rules 3 and 4 we can abstract further information about rule behaviour: (5) rules help us make sense of organizational life, (6) rules control behaviour, (7) rules are deliberately created and (8) rules arise out of situations.

5 *Rules as sense-making phenonema.* When we enter/join an organization for the first time, it is like attempting to play some game in which you only have a smattering of knowledge of how the game should be played. In a study of a Canadian distance education university, Sharon McGuire (1988) shows how a new faculty has to cope with a very different set of rules from that applied in more traditional universities. In the process of learning and coming to terms with the rules, the faculty members are seen as initially frustrated and confused and only able to gain an understanding of what they and the organization is about after a fair bit of interaction with and through those rules. In Strauss' case 'negotiated order' actually refers to the way people come to settle on a view of their organizational reality that then helps them to make sense of what is going on. This extends in the case of the patients to making sense of their illnesses:

When patients are closely observed 'operating around' the hospital, they will be seen negotiating not only for privileges but also the precious information relevent to their own understanding of their illness. (Strauss *et al.*, 1978, p. 313)

The work of Ervin Goffman (1957, 1959, 1984) has indicated that patients in mental institutions learn to become patients – they learn the rules of how a mental patient is supposed to act and, once learned, they are more effectively able to interact with other actors in the organization.

Zimmerman (1978) and Schall (1983), from different perspectives, both argue that it is not a simple learning of the rules themselves that help in the sense-making process but, rather, the existence of rules that can be drawn upon to define a particular situation. In order words, the relationship between rules and sense making is rather a complex process. Zimmerman's approach challenges the 'traditional perspective' which views the product of organizational activities as being 'administratively rational'. Through studying the actual rule-use activities of receptionists in a district office of a Metropolitan County Bureau of Public Assistance, Zimmerman (1978, p. 263) indicates that:

the 'competent use' of a given rule or a set of rules is founded upon members' practical grasp of what particular actions are necessary on a given occasion to provide for the regular reproduction of a 'normal' state of affairs. A feature of the member's grasp of his everyday affairs is his knowledge, gained by experience, of the typical but upredictable occurrence of situational exigencies that threaten the production of desired outcomes.

Hence:

the notion of action-in-accord-with-a-rule is a matter not of compliance or noncompliance *per se* but of the various ways in which persons *satisfy* themselves and others concerning what is or is not 'reasonable' compliance in particular situations. Reference to rules might then be seen as a common-sense method of accounting for or making available for talk the orderly features of everyday activities, thereby *making out* these activities as orderly in some fashion. (Zimmerman, 1978, p. 261)

Schall (1983, p. 560) is concerned with the communication-rules, i.e. 'tacit understandings (generally unwritten and unspoken) about appropriate ways to interact (communicate) with others in given roles and situations'. Schall argues that communication-rules signal definitions of a situation that have an important impact upon how rules are chosen for enactment of that situation:

'Definition of the situation' here means an actor's interpretation or belief about 'what's going on here', an attributional labelling of the interaction context. The definition may be based on role, goal, event, or locus and will vary in specificity ('this is a mother-to-daughter matter'; 'this is a chance to get a promotion'; 'this is a performance review'; 'this is our company'). The definition inferred will activate compliance to rules seen as appropriate to that kind of situation. (Schall, 1983, p. 561)

In the work of Zimmerman and Schall, we are reminded that action involves actors and structures. Established organizational rules help us, at one level, to reach a certain understanding of 'what is going on' but, at another level, the various actors in interaction are making choices about which rules are appropriate for the understanding of a given situation.

6 *Rules of control.* The work of Stuart Clegg is central to a rules approach to organizations. As Clegg reminds us, organization is about control. Organizations, by almost any definition, are established to achieve more or less specific ends or goals. In the process of establishing, maintaining and operationalizing goals, people stand in different relationships. These are those, who by reason of ownership (founders, owners shareholders) or management responsibilities (managers, directors, leaders), are directly concerned with goal-related activity, ensuring that organizational goals are strived for and achieved. This usually involves the employment of others whose task it is to carry out goal-related activities. For this latter group – non-managerial employees – organizational goals are more likely to be their means of achieving a variety of other ends (e.g. wages, salaries, employment status). Throughout the history of organizational development and the development of organizational and management theory, it has been assumed that employees need to be motivated and controlled in order for organizational ends to be met (Clegg and Dunkerley, 1980). Whatever the truth of the matter, systems of control are a central feature or organizations. For Clegg (1981, p. 545):

Control in organizations is achieved through what may be termed 'rules'. These rules are not necessarily formally defined by members of the organization, although they may be. They do not depend on the members' cognizance of them for their analytic utility. 'Rules' is meant merely as a term by which one can formulate the structure underlying the apparent surface of organizational life.

Clegg identifies six major forms of, what he calls, *selection rules*: extra-organizational rules, technical rules, social regulative rules, reproduction rules, strategic rules and state rules. Briefly, his argument is that different degrees and configurations of the major areas of rules compose organizations in different ways. State intervention (*state* rules), for example, is likely to differ in form and degree into the affairs of a hospital as opposed to an art gallery. *Extra-organizational* rules refer to the way that social values about the relative worth of men and women, and of different ethnic groups are translated into organizational rules about who is employed and who is not, who is allowed to do what, and who is paid what (with female and non-whites usually assigned to the relatively less paid, lower-status positions). *Technical* rules refer to the way the process of production acts to control the employee, e.g. as witnessed in assembly line production, or in a system of carefully laid down rules of procedure such as that carried out in MacDonalds' hamburger joints. *Social regulative* rules refer to control through more subtle, 'hegemonic' means such as company efforts to create a 'strong' organizational culture in which employees are made to feel part of the organization. *Reproduction* rules refer to the way that management and organizational theory has tended to reflect the status quo – the interests of those in control – and in turn provided new ideas for the maintenance of control, e.g. as witnessed in the debate on organizational culture (Ouchi, 1981; Deal and Kennedy, 1982; Davies 1984).

Stategic rules to refer to the influence that powerful organizations (multinationals, company towns) can have over a given community. In the example of the company town, the organizational rules of control stray way beyond the boundary of the particular company. A good example is the relationship between the mills of Sir Titus Salt and the town of Saltair in the nineteenth century. Salt insisted that his employees attend church on a regular basis and that they remained temporate. Failure to comply with these and many other rules led not only to dismissal from the mill but from the community – Salt owned the houses in which his employees lived.

7 *Rules as deliberately created phenomena.* Within organizations, as we have discussed at length, rules achieve a number of ends, including control, clarification, guidance, etc. It is second nature within organizations to establish a far-ranging set of rules to attempt to achieve co-ordination and control. Usually, those rules are written down, deliberately laid out for all to see and follow. Bureaucratic organizations are classic examples of carefully laid out systems of rules. Indeed, Max Weber predicted that the very efficiency of bureaucratic ways of organizing lay in the existence of clearly defined rules. The organization member, according to Weber, was more likely to follow organizational dictates if he or she could see that they arose out of and conformed to a set of rationally based rules.

Gouldner links bureaucractic rules directly to control, arguing that 'rules are a form of control that will be used when alternative forms are no longer possible, and bureaucratization is not simply the rational introduction of a technically efficient, objective organizational structure, but as a result of, and a stage in, the conflicting relationships that characterize industrial organizations' (Salaman, 1983, p. 144).

Organizations differ, of course, in the degree to which they attempt to impose written rules on the behaviour of employees. Burns and Stalker (1961), for example, have indicated that in situations of market uncertainty, employers are more likely to rely upon less formal rules in order to allow their employees the flexibility required to deal with changing conditions. The extent to which an organization employs professions may also downwardly influence organizational reliance upon written rules. Hall (1978) suggested that the socialization process in the making of a professional acts to provide a set of internal rules of control. Thus, the imposition of bureaucratic rules upon the work of certain professional groups may lead to conflict (Padsakoff *et al.*, 1986), because professionals expect a degree of autonomy.

8 *Rules arise out of situations.* An emphasis upon rules and rule-bound behaviour throughout much of the organizational and management literature has given rise to a view of the *rational* organization. Yet, clearly, as we have seen through the examples discussed throughout this chapter, the deliberately formulated rules of an organization form only a part of a given reality and do not necessarily (or usually) conform to a direct representation of that reality. In Sudnow's study, we saw that the written penal code serves as a background to a series of negotiated rules. The penal code was important in serving as the context in which decisions were taken but did not serve as the final word. Likewise, Zimmerman's case indicated that

bureaucratic rules were open to interpretation. In this case, receptionists were required to filter clients through to case workers according to laid down rules but, in fact, in the face of a number of circumstances, they acted in a way that met those circumstances while appearing to satisfy the rule. In short, they reacted to circumstance according to a different set of rules than the ones that were laid down:

> Receptionists' practical interests in the trouble-free development of the workday reflect their knowledge that things sometimes go awry and that they are accountable to others in the setting for their efforts to manage the course of work to minimise disruptions and control departures from routines. (Zimmerman, 1978, p. 257)

In any given organization, attempts to enact a rational pattern of behaviour is generally bounded by time and resource commitments (Daft, 1989) that make it almost impossible to follow a given set of rules. Rule interpretation is also a crucial factor in the way an organization actually operates. To quote Blau:

> A bureaucratic procedure can be defined as a course of action prescribed by a set of rules designed to achieve a given objective uniformally. Agency-wide rules must be abstract in order to guide the different courses of action necessary for the accomplishment of an objective in diverse situations. (Blau, quoted in Salaman, 1983, p. 146)

It is well known that attempts to enforce or strictly adhere to bureaucratic rules can be disruptive (Merton, 1949): the *work-to-rule* tactic of industrial relations is a recognition of that fact. As Douglas has put it:

> Anyone who starts with the abstract rules and hypothesizes what the concrete, situational uses will be, or what the social actions of those expressing the abstract rules will be, is almost certainly going to be wrong. (Douglas, quoted in Salaman, 1983, p. 149)

A large body of rules – written and unwritten, explicit and implicit – arise out of the interactions of organizational members as they attempt to deal with on-going problems.

Subjecting our rules analysis to yet further scrutiny, it would seem that: (9) rules are not necessarily universally held, (10) rules are not always known, (11) rules are not always understood, (12) rules are resisted and (13) there are spaces between rules.

9 *Rules lack universality.* As organizational members differ in their relationship to goal-related activity, it is likely that they also differ in their relationship to organizational rules. The Hawthorne Studies provide a classic example (Rose, 1978). In a study of the 'bank wiring room', researchers found that, despite organizational norms of maximization of effort, groups of employees developed their own – informal – norms for the restriction of output. Gouldner's (1954) study of bureaucracy found that the rules often served to signal minimally acceptable levels of performance, i.e. rules could be used to decide how low a level of performance a person could get away with doing. People enter organizations with different objectives and understandings and often negotiate over rules to achieve their own given ends.

People comply with rules for a number of reasons. Agreement with the rules is only one reason. Etzioni (1961) suggests that compliance will vary according to the organization. Thus, where the organizational goal is *order* (e.g. prison), compliance will be based on coercion. In business organizations where the goal is *economic*, compliance is more likely due to *utilitarian* considerations (i.e. a rational weighing of reward/punishment). And in organizations where the goal is *cultural* (e.g. churches, political parties), compliance will more likely be *normative*. Clegg (1983) and Giddens (1982) suggest another, more profound, reason for rule compliance: a human need to feel that you know, in the profoundest sense, what you are about. As Clegg (1983, p. 116) puts it: 'people continually recreate institutionally located and taken-for-granted typifications because of existential dread: the fear of uncertainty and chaos that lurks in the world'. It is what Giddens has in mind when he talks about *ontological security*.

10 *Rules are not always known.* As Clegg points out (see above), rules do not 'depend on the members' cognizance of them for their analytic utility'. Organizations are composed of a number of different areas of rules and these sets of rules impact upon different organizational groups in different ways. Take, for example, McGuire's study of the Canadian distance education university. The new faculty members are seen as taking a considerable time in coming to terms with and understanding the rules of the game and yet, in the meantime, they are able to function within the organization and present a series of pictures of accomplishment along the way. The new faculty members in this case acted according to the expectations of some of the rules without an awareness of the existence of those rules or what exactly they had to say.

11 *Rules as misunderstandings.* Another feature of the non-rational character of rules is the fact that they are always open to interpretation. In order to be extant they need in some way to be active and activated. This occurs through the myriad of organizational interactions which, at the bottom line, involves a series of rule interpretations. Through the process of interaction, understandings about rule use are arrived at. Understandings, however, are never a simple process and, from time to time, organizational behaviour can arise out of misunderstandings. The history of organizations is littered with crucial incidents and actions that arose out of misunderstandings.

12 *Rules are resisted.* An essential element in any organizational life is a series of negotiations over the rules. In a vast number of ways, organizational members informally negotiate over the rules they are presented with. A variety of tactics are employed, ranging from deliberate misunderstandings to downright refusals. The processes of negotiation and control imply disagreement and resistance. Indeed, it is through a range of resistance that rules are arrived at, are more or less maintained, or are either modified or changed. Organizational rules, in other words, are not straightforwardly the pronouncements of the dominant. They reflect varying levels of negotiated outcomes.

13 *Rules and spaces.* From the work of Ervin Goffman we can see that within

organizations – including total institutions – not all behaviour can be attributed to rule orientation. There are spaces. Goffman (1959) gives the example of the waiter who is expected to *perform* according to well-understood rules when in the *front*, i.e. when serving in the restaurant, but who appears to take on a different character when off-stage or in the back of the restaurant and out of public view. Likewise, Goffman's (1984) study of asylums reveals the spaces in which the patients are able to escape from time to time:

> In Central hospital, as in many total institutions, each inmate tended to find his world divided into three parts. . . . First, there was the space that was off-limits or out of bounds. . . . Second, there was *surveillance space*, the area a patient needed no special excuse for being in, but where he would be subject to the usual authority and restrictions of the establishment. . . . Finally, there was space ruled by less than usual staff authority. . . . [Here] inmates and staff tacitly cooperated to allow the emergence of bounded physical spaces in which ordinary levels of surveillance and restriction were markedly reduced, spaces where the inmates could openly engage in a range of tabooed activities with some degree of security. (Goffman, 1984, pp. 203–205)

We can note that Goffman's discussion here of what he calls *free places* refers to physical as well as authoritative spaces, but we can also note that such spaces are more often than not spaces *created* by the rules and not just areas on which the rules are silent.

So far we have considered organizational rules at the level of the organization itself; however, as we stated in the previous section on ways of viewing organizations, it is important to see the organization as part of a series of broader interconnections. Organizations can and do have their own peculiar areas of rule development, but in a broad context of organizational development. As our discussion of the work of Clegg makes clear: (14) rules are historically established, (15) rules intersect in the establishment of organizational rules and (16) organizational rules are informed by broader meta-rules.

14 *Rules as historical phenomena.* A major problem with ethnomethodological approaches to organization lies in the fact that they fail to account adequately for historically established relationships. The very term structure implies that a series of interactions and understandings have, *over time*, cohered into some kind of pattern. Berger and Luckmann (1984, pp. 70–72) provide a useful account of the relationship between interaction, structure and history:

> All human activity is subject to habituation. Any action that is repeated frequently becomes cast into a pattern, which can then be reproduced with an economy of effort and which, *ipso facto*, is apprehended by its performer *as* that pattern. . . . Institutionalization occurs whenever there is a reciprocal typification of habitualized actions by types of actors. Put differently, any such typification is an institution. . . . Institutions further imply historicity and control. Reciprocal typifications of actions are built up in the course of a shared history. They cannot be created instantaneously. Institutions always have a history, of which they are the products. It is impossible to understand an institution adequately without an understanding of the historical process in which it was produced.

Clegg (1981, p. 546) agrees, arguing that 'the organization is a historically produced object':

> Rules are the fundamental organizing principles underlying decisive breaks of or interventions into control of the labour process. Each rule represents a distinct and historically evolved principle of organization that is embedded in the actual functioning of the organization.

The question of the historical significance of rules was raised very significantly in the early debates around the notion of organizational culture. When Japanese companies began to compete successfully in the US market, a number of US companies sought answers in the management structures of the Japanese firms (Lee and Lawrence, 1985). This in turn led to a number of US companies attempting *unsuccessfully* to emulate Japanese management structures and styles. As William Ouchi (1981) was to point out, Japanese management structures reflected the broad Japanese culture, established over centuries. Clearly, it would be foolish to attempt to supplant such a style in a different (US) cultural context.

15 *Rule intersection in the establishment of organizations.* Each organization is unique in so far as it is composed of a particular configuration of rules. As Mills (1988b, p. 360) puts it: 'the very configuration of such "rules" of behaviour . . . distinguishes one social or organizational group from another; it is an essential part of their cultural identity'.

Returning to Clegg's selection rules (outlined above), we can see that the state is likely to intervene in one organization (e.g. hospitals) differently from the way it intervenes in another organization (e.g. florist shops). State rules will differ in type from one organization to another. Rules of adequate health care will be felt within a hospital, whereas the rules of adequate protective custody will be felt in a prison. Technical rules will also differ in the way they impact organizations. Computerization, for example, impacts some organizations to a great extent (banks) and other organizations very little (health clubs). This can lead to different configurations with very different implications for the way we understand activity within each organization. Take, for example, the contrast between Canada's 'open university' (Athabasca) and other traditional universities in that country. State (governmental) rules will intervene in more or less similar ways, but at Athabasca – with its emphasis upon distance education – computerization is a crucial part of the organizational infrastructure as opposed to many other universities where it is only a part of the operation. In effect, this confronts Athabasca faculty with a unique set of rules for running and coping with 'the system'.

16 *Organizational rules are informed by meta-rules.* Clearly, when we enter into any organization we are not at a total loss. We may not know the particular *rules of the game* but we do have a fair understanding of how games are played. The work of Henryk Sterniczuk (1988) indicates how the social values and institutions of a given country influence the rule formation within organizations in that country. Comparing communist with capital societies, Sterniczuk (1988, p. 3) argues that 'organizations are deep-rooted phenomena of society's political economy', and he

goes on to outline some crucial ways in which the organization of that political economy influences organizational developments (Fig. 1.4)

It would appear that we enter organizations with fairly well-developed rules about what an organization should or is likely to look like. Gorbochev's introduction of *glasnost* into Soviet life is, in fact, from our perspective, a way of changing outdated organizational rules by changing the way Soviet people think about social life in general.

Fig. 1.4 Some elements of a comparison of a business organization and its environment in communist and market-democratic systems (adapted from Sterniczuk, 1988, pp. 4–5).

	Communist system	*Market-democratic system*
1 A creation of a new organization	strong state restriction; precisely specified rules of new organization; once created an organization is relatively free from constraints for survival	mostly free from constraints; strong competition for survival
2 A necessity for rationalization of a creation of new organization	social needs expressed in terms of ideology, current state policy and very seldom an opportunity for financial gains	lack of necessity of rationalization of needs for creation of new organization
3 System of organization's performance appraisal in society	artefact; created by state authority; subject to changes according to current interpretation of ideology, policy and a meaning of social needs and tensions for survival of political state's elite	market type of feedback
4 A meaning of the law and formal rules for organizations and individuals' behaviour	the law and formal rules as a legal means of state domination; organization reaction to the state law and formal rules; bargaining and games, individual reaction to the state law and formal rules: constraints of freedom and behaviour; games	the law and formal rules as legal means for limitations of freedom of choices: both state authorities and private organizations; organization reaction to that constraints games or follows individual reaction: follows or games
5 Functions of an organization in	multifunctions: – organization of political	production/service and distribution

Fig. 1.4   *continued*

	Communist system	Market-democratic system
institutional system of society	control of human behaviour according to ideology and policy of ruling elites; production/service and distribution; distribution of social justice in structure of society	
6 Relations to an environment	a domination of hierarchical relations; – an organization as an element of the state's organized system (based on hierarchical subordination)	a domination of horizontal relations; – an organization as an independent unit of societal-economic system
7 Character of bureaucracy	public; a manager as state's official	private; a manager as official representative of owners or having authority from owners' delegation
8 Legitimate knowledge for organizational members decisions and actions	a part of systematic knowledge legitimated through ideological and political criteria of ruling elites	systematic knowledge
9 Relation of state authority and civil society	– constant struggle of a social order and order controlled by state authority; – order based on struggle for changes coming from both state authority and civil society; – deep feeling of illegitimacy of social, political, ideological reality (also from both sides' viewpoints)	– a dynamic equilibrium between state administration; society's representatives and civil society itself; – order based on legal culture property rights principles of systematic knowledge – a domination of conservative perception of social order as legitimate
10 A meaning of an organization for an individual	a source of meaning, social status, money and self actualization; a place of political participation in society; a place for self-expression in public life	– a source of meaning, social status, career, money and self-actualization, – membership: limited in time and space; calculative

Finally, any analysis of organizational rules must keep in mind that rules are *gendered*, i.e. that rules are created out of sexually differentiated ways of being; thus (17) rules are gendered.

17 *Rules as gendered phenomena.* Gender is a culturally created phenomenon, developed through a series of rules that operate at different levels. At the most fundamental level, we acquire a set of meta-rules through which we come to view a whole series of other rules:

> From very early in life children learn to 'read' or understand social rules of behaviour through what might be called *master rules*, i.e., sense is made of each of a number of rules by reference to a broader, more-or-less coherent class of rules which coalesce in notions of gender, of class, or race, and so on . . . (Mills, 1988a p. 9)

The development of identity indicates meta-rules are developed, and maintained or rejected through the whole process of interaction. In other words, we may enter into organizations as more or less gendered persons but the process does not stop there. Organizational rules themselves can influence how we are viewed and how we view ourselves. As Goffman (1984, p. 170) expresses it: 'organization can be viewed as a place for generating assumptions about identity'.

If we look back at our early example from the movie *The Accused*, we can see that the victim's involvement with the legal process had serious consequences for her sense of self. The legal process centred upon the criminal *act* itself, rather than on the *effects* of that act. Hence the defence lawyers were concerned to restrict the charge to some form of rule breaking that did not carry with it the stigma of 'sex crime'. The prosecution, from a concern to see the accused jailed, agreed to a different description of the act. From the victim, however, the charge sent a signal to her and to people at large that herself in particular, and females in general, are sex objects and that that is somehow all right as long as no *real* physical harm is done. The rape – in this case – is only a part of a general process that serves to signal the worth of the victim and, beyond that, to women as a class of person. The legal case and its outcome – tied as it is into broad social processes of legitimation – send the more important signals about the relative social worth of women in relation to men. Actual legal pronouncements, across a range of civil and criminal acts, are too often similar in their outcomes (Khan and Mills, 1989). Within the realm of organizational analysis, it is only just now beginning to be recognized that organizational rules – ranging from attitudes to sexual harassment through to exclusion of females from whole areas of work and levels of management – play a vital process in the construction of gender:

> It often makes a great deal of difference if you're a man or a woman! Many organizations are dominated by gender-related values that bias organizational life in favour of one sex over another. Thus, as many feminist writers have emphasized, organizations often segment opportunity structures and job markets in ways that enable men to achieve positions of prestige and power more easily than women, and often operate in ways that produce gender-related biases in the way organizational reality is created and sustained on a day-to-day basis. This is most obvious in situations of open discrimination and

various forms of sexual harassment, but often pervades the cultural of an organization in a way that is much less visible (Morgan, 1986, p. 178)

Exploring organizational rules

A focus upon organizational rules achieves several things. In revealing the rules character of organizations, we are provided with a way of freeing organizational behaviour from dominance; of coping with individual and organizational uncertainty; of development ways of *reading* and clarifying a range of organizational situations; and of providing leadership and direction within organizations.

Rules, in the broadest sense, are outline steps for the conduct of action, and depending upon combinations of circumstances and actors, those steps will be experienced as controlling, guiding and/or defining. Within organizations, rules as controlling are more likely to form the framework within which other rules will arise; organizations being primarily formal arrangements of people around goal-centred activities that members are expected to more or less engage in and conform to. In Chapter 2, we indicate the ways in which organizational rules (witnessed in particular in hierarchical arrangements and communications) shape decision making and the exercise of power, and how they mark out the boundaries of the organization itself.

In Chapter 3, we examine ways in which people become effective organizational members through a process of induction, socialization and negotiation of rules – expressed as 'ways of doing things', 'formal rules and regulations', 'mission statements', 'goals and targets', etc. And we examine some of the implications of these processes for human experience, identity and being.

Chapter 4 specifically deals with the way in which implicit assumptions about gender and sexuality inform organizational behaviour, culture and control.

In Chapter 5, we examine the question of change within organizations, examining the way that change involves both the development of new rules and the reaffirmation of old rules.

Chapter 6 looks at conflict and the rule system, examining rule-based theories of organizational conflict. We pay special attention to conflict between groups within organizations.

Chapter 7 examines rules about other organizations, i.e. the fact that several organizations have fromal rules about the way that organization members can and should relate to other organizations. For example, the Vice President of Coca-Cola (Sergio Zyman) was disciplined by the President of the company for drinking Pepsi. Some of the rules governing contact and competition between organizations reveal much about the culture of the organization.

Finally, in Chapter 8, we discuss rules about rules. We bring together several themes of the book and suggest some of the implications of our analysis of rules in organizations for the study of organizational behaviour and the practice of organizational consulting for organizational development.

2

Rules, roles and boundaries

Introduction

Chapter 1 examined a variety of paradigms within which organizations have been viewed. In addition, a number of ways of viewing the construct 'rules' were introduced. One generalized view sees rules as the formal requirements of an organization which seeks to determine and shape the actions of individuals and groups in that organization. As such, rules are seen as mechanistic, functional and deterministic and are exemplified in bureaucratic organizational types (Weber, 1922) and in Taylor-like formulations of organizations. The task of the researcher looking at such rules is to examine their origins and status in the organization (Lebas and Weigenstein, 1986). In addition, researchers look at the way rules are broken and the consequences of such rule breaking (Brady, 1987).

A second generalized view of rules within organizations can be referred to as an interactionist view. From this viewpoint, rules are seen as the way in which individuals interpret their own actions and the actions of others. Rather than being a set of statements intended to determine the appropriateness of an action, this view sees rules as the explanations an individual provides for themselves and others which 'cover' their actions in the workplace (Bittner, 1974; Strauss *et al.*, 1978). In this formulation, organizations do not have a rule-set, but a variety of rule-sets which compete with each other for position and power at given moments in the history and development of the organization. To use Levi-Strauss's term, they are '*bricolages*', composed of 'secondhand bits and pieces of rather general notions and traditions of how to go about things, each having its own semblence of logic and legitimacy' (Burns, 1981). To make sense of the organization, individuals and groups of individuals have to make their own 'rules of sense' which provide them with a framework for action within the organization.

In this chapter, we wish to examine this interactionist view of rules in depth and look at a particular conceptualization of these rules. The ideas in this chapter owe a great deal to developments in constructivism (Watzlawick, 1976, 1984; Maturana,

1988) as well as to developments in the practice of family therapy (Murgatroyd and Woolfe, 1985) and reversal theory (Apter, 1982, 1988a). We shall also introduce a model of rules as a heuristic tool for examining the interactionist nature of rule practices within an organization. In doing so, we elaborate on earlier contributions to the literature of organizations (Murgatroyd, 1984, 1986). Throughout this chapter, we regard organizations and groups as synonymous terms – an organization is a relational dynamic group. It is also assumed that the rules we refer to are the rules which are seen by an individual as either explicit or implicit in their action or in the action of others. These rules can concern rules for self-behaviour or self-thought, rules about relationships with others or rules about adaptability and conformity.

The phenomenology of individual rules

Each individual develops their own rule set. For example, individuals develop rules about what clothes are appropriate in different situations or how to address strangers or how to write a document which seeks to be critical of some action taken by another. While each individual develops their own rules – *rules are phenomenologically grounded* – it is clear from observing actions in organizations that there are structural patterns in the rules developed by individuals. That is to say, rules tend to cluster around patterns (e.g. in an organization there are patterns of rules about clothes, addressing strangers or writing a critical document) and individuals tend to structure their rules in terms of these patterns. Thus, though rules are phenomenologically grounded, they are structured in terms of patterns of social experience.

Experience is patterned in three ways. First, it is patterned by previous experience, i.e. by the historiography of the person. What has worked in previous situations will be used as a frame for the development of a rule for new experiences. This idea is the cornerstone of several types of social theory, including behaviourism, constructivism and structuralism. It suggests that individuals develop rules to make sense of the world as they experience it, and in doing so seek to make connections to their own previous experiences (hence the reference to historiography). Rules are thus cumulative.

To illustrate this, consider how individuals behave when being interviewed for a position within an organization. They prepare themselves in a particular way, present themselves in a particular way and answer questions asked in a particular way. The same person will behave in very similar ways between one interview and another, possibly making slight changes to the general pattern of their interview behaviour. If subject to analysis, this patterning of behaviour could be expressed in terms of 'my rules for interviews'. What most shapes the repetition of behaviour is success – 'if dressing like this and answering questions in this way secured my last position, then this *is* the rule-set for my next interview'. We use this illustration to show that rules for action are shaped by experience and as such are cumulative.

Our key point is that individuals seek to make sense of their experience by constructing rules to explain their experience to themselves*.

The second way in which experience is patterned derives from the attempt of the individual to reconcile their actions with the perceived expectations of those with whom they interact. This takes two forms. First, individuals tend to conform to group norms when they seek support or desire confirmation from a group. Several studies reflect this, most notably those by Goffman (1961), Asch (1958), Milgram (1963) and others (see Kiesler and Kiesler, 1976). Similar findings concerning the willingness of one person to conform to the perceived rules of another derive from the study of interactions between a powerful and less powerful person (see, e.g. Jones, 1964). Secondly, when the individual seeks to rebel from the norms of the group or to change the rules of the group, they can be seen to be making escape attempts (Cohen and Taylor, 1976) or of being negativistic (Apter, 1982). In both cases, the individual should be regarded as responding to their perception of the rules of others.

The third way in which experience is patterned relates to the way in which an individual perceives an action to be socially desirable at a more general level. For example, as a parent, our actions are shaped not just by our experience of being a parent and of the way our parents dealt with us as children, but also by our assumptions about how parents *should* behave, with this 'should' being derived from our understanding of social and cultural norms in our society. Similarly, our actions as managers or employees are shaped by a conception of what actions it is generally appropriate for us to take as managers or employees in a particular type of organization.

These three layers which the individual has to relate their rule-set to – self-rules, social rules and societal rules – represent a complex social world *within* the individual. For each of these layers centre on the interpretations made of the world and experience by the person developing their rules. At the level of theory, these assumptions lead to the view that the individual is a *closed system* which regulates itself and reproduces its actions through the development and transformation of rules for action. As such, the individual should be regarded as an autopoetic system (Maturana and Varela, 1972), which is continually struggling to make sense of contradictory information, demands and requirements as the individual seeks to engage in social action. Such systems are characterized by autonomy and individuality and the search for self-understanding. They are not affected psychologically or socially by events, but are affected by their reactions to and beliefs about such events (Ellis, 1962), especially where such a reaction challenges the validity of their own rules and patterns of rule transformation.

---

* Note that these rules for action need not be behaviourally determined. Some people behave in a way in interviews that does not secure them the job, but gives satisfaction to the person. Thus, a person who is seeking to make a point about an organization may choose to behave in such a way as to ensure that they are not employed: their satisfaction derives from having been able to make their point. If anything, the rules for action as we envisage them are more constructivist than behavioural.

The phenomenology of organizational rules: culture and the individual

This layering of constructions of the phenomenal world by the individual affects our understanding of an organization. As Morgan (1986) has noted, organizations can also be thought of as autopoetic systems. They develop internal rules (formal and informal), they have their own view of their markets and activities, their own 'culture' and their own way of dealing with rogues, rebels and challenges. They behave within the terms in which they think organizations of their size and kind should behave, they conform to their own norms for behaviour. Furthermore, when looking at the 'external' [*sic*] sources of challenge or threat to the organization – including, for example, new entrants to the industry, poor suppliers or powerful suppliers, new product developments from competitors, the powers of the consumer or the actions of government (Porter, 1985) in the case of a business organization – these have to be understood in terms of the way in which these challenges or threats are *perceived, constructed* and *understood* by those in that organization. That is, the organization is largely a world unto itself and is affected by the perceptions held by individuals within that organization of the events which take place beyond its boundaries.

To give an example of organizations as closed systems, consider the actions of the British Cabinet between 1932 and 1934. Despite warnings from their own Ambassadors in Berlin, Churchill and others, the British Government chose to believe that Adolf Hitler was not building a strong military force in Germany* and that his intentions in Europe were peaceful (for an account, see Manchester, 1988). While the Cabinet was presented with evidence that reflected the exact opposite of their position, their own construction of the meaning of the data presented to them was one which sought to maintain continuity of belief. A similar pattern of construction can be seen to have occurred at the executive level within Coca-Cola during April 1985 when they launched 'New Coke' in the USA to a wave of protest – the executives chose to construct the meaning of this reaction in a particular way, i.e. as an expression of considerable interest (Oliver, 1986), at least for a short time. In both of these cases, the organization had to change some of its personnel in order to achieve a complete change of construction. A third example which makes this same point concerns the actions of Oliver North in relation to the Iran-Contra dealings in 1986–7. While his actions were illegal, his belief in his mission made him and others who supported his actions at the highest levels of the US Government immune to differing constructions of the actions in which they were engaged. Finally, those who established and ran Osborne Computers took a particular view of their fortunes and refused to be affected by outside advice or evidence of failure – their confidence in their own construction of their actions was supreme (Osborne and Dvorak, 1984). Indeed, according to many who have written about entrepreneurship (e.g. Kao and Knight, 1987), such faith in the members'

---

* See Baldwin's speeches to the House of Commons, 8 March 1934 and 22 May 1934, reproduced in Hansard.

construction of the phenomenal world is an essential factor in determining the success of new business ventures.

In presenting this view of organizations as autopoetic systems, where the meaning of events is socially constructed *within* the organization, what is being proposed is that the organization is more than the sum of its individual members' actions and thoughts: the organization has a culture, values and belief systems which are in turn expressed through interactions and customs. Organizational members construct their rules concerning their own individual actions within the organization in terms of their understanding of this culture and its related customs, values and beliefs systems. In this way, organizations are more than the sum of the rules of those who constitute the organization.

This becomes clear when particular organizational events are examined. For example, a merger between two organizations creates tensions between two groups of staff, even though they may both be concerned with the same activities and services. Walter (1985) examines this phenomenon in detail. He suggests that the issue for study revolve around two sets of actions: (1) those which relate to freedoms, self-esteem and equality, and (2) those which relate to control, performance and primacy. While there are different types of mergers and acquisitions*, they each produce strains and stresses – they each challenge the rules which individuals have formulated to guide their actions in relation to the organization of which they are a member and the roles assigned to them in that organization. While value differences are at the root of many of the issues which individuals find themselves dealing with, these are most often expressed in terms of 'property' rights (control, performance and primacy). These tensions are clearly evident not just to company insiders, but often to customers. It can take up to 5 years for a company to settle (i.e. for new rules and roles to be established) after a major merger or acquisition (see also O'Day, 1974). In these ways, then, we can see that the rules which individuals develop to govern their own actions are shaped (in part at least) by cultural and normative features of the organization in which they are part.

A second example of the way in which critical events in the cultural history of the organization can shape actions within it concerns issues of succession. The organization has to adapt to the experience of new members and the new members have to adapt to the culture of the organization. This is most dramatic when the Chief Executive Officer (CEO) changes, but can also be dramatic for a sub-unit which experiences personnel changes. One case study that has been widely written about concerns the arrival from Pepsi of John Sculley as CEO and President of Apple Computers Inc. and the subsequent departure of Apple co-founder, Steve Jobs. While there are many aspects to the dynamics of this particular interaction, the succession of Sculley was an event which might be described as a 'cultural epiphany†' (at least to some), which involved the establishment of a clear set of

---

* Walter (1985, p. 311) identifies four: vertical, horizontal, concentric and conglomerate.

† We are grateful to Dr Peter Chiaramonte for his suggested use of this phrase.

cultural norms, not subject to whim or transience, which in turn enabled individuals and groups within Apple to develop rules and roles and stabilize a very complex organization (see Sculley with Byrne, 1987). The same might also be said for the arrival of Lee Iacocca at Chrysler in 1978 (Gordon, 1985). While culture is dynamic and shaped by the historiographies of those who comprise the organization, cultural traditions shape (but do not necessarily determine) the actions and reactions of individuals.

A third example of the way in which the culture of an organization affects the actions of individuals within it concerns the stages of development of an organization, the natural process of development and transition which occurs as organizations both grow or shrink in size and as they develop experience and competencies in doing what they do (Greiner, 1972). There are many studies of such transitions (e.g. Cameron and Whetton, 1981; Kimberley, 1979; Miles, 1980). Most point to the same conclusion: change in the leadership of the organization, especially when the organization is aware of performance failures, constitutes the most frequent transition event that carries major implications for the culture of the organization itself (de Vries and Miller, 1986). Other transition events, such as relatively poor performance in one year over another, an innovation or change in operational methods, can also affect the cultural norms of the organization and thus require individuals to develop new rules and roles.

Personal boundaries and group relationships

While cultural patterns can be seen to represent a framework within which individuals within an organization determine the entity of that organization and are so enabled to distinguish between one organization and another, it is not being suggested that *all* who participate in an organization share the exact same cultural understanding or values or hold them with the same degree of intensity. Nor is it suggested that cultural explanations for organizational identity are in and of themselves explanations for the social actions of individuals within organizations. There is a need to understand both the nature of organizational learning (Argyris and Schon, 1978) and the nature of individual differences and motivation (Apter, 1982). It is, however, important to recognize that two kinds of implicit cultural rule-sets do act to shape action.

The first are the cultural rules which relate to both boundaries and relationships. A boundary marks the identity of a group of individuals within the organization. For example, in our own university, there are executive officers and other 'suits' who make decisions at the highest level of the organization; there are the staff in the different faculties, each of which have boundaries around them; there are support staff working in service units, and so on. Each has their own boundary which is defined not simply in terms of organizational sub-grouping or the task-culture, but also in terms of appropriate and inappropriate behaviour, levels of responsibility (action limitations) and ability to manage time. In other organizations, the number and variety of groupings may vary according to organizational size and the nature of the organization.

Within the boundary of a group, rules about the nature of relationships pertain. In looking at the patterns of relationships within a group, several types of group can be observed and a variety of group styles described. Four particular forms of relationship patterns will be used in this chapter to introduce the idea of structural rule patterns. These four relationship types are derived from a theory of structural organization within families as exemplified in the work of Salvador Minuchin (1974, 1984) and his co-workers (Minuchin and Fishman, 1981), Jay Haley (1976) and the Milan School of Family Therapy (Palazzoli *et al.*, 1978) and elaborated by Sprenkle and Olson (1978).

The starting point for looking at relationships within a group is the idea of *cohesion*, i.e. the extent to which there is a bonding of identities within a group and the extent to which this bonding is perceived to limit in some way the autonomy of individuals within the group. A group derives its strength from the extent to which similar goals and ways of working are shared by the group and from the unique qualities which each individual brings to the group, but the bonding of the group can act as an inhibitor of individual action, unless the individual perceives an action to be appropriate in the context of the group.

This observation has led Minuchin (1974, esp. p. 54) to suggest that group cohesiveness can be regarded as something which is experienced in different ways in different groups. He suggests that in looking at cohesiveness there is a continuum between highly cohesive groups which have very weak levels of individual autonomy within the group (*enmeshed groups*) and, at the other extreme, a group in which there is an extremely high level of autonomy and very little cohesion (*disengaged groups*). Between these two extremes are two other more moderate relationship patterns, at least according to Olson *et al.* (1979): *connected* and *separated*. A connected group is one in which there is a degree of commitment to the group, but where individual autonomy is also protected; a separated group is one in which individual autonomy is more important than the coherence of the group, but the group has a degree of identity which is stronger than that of a disengaged group. These four kind of group identities can be shown as a continuum (see Fig. 2.1).

Let us look at examples of each of these kinds of group. An enmeshed group is one in which group identity is strong and individual identity is weak, i.e. a group where the boundaries between individuals within the group can be said to be porous or sponge-like. It is a group in which individual pride and satisfaction comes from

enmeshed . . . connected . . . separated . . . disengaged
high group cohesion   low group cohesion
low individual autonomy   high individual autonomy

Fig. 2.1 Four points on the cohesiveness dimension.

the achievement of a high level of group cohesion, in which individual identity is located in the persona of the group. A sports team that is working like a machine, with individual actions being performed according to some prearranged patterns of teamwork, would be one example of a group in which enmeshment could be seen to occur. Another would be a choir performing a choral work with precision and perfection. Enmeshment in these cases is visible to others. Most often, however, enmeshment is something that is felt rather than seen. It can occur in any organization in which the goal or purpose of the group acts in such a way as to sublimate individuality. For example, a number of religious cults seek to reduce individuality to a minimum in order to stress the importance of collectivity, as do some political movements. Or a group which has everything invested in some collective achievement, such as the workers' cooperative in South Wales working on the design and development of computer software, is a group in which enmeshment is felt by group members. One of the South Wales group said that all of his satisfactions and feelings of worth came from the collective achievement of the group, while another said that he had 'stopped thinking of himself as important' and started thinking of the group as the source of satisfaction.

At the other end of the cohesion continuum is the group that is disengaged: it is a group in name only and is characterized by the egocentric behaviour of individuals within it. One example of this would be a small law practice in which each partner had very different legal areas of work and the group existed merely as a convenience for marketing and administration. Another could be a production line in which each production worker had such a unique task that, even though each was dependent upon others, the experience of work was one which was private and isolated. The characteristic feature of this form of group experience is that the self is located within the person and their own roles, tasks and identity rather than in the persona of the group.

Between these are the connected and separated forms of group relationship. A connected form of group relationship is common to many organizations. For example, a small entrepreneurial firm in Cardiff which repairs electrical equipment has a high degree of connectedness – individuals feel a loyalty to the firm and its ways of working, they share ideas and 'secrets', cover for each other when someone is ill or is away for some reason, have a group social life and yet there is also a great deal of individual pride and a respect for individual achievement. Some of the school organizations with which we have been associated can also be described in this way (see Reynolds, et al., 1987). An example of a separated organization is the Department of Psychology at a university in Norway, where individuals pursue their own research interests and share findings, equipment, facilities and have some common interests – a small group within the department plays cards once a week – but individuality and self-pride are more important to members than the achievements of the department as a collective.

If these four sets of relationship patterns (four key points on a continuum) are seen as acceptable descriptions of relationship patterns in groups, then each can also be seen to involve different sets of implicit rules for communication. For example, in an enmeshed group, self-disclosure is high, whereas in a disengaged group, self-disclosure is rare (Jourard, 1971). In an enmeshed group, the distress one person might experience over something is quickly shared by other group members (sometimes to the point at which all group members experience the same symptoms of distress as the identified 'patient': see Palazzoli *et al.*, 1978), whereas in a disengaged group, distress is merely acknowledged. In communicating a success to an enmeshed group, a member will seek to show the benefits of this success to the group, whereas in a similar situation with a disengaged group, the personal achievement will be presented as such, with group members being asked to draw the obvious conclusion that what is good for the individual is good for the group. The different kinds of myths, rituals and rules of these four kinds of group will reflect the differing nature of cohesiveness within these groups.

We have presented these four group types as if they were both discrete types and readily recognizable. In fact, as the Milan group have pointed out (Palazzoli *et al.*, 1986), groups of any kind present a relational organization that is very hard to read and decipher. They give several examples of how cohesiveness is shown in the games organizations play with consultants. One concerns an entrepreneurial company involved with the development of new technology. Following a period of rapid development and growth, it was necessary – according to the shareholders and bankers – to streamline the company. The two major shareholders and founders of the company eventually agreed with the Board to streamline the company and appoint consultants. However, the consultants that were appointed had no experience with this particular task and recommended, with the full support of the workforce, that no changes be made. While the Board were given the impression that there was widespread support for change, those with most at stake (the founders and the workforce) had conspired to ensure that no changes would actually take place. To do this the workforce and founders needed to have connected/enmeshed qualities which facilitated the promotion of a particular view of the organization – one which was both successful and well managed and yet efficient. Palazzoli *et al.* (1986) note that such games are often revealing of the way in which a group functions.

Another critical indicator of group cohesion is the language used by group members to talk about the group. As Sproull (1981) notes, the way in which beliefs about a group are shaped is through the language of the group and the language used by group members to talk about the group. Key features to look for in the language used by group members about the group are the extent of shared meaning and common-phrasing to describe group events and actions (enmeshed groups have a higher degree of commonality than disengaged groups: see Pondy, 1978). Not only does language indicate how an individual thinks about a group and their place within it, but language shapes beliefs about the group. Furthermore, by facilitating the creation of belief-systems within a group, language can help to establish and maintain the emotional climate of a group (Edelman, 1964). Indeed, some have argued that the use of language can, *of itself*, affect sentiments and emotions independently of any substantive actions (Pfeffer, 1981). Thus the language of a group and its members can be most revealing in understanding both the nature and extent of its cohesiveness.

Finally, the non-verbal interactions within a group are also revealing of the extent and nature of cohesiveness. The basic features of non-verbal communication have been examined and reviewed by Knapp (1980), Argyle (1975), Ruesch and Kees (1956) and others. Groups can be seen to differ in the extent to which verbal and non-verbal language communications are contradictory, in the extent to which messages are carried within the group in a non-verbal way, and in the way in which non-verbal signs are used to complement verbal messages and in the extent to which non-verbal signs are used to regulate and enforce the communication rules of the group. In disengaged groups, contradiction and substitution are frequently seen, whereas in enmeshed groups, complementary and regulating non-verbal behaviours are common. These assertions are based on a reading of the literature of discourse analysis (Eemeren *et al.*, 1987; Potter and Wetherell, 1987; Stubbs, 1983).

Using language, non-verbal behaviour and games, individuals can show that they understand their place in a group and the group itself can show how they expect members to act and behave. Different kinds of group reflect different levels of cohesiveness, each level representing a different rule-set which shapes individual action. An individual is capable of developing a complex set of associative inference rules for their behaviour in a particular group (Cook, 1971). These are constructed by means of experience (induction), construction, analogy and the recognition of perceived authority (Sarbin *et al.*, 1960). Let us look at examples of each of these roots for the construction of rules:

1 *Experience (induction).* If the individual consistently notes that the group always acts in a particular way under specific circumstances, the individual will recognize the rule of behaviour for this circumstance. For example, when a group member makes a significant contribution to the group, there may be a rule that states that this contribution should be recognized by applause and cheers, or there may be a rule that states that the contribution should not be acknowledged at all. With experience, an individual group member will 'learn the ropes' of the group.

2 *Construction.* These are the rules that individuals invent for themselves. For example, an individual may think that women's contributions to a group are always in support of the actions of males. Such ideas often have no foundation in fact but, if shared by many group members, these rules can become normative. Because they are irrational, i.e. they have no foundation in fact or they do not arise logically from a review of all the available sources of information, they tend to be rules which, if shared by the group, are difficult to change.

3 *Analogy.* While individuals are capable of behaving in very different ways in different groups (Skynner, 1987) and of changing their system of rules and beliefs (Bonarius, 1965), they also seek to bring some stability into their actions through being able to use similar rule-sets in different environments. Individuals, therefore, seek to develop rules by drawing analogies between the appropriate actions in one situation and transferring these to another. This applies to within-

group (using past practice as an examplar for current action) and between-group (what worked in group A should also work in group B) analogies. To give one example, individuals who use humour to reduce conflict within a group are likely to use this same technique across the groups in which they are involved.

4 *Authority.* There are two kinds of authority which give rise to rules within groups. The first is external to the group and concerns the authoritative statements made by others which an individual accepts as true. For example, an individual may accept the US Surgeon General's statement that inhaling the cigarette smoke of others increases the risk of cancer, and this in turn leads the individual to refuse to work in groups in which others smoke. A second kind of authority arises within the group – the authority of group norms and established procedures. A great deal of research has been conducted in this field (see Krech *et al.*, 1962), and the results suggest that as group norms emerge over time they become increasingly implicit and complex and carry more authority: newcomers must therefore master this authoritative rule-set so as to 'fit in' to the group.

Through experience, construction, analogy and authority, an individual develops rules for being in a group and these rules will in turn reflect the nature and extent of that group cohesiveness.

Responsiveness and adaptability

The cohesiveness continuum aids our study of relationships within an organization and the rules that shape interaction within that organization. But this is just one of two critical dimensions in our understanding of complex organizations. The other dimension relates to the way in which a group responds to conflict, change or uncertainty: the extent to which the organization is adaptable. Throughout, we use the words group and organization as if they were synonymous.

Within an organization, there is a dynamic tension between the pressure to change (genesis) and the pressure to remain the same (stasis). A business that has found a successful way of producing a product, marketing it and making a profit is likely to want to preserve its operating methods and retain its ways of thinking, rather than make modifications or wholesale changes: 'if it ain't broke, don't fix it'. In contrast, an organization that is new to a market will seek to change and modify its actions in response to its perceptions of the market so that it can become increasingly effective. In both cases, the pressure to change will be felt. In the case of the established firm, this will result from changes in the competitive environment, changes in the nature and cost of supplies, the emergence of new technology, the possibility of new entrants to the market or changes in buyer behaviour. In the case of the new organization, all of the pressures just mentioned together with the internal pressure to improve and become more efficient will drive demands for change.

How will an organization manage the tension between stasis and genesis, between stability and change? How *adaptable* is the organization? To simplify the approach to this complex issue, Olson *et al.* (1979) suggest that there is a continuum of responses to this question which can be used to study a family, group or organization. The extremes of this adaptability continuum are *rigidity* (change is not tolerated and stasis is maintained at all costs) and *chaos* (change is embraced and frequently implemented, but with no plan or attempt to manage transition – the organization is in a state of cultural revolution with change being something that can be initiated at any point in the organization). Between these two extremes are two more moderate positions: *flexibility* (change is welcomed but is implemented with an eye to both constant improvement and maintaining the adaptability of the organization) and *structure* (change is entered into when necessary and with care to show the link between past practice, such change will only occur after a careful review and scrutiny and with the support of those in authority). We can show this on a continuum as follows:

```
chaotic  . . .  flexible  . . .  structured  . . .  rigid
hypergenesis                                        extreme stasis
```

Fig. 2.2 Four points on the adaptability dimension.

Let us look at some examples of these different kind of responses to change, challenge and uncertainty.

By tradition, Swiss watch manufacturers prided themselves on refining mechanical (clockwork) watches and saw themselves as manufacturers of time-pieces. They ignored the development of digital technology, despite the warnings of some in the industry. When the first digital watches began to appear on the market, Swiss watch manufacturers saw them as being inferior, and therefore not a threat. They did not change their products, their marketing strategy or the understanding of their core business. This rigid response to developments in the market (challenges and changes) led to a major loss of business and almost to the total collapse of the Swiss watch industry. Only by redefining their business in terms of fashion accessories and because of their exclusivity (e.g. Piaget, Rolex) did the industry survive. Many smaller and medium-sized manufacturers, however, failed because of their rigid response to the market environment.

Simiarly, between 1970 and 1980, the Xerox Corporation hoped to maintain its competitive position without investing in new technologies, new marketing strategies or new ways of working. Prior to 22 April 1970, Xerox had no major competition. Indeed, the 2nd Circuit US Court of Appeal recognized that Xerox had an absolute monopoly in plain paper copiers between 1960 and 1970. However, with the entry of IBM into the copying machine business, the fight for the market share began. Rather than respond to its new position as a competitor, Xerox responded rigidly by seeking legal sanctions against its competitors, a strategy aimed at maintaining its market position by ruling out (literally) any new entrants. Consequently, Xerox became increasingly vulnerable: it faced anti-trust suits from several companies, it lost its market share, it spent millions on legal costs (one case alone cost the company $23 million) and it failed to provide resources for new product development. Their marketing executive at the time observed that 'we had nothing but refried beans in the marketplace. . . . I was out there with a rusty bayonet and an empty rifle' (Jacobson and Hillkirk, 1986). When the competition was most severe, the company 'froze' – it was a rigid response. Consequently, the company's share in the $25 billion market fell from 82% to 35% and, in less than 10 years, the market was open to new competition.

These two examples of rigid responses can be contrasted with two examples of chaotic responses to challenge, change and uncertainty, both of which come from the computer hardware industry. In July 1981, the Osborne Computer Corporation shipped its first computers to an eager market. Just over one year later it was selling $10 million worth of computers a month, a phenomenal success story. Things improved further. In its first full fiscal year, ending in February 1983, Osborne's net revenues reached $100 million: it had become one of the fastest growing companies in North America. In September 1983, just 26 months after its first product was sold, Osborne filed for bankruptcy. Writing about the company, Osborne and Dvorak (1984) point to a variety of reasons for this dramatic failure:

> Turning to staff, systems and organization, two conflicting influences need to be considered:
>
> 1 In the absence of a cohesive organization, people work at cross purposes generating confusion instead of results – which is bad.
> 2 Within the intoxicating environment of unrestricted and rapid growth, many capable people acquire a will to succeed that borders on missionary zeal. They achieve spectacular results beyond reasonable expectation – that is good.

Their diagnosis for the failure of the Osborne Computer Corporation is the absence of control over developments and responses within the company (chaotic response to change), which in turn led to the lack of cohesion among the workforce. The very name of their book describing these events – *Hypergrowth* – is indicative of this. Interestingly, the account they provide has as its underlying theme the tension between stasis (regulation and control to maintain stability) and genesis (the missionary zeal which facilitates rapid change and improvement).

Similarly, the success of Apple Computers is legendary. It was the first major computer hardware manufacturer to challenge IBM's position, achieving Fortune 500 status shortly after it was founded. For a considerable period of time, Apple dominated the home and personal computer market and currently dominates the market for desk-top publishing systems. It is, and has been, a remarkably successful company. For a period of time, however, it was in trouble. The problems began in 1984 with tensions between two divisions (groups) inside the company – the Apple II group which was the mainstay of the business, contributing 70% of all Apple product sales, and the Macintosh group which was new but was the focus for a great deal of attention and resourcing. This tension escalated to tension between various management factions, focusing around Steve Jobs (the co-founder of Apple) on the one hand, and John Sculley (the recently recruited CEO) on the other. When faced with a sudden and unanticipated drop in sales of the Macintosh and dissaffection from the Apple II division, management's response was seen and perceived as chaotic. At one point, the Board of the company changed the status of Steve Jobs and at another there was an attempted rebellion by managers. The issue was settled, after many restless and chaotic months within the company, by Steve Jobs leaving the company and full executive authority passing to John Sculley. Sculley's account (Sculley with Byrne, 1987) makes clear that the experience was perceived by the workforce, both intellectually and emotionally, as being chaotic.

The response of General Motors (GM) to their difficulties in re-tooling and reorganizing the company in order to respond to more intense competition from Japan and Europe represents a more structured approach to dealing with change, challenge and uncertainty. For a considerable period in its history, GM was 'one of the most insular and inner-directed companies around' (Burck, 1981). From a period of rigidity and stagnation in the early 1970s GM became one of the most dynamic and strategic companies in car manufacturing. They changed their Board by bringing in new and 'not from the company' Board members and also, for the first time, employed several executives from outside the company with the express mandate of modernizing and re-tooling the company. This included investing in new technology, reshaping the design of the cars for the US market (especially in the light of the new demand for fuel efficiency), integrating international sales with the US sales division, downsizing the fleet and modernizing the personnel arrangements in order to promote greater cohesion, and a more structured and strategic approach to change. In her description of these developments, Kanter (1983) emphasises the drive for cohesion among the workforce and the drive for a structured and managed approach to change. This was achieved through two strategic missions within the corporation: to improve the quality of the products sold while at the same time improving the quality of working life. By the early 1980s, GM was an extremely successful car company which had a structured approach to change. They were used by Peters and Waterman (1982) as an example of an innovative company.

As an example of a flexible approach to change, challenge or threat, we cite a UK company, Lifeskills Associates. Lifeskills was founded by two staff at the University of Leeds as a training, consulting and publishing company. Its primary focus at its inception was the development of materials and training strategies in the field of careers guidance and social skills training for school and college pupil populations. A flexible approach to development within the company has led it into several other fields, including training for service management development within large corporations and the production of customized time-management systems for corporate clients. While retaining its original focus as a key feature of its business, Lifeskills has grown in a flexible way in response to strategic opportunities. The company has been so successful that it is now the subject of several takeover bids by other organizations.

These vignettes suggest that these categories of response to change, challenge or threat can be identified through case studies of specific organizations. The point to note here is that these response patterns are cultural features, they are part of the rule-set of the organization. Individuals within these organizations, in considering whether to propose or encourage a particular change strategy, make their decision in the light of their understanding of the implicit assumptions about change extant in the organization at that time.

Two points are also worth noting from these short case studies. The first concerns the nature of the adaptability changes within the organization: it is not fixed for ever. This is especially true in non-monopolistic businesses which have to be responsive to market pressures, changes in supplier arrangements, new technology developments, changes in consumer behaviour and government regulation. Apple Computers, for example, went through a chaotic period and came out as a structured change organization within a relatively short period of time. Rules concerning adaptability can change, though most often these changes are the result of changes in either the external environment or in personnel within the organization (Kanter, 1983). Secondly, what determines adaptability is not the external environment or the new personnel coming into the organization, but the willingness of individuals to change their ways of working or ways of thinking about tasks and routines within the organization (Imai, 1986). The implications of this last observation is that adaptability is grounded in the rule-assumptions of individuals within the organization.

Sixteen types of organization

When these two dimensions of organizational life – adaptability and cohesion – are combined, the emergent matrix provides descriptions of 16 types of organization, as Fig. 2.3 shows. Each type can be regarded as presenting a rule-set or 'frame' (Goffman, 1974) for shaping members' actions and beliefs about the organization. The model can be used to examine both the organization as a whole or its subsets. Before elaborating on the utility of this matrix, five key points need to be made.

1 Each cell represents a complex rule-set which individuals, find guides and shapes their actions. An organization or group operating within one of these cells has particular patterns of rules and ways of working which, when examined,

	Chaotic	Flexible	Structured	Rigid
Enmeshed				
Connected				
Separated				
Disengaged				

Fig. 2.3 Sixteen types or frames for organizational rule-sets.

constrain or inform individual action. Each cell can thus be regarded as a rule-set or 'frame'.

2 The matrix can be used to describe either an organization as a whole – such as GM, Lifeskills or Apple Computers – or parts of these organizations – the truck division of GM, the publishing division of Lifeskills or the LaserPrinter division of Apple. That is, the matrix can be used to examine and define groups or subgroups. When it is used to examine subgroups, a valuable contrast can be drawn between the subgroup and the larger organization. For example, a description of a subgroup within the 3M Corporation provided by Nayak and Ketteringham (1986) suggests that it was flexible and connected, whereas the larger group of which this was a part was more structured and separated. Some of the tensions and issues faced in seeking acceptance of new product processes or ideas can be seen as a function of these differences.

3 The categorization of a group or organization in terms of this matrix does not act as a firm predictor of the behaviour of individuals within the group at all times. Individuals can be rogues within the group or token-rogues, and groups can change their structural dynamics at any time. What the categorization does is to identify the dominant transactional forms within a particular frame.

4 Some of these organizational types or frames are likely to produce dysfunctional behaviour in either individuals or overall organizational performance. The four corner frames (chaotic–enmeshed, chaotic–disengaged, rigid–enmeshed and rigid–disengaged) are organizational types least likely to facilitate survival in highly competitive environments and most likely to be difficult to work in from a quality of working life point of view. These propositions come from studies of family dynamics and small groups (Sprenkle and Olson, 1978; Russell, 1979), but are also based on studies of entrepreneurship (Kao and Knight, 1987).

5 The rule-sets implied for each cell in this matrix are the rules as perceived by the individuals who form the group being studied. They are not imposed rules – organizations which are very rigid and enmeshed can still have within them subgroups which are connected and flexible, thus suggesting that organizational culture does not need to be overpowering – a fact demonstrated by successful worker buy-outs of organizations, such as Avis Rent-a-Car (Kirkpatrick, 1988). Furthermore, this insight suggests that each organizational type has the potential to become another organizational type through a process of relationship changes and renewed adaptability.

Organizational types and individual action

The previous sections have developed the proposal that implicit organizational rules relating to cohesiveness and adaptability are central to an understanding of organizational dynamics and the actions which constitute the daily life of the organization. In this section, we wish to examine the implications of these observations for our understanding of the phenomenology of organizational life.

A great deal of organizational life is routine and repetitive (Pfeffer, 1982). At the moment at which these routine tasks are being performed, the complexities and dynamics, intrigues and uncertainties of the organization are often not uppermost in the minds of an individual. It appears that many actions and processes undertaken within the organization are triggered as routines and, at these points, the process or transaction is largely non-cognitive, i.e. the action or transaction is performed in a script-like way (Abelson, 1976; Langer, 1978). In short, action in repetitive tasks is dictated as much by habit as by thought. A similar conclusion about the routine of organizational life has been reached by Collins (1981). In a powerful contribution to the theory of social organizations, Collins argues that cohesiveness and a feeling of belonging – gained by the performance of belonging rituals – shape a great deal of the day-to-day behaviour of organizations. For Collins, task-performance is a physical demonstration of belonging – failing to perform a routine task in a routine way disrupts cohesiveness and makes a group dysfunctional. Satisfactory performance of routines provides the individual with a source of positive affect or 'self-tone' (Apter, 1988a).

While there are other views of this phenomenon – the satisfactions derived from the maintenance of rituals and routines – it is interesting to note that the main alternative viewpoint places emphasis on seeing the routine in terms of the way in which the individual locates and translates the meaning of a particular action (including a repetitive action) in terms of the causal map of the organization constructed by the individual (Weick, 1979). If individuals do indeed seek to locate the meaning of rituals in some larger schema of the organization (and the work of Collins casts doubt on this), then the map itself is only called into question at critical times.

Moments of truth

This leads us to another construct now being used in the field of service management and quality assurance, i.e. moments of truth. A moment of truth occurs in an organization when the identity of the organization – its very purpose and functioning – is at stake in some way. For example, when an airline which markets itself as 'British Airways – The World's Number One Airline' fails to arrive on time and fails to deliver a passenger's luggage to the correct destination, these are moments of truth for this airline and its customer. The baggage attendant at the moment of complaint recognizes both that there is something wrong with the airline's routines and that at that moment he or she *is* the airline as far as the customer is concerned. A moment of truth can be defined as *a critical incident which exemplifies for those concerned the cohesive and adaptive qualities of the organization as expressed in the performance of some particular task or action.*

At a moment of truth, an employee is able to recognize either the success of the organization's preparedness for such a moment and obtain a positive sense of belonging, or he or she recognizes the ill-preparedness of the organization and feels self-doubt and/or uncertainty about the organization. At such moments, questions about levels of peer support, ability to make decisions without complex approvals and the ability to act are uppermost in the minds of the worker. At such moments, the experience of the organization and its complexities are significant for the employee.

Before exploring the theoretical and practical implications of this construct as one in which the cohesive and adaptive properties of an organization are immediately available to an employee, it may be useful to examine the origin of the construct itself. Developed by Jan Carlzon, the President and CEO of Scandinavian Air Systems (SAS), as a means of communicating the service imperative of the airline to all of his employees, the construct is becoming central to the way in which service organizations seek to manage their enterprise (Albrecht and Zemke, 1985). In 1981, SAS posted a loss of $8 million. Under Carlzon's dynamic leadership and a campaign aimed at improving the quality of the moments of truth – changing the meaning of interactions between staff and customers, enabling staff to be more adaptive and creating a more cohsive corporate culture – the company posted a gross profit of $71 million in 1982 on sales of $2 billion. All of this occurred during a major recession in the airline industry worldwide, with industry-wide losses of approximately $1.7 billion per year between 1981 and 1983. Critical to the success of the strategy developed by Carlzon was the widespread acceptance of the construct of a moment of truth within the company.

Since this time, the construct has been developed and refined (Albrecht, 1988; Juran, 1988) to be a particular way of looking at transactions both within organizations and between organizations and their customers. It is becoming a device for looking at the moments in the life of the organization at which attempts are being made to reconcile the consensual needs of stakeholders (Dermer, 1988) in the organization. That is, the use of this construct implies that the task of management is to facilitate positive moments of truth for customers and employees – management is capable only of acting as a participant (albeit a critical one) in an ongoing process. In this respect, organizations can be seen as a set of negotiated outcomes (Murray, 1978) or pluralistically determined coalitions (Cyert and March, 1963) acting within ecologically determined fates (Hannan and Freeman, 1984). Not all activities within an organization are known to management (Mintzberg, 1978) and a great deal of autonomous activity takes place with organizations. The critical question is how these activities are sustained and accepted within the dynamics of the organization. They can become critical at a moment of truth.

By looking at moments of truth rather than the objectives and the structural maps of organizations provided by managers, it becomes possible to examine the way in which individuals within the organization perceive both their autonomy (as a feature of cohesiveness) and their ability to act independently (as a feature of adaptability). Looking at moments of truth provides a starting point for the analysis of the consensual rules used by organizational members to define their place and limits to action in the organization. A detailed scrutiny of the moment of truth can help our understanding of the type of organization we are observing.

As Dermer (1988) has noted, what is interesting about looking at organizations in this way, is that the focus upon moments of truth and the issues that these moments give rise to enables the researcher to study both the formal (explicit) and informal (implicit) rules which govern not simply the actions taken at these moments but also the coalitions formed in order to be able to act on these moments (Diesing, 1962). Rather than focusing upon the power of named managers and executives, looking at organizations in this more pluralistic way enables and encourages us to look at the multiple rationalities and related rules within an organization and to seek to understand the organization in terms of the way in which the network of related rules used by related groups shapes organizational behaviour (Bacharach and Lawler, 1980).

At the level of the individual, looking at their experiences of these moments of truth and their assumptions about what they are and are not able to do at these moments is indicative of their explicit and implicit rules about the organization. In particular, these moments and the issues they give rise to for individuals enable us to examine the cohesiveness of that individual's relationships with significant others associated with that moment and the extent to which they feel able or unable to act. Detailed explorations of these moments of truth within the organization facilitates the study of rules.

In addition, these moments permit a detailed study of the role and nature of management within organizations. In terms of the 16 organizational frames described above, it is possible to regard the task of management at a particular moment in time as either maintaining the 'frame' of the organization's dynamic rules or seeking to change that frame, where a 'frame' is defined in terms of the transactional patterns associated with one or more of the 16 types of organization identified (Dermer and Lucas, 1986). That is, because organizations can be thought of as having many different rationalities and groupings (Silverman, 1970; Van Maanen, 1975; Weick, 1977), the task of management is to promote a sense of commonality and purpose through consenual management or conflict resolution. Managers seek to aid rule identification at such moments.

Finally, focusing upon moments of truth and the ways in which individuals act during them can draw attention to the inconsistencies and contradictions of organizational life and the rules which operate within the organization. This can take the form of both individual inconsistencies – the same person acts in different (sometimes opposite) ways at similar moments of truth – and organizational inconsistencies – the organization has dysfunctional or contradictory rules at such moments. These inconsistencies can affect the way in which the individual experiences the organization and can also act as challenges to the frame of the group or organization. They can also be a major source of organizational conflict and tension.

Moments of truth as rule indicators

Having introduced the construct and outlined its value to any analysis of organizations based on rules, it is incumbent upon us to examine some moments of truth so as to demonstrate their value in revealing the implicit and explicit rules of organizations. The vignette we have chosen is one in which a manager is faced with a significant challenge to her unit due to the budget process.

The organization from which this case derives is a public service organization with a variety of functions. During each phase of the budget preparation, the managers are asked to make presentations to the executives about the needs of their department and the likely budget requests they will make once the budget process begins proper. This reveals an implicit power rule: executive officers have a right to understand and anticipate what managers will present formally prior to its formal presentation – executives will not be ambushed by managers.

Following this presentation, the top team sets resource expectation levels (RELs) for each unit within the organization. These RELs specify what kind of budget bid a unit can make. There are three categories:

1 *Resource reduction*: the unit will be asked to present a reduced budget.
2 *Stable resources*: the unit will be asked to manage at the same budget level as in the previous year.
3 *Strategic allocation*: the unit may bid for additional resources for specific activities linked to the organization's strategic plan.

It is a firm rule of the budget process in this organization that RELs cannot be breached once set either by managers or by executive officers. It is noted by some managers, however, that because the executives set this rule they can also modify it as the budget scenarios unfold, i.e. there is scepticism that the rules set will be adhered to if contingent factors are fully taken account of.

During the REL process, the manager of the support services unit is told that she is a stable resource unit *only* if she can produce a budget plan that will be stable over a 3-year period and yet cope with an annual growth of activity of some 10%. That is, while others who demand services from this unit are able to increase their demands upon it, she is told that she has to continue to provide these services without loss of quality and with the same dollar amount (adjusted only for inflation) over a 3-year period. An interesting challenge, to say the least. It is even more interesting when it is realized that this unit is the only unit in the organization that is asked to develop a budget of this kind; all of the other units are either stable within existing levels of money and activity or growth through strategic allocation.

For the support services manager, the receipt of this REL designation (which was set by memorandum rather than through a personal meeting) provides a major challenge in the following ways:

1 The designation in itself means that the unit will falter in its ability to perform current tasks, because the inflation adjustments do not cover the full cost increases over the 3-year period.

2 The designation implies that the task will be politically difficult to fulfil, i.e. in order to submit an appropriate budget under this budget rule, she has fundamentally to change some aspects of the ways in which her unit works, changes which will be resisted by her staff.
3 The designation also implies a level of managerial accountability that she has hitherto not had to comply with. What she has to do is to maintain quality with less resources, *or else* face more direct intervention by the executives.
4 At a personal level, the unit manager feels that she has been singled out, and that this budget rule should apply to all of the other units. She feels that the integrity of her unit is challenged by the designation and therefore that her integrity as a manager is also being challenged.

In an interview with the support services manager on the day the REL memorandum was issued, she said:

> I feel as if my place in the organization is being questioned and that I am a suspect in a crime that I have not committed. They [the top team] seem to want me to do something but they leave me guessing as to what it is. Meanwhile, my own staff want me to resist this 'thing' that they think the top team want me to do, but they don't know what this thing is. When I received the REL memo I wanted to just hand in my resignation – it seemed to me that the rules of the budget process were unfair and that I had been asked to do mission impossible. Yet if I resign, I am playing into their [the top team] hands. I am not sure that I belong and I am not sure that I can adapt to their way of thinking, since I am not sure what it is!

In this one paragraph the nature of the moment of truth for this manager is revealed: it is a moment in which her place and the place of the unit in the 'scheme of things' within the organization is seen as problematic. All the nuances of the situation are experienced vividly, and a real dilemma of conscience faces her. She struggles with the issues of belonging (cohesion) and responsiveness (adaptability), and the extent to which others want her to belong and respond and the price she will have to pay with her own staff for belonging and responding. For her, the rules of the organization have been changed, and she has to question the meaning of the new rules in terms of her belonging and willingness to be adaptable.

This one moment is a major moment of truth for this one manager. We chose to examine this as a critical incident, because it is revealing of the way in which questions about cohesion and adaptability can arise. But not all moments of truth are as major as this one. They can arise when routines fail or when some small event leads some members of the organization to question the nature of the organization itself. For example, a company recently sent a memorandum to all of its employees pointing out that its insurance arrangements did not cover the presence of children on the premises and asking all staff not to allow children into their areas (the organization did have a day-care centre on site and it acted as a public building for some of its functions). The problem was correctly identified – inadequate insurance cover – but the solution was a new problem rather than a solution. The memo led to an informal protest – on the next school half-day holiday in the area, most of the staff brought their children to work. Rules were advanced, challenged and eventually repudiated in this case. The intention of the writer of this memo was not to encourage employees to question the organization, but to 'solve a simple insurance problem'. Yet for some in the organization, the memo challenged the identity of the organization itself.

These are the moments in the life-cycle of an organization at which the moments of truth are especially sensitive. These include:

- The succession of a manager or supervisor.
- The takeover of a unit by another unit or organization.
- Annual merit pay decisions.
- Promotions and recruitments.
- Terminations of staff and the understanding of the issues associated with termination in each case or category of cases.
- Resource allocations.

At these times, the nature of the implicit rules of the organization often become explicit for a short time. As they do, the numbers of moments of truth increase in the experience of affected individuals and these moments can act together to reshape the person's experience of the organization.

Boundaries

Up to this point it has been suggested that individuals construct meaning through their experience of organizations and that these meanings are framed in terms of questions and cohesion and adaptability. By looking at the relationship quality of the organization and its responsiveness to threat, challenge or change, it is possible to discern some of the rules which shape and mediate action within the organization.

By suggesting that there are 16 basic frames of organizational dynamics from which an analysis of the cohesiveness and adaptability can begin, it is also possible to see these 16 types as relating to subsystems of the organization. For example, in one organization, the accountants were thought of as very enmeshed and rigid, whereas a group of people working in marketing were thought of as flexible and connected. Furthermore, these 16 types are not fixed and static but a basis for reviewing the dynamics of rules within an organization.

If an analysis of organizations begins from the framework outlined here, then it is also necessary to look at the nature of boundaries within an organization and between one organization and another. A boundary is the extent to which one rule-frame or subsystem is permeable to others who wish to enter it from another frame. Putting this simply, a boundary refers to the definition of who participates in a subsystem or frame and how they participate (Minuchin, 1974). If we begin with the assumption that participation within one frame (e.g. enmeshed-rigid) requires context-specific responses from members which display their understanding of the implicit rules of this frame, then we need also to understand the rules by which others are excluded from this frame. That is, we need to understand the boundary marking actions that delineate membership and actions in this frame.

There are many ways in which individuals or groups mark boundaries between themselves and others. Among those most frequently cited:

- The way in which physical arrangements are made within an organization to delineate group areas or personal space can be regarded as boundary markers. This applies to both the formal arrangements and to informal ones (i.e. seating at meetings).
- The language people use when addressing each other can be indicative of boundaries (the use of 'we', 'them' and 'they' are especially revealing).
- Turn-taking in conversations and meetings can reveal something of status and power issues associated with particular groups: this is especially revealing for within-group boundary issues.
- Linked to turn-taking is the role of interruption and simultaneous talking in group situations: this can be most revealing of status, power and the implicit frame-rules during a meeting.
- Generational boundaries – between old and new organizational members and between upwardly mobile and downwardly mobile staff, for example.
- Alliances and coalitions over specific issues within and between groups can be most revealing in terms of determining how porous a boundary between one frame and another really is.

To some extent, the cohesion dimension described earlier is a statement about boundaries between people within a subsystem: disengaged individuals or groups have inappropriately rigid boundaries, whereas enmeshed groups have diffuse boundaries. It is important to note that what is being described by these terms is not functionally but transactional style.

Indeed, this last point is the subject of some research in terms of organizational effectiveness. Lawrence and Lorsch (1967a, b), in an imaginative study of organizational structures and performance, suggest that the transactional styles of subunits within organizations may need to vary between subunits because of the nature of their particular environments. Further, the transactional style and adaptability of the organization as a whole varies according to the industry and its environment. Thus there is no optimal deisgn for an organization: the design is a function of a variety of situational determinants.

A profusion of frames

Individuals can be members of more than one frame when they participate in organizational life. Indeed, each frame can be seen as a subsystem and individuals can be members of one or more subsystems, i.e. they can have multiple identities within an organization.

This is an important point. Returning to an earlier example, an accountant can be rigid and enmeshed while with his colleagues, but can change his frame when in another context and in the absence of his colleagues. While he may seek to be consistent between frames over certain issues, he may also appear to be inconsistent between frames on others. Indeed, there can be subsystems within subsystems – some of the accountants may be enmeshed and rigid but others may work from a different frame. An individual may move between these systems with some regularity, depending on the situational determinants for that person at that time.

In this way, it is possible to see the 16 frames presented earlier as a basis for looking at organizations as dynamic entities in which the behaviour of individuals is itself dynamic. This leads us to issues about rule consistency and congruence. When an individual changes his or her frame either within a subsystem or between one system and another, they may experience some internal conflicts and stress. They may also face challenges by their new or old frame colleagues. What is being undertaken by the individual who switches frames is a process of self-typing (Klapp, 1962) which depends crucially on experiences of success and failure in organizational survival and upon the power and consequences of differential association (Strauss, 1959).

Conclusion

This chapter has examined the implicit and explicit framing of rules in relation to two key dimensions of organizational life – cohesion and adaptability – and has proposed that organizations can be viewed in terms of 16 types or frames involving varying degrees of cohesiveness and adaptability. It has been suggested that these 16 frames for action are phenomenologically grounded and that these frames become critical at moments of truth within the organization. It has also been suggested that organizations typically involve multiple frames and that, because of this, organizations should be regarded as pluralistic and consensual. In such pluralistic organizations there are many opportunities for inconsistency and conflict and these are most likely to become apparent at a moment of truth. Furthermore, the inconsistencies and multiplicity of frames within an organization are likely to be reflected in the inconsistency of individual action and frames.

The implications of these ideas will be more fully explored in subsequent chapters.

— 3 —

Becoming an organizational member

Introduction

'Joining' and 'becoming' are key constructs in the understanding of individual actions in organizations. 'Belonging' is a central idea in the understanding of organizations as cultures (Ott, 1989). Generally, these three constructs are seen as elements in a process of socialization. In terms of rules, socialization can be seen as a process by which an individual masters the rules of the organization, and in so doing adjusts to them; equally, it is the process by which the rules of the organization are revisited by existing players in order that they can be adjusted or reinforced so as to take account of the arrival of a new player (or players) and the subsequent need to integrate a new person or group of people into the organization.

There are a variety of responses to the question 'What *is* the process of socialization in an organization?' When analysed, these responses can be looked at in terms of four models of the relationship between the person and the organizational environment (the 'person–environment fit'). These are:

1 The *mechanistic model*, in which the person is seen as constantly responding to their environment, with behaviour being caused by environmental factors – this is a form of extreme behaviourism.
2 The *organismic model*, in which the individual uses some generic rules of development (shaped in part by physical and social factors) as a basis for their creation of purposes within their work environment, these 'rules' being essentially stage-order rules of the kind described by Erickson (1959).
3 The *contextual model*, in which an individual strives, through their daily action, to give meaning and substance to their existence without necessarily having a particular end-view in mind; and
4 The *systems model*, in which the relationship between the individual and their environment is seen as an iterative process by which the individual absorbs the rules of the social system until they become effective as self-motivational forces – the individual is a replication of the social system through their actions.

Four psychological approaches

These four basic models provide a starting point for a variety of ways of understanding the psychology of socialization. Again, there are essentially four epistemological models from within which socialization processes have been examined by psychologists: (1) theories of social learning; (2) psychoanalysis; (3) developmental approaches; and (4) ecological theories.

Social learning theory has passed through a number of forms since its early development within behaviourism (Skinner, 1938). In contemporary forms, social learning occurs as a direct result of the experience of successful adaptive behaviour in response to a particular social stimulus, but is mediated both by cognitive processes (Macoby and Martin, 1984) and by the experience of interpersonal relationships and social influences (Bandura, 1986), of different potencies. Through their attempts to construct systems of rules by which they may engage in adaptive coping as opportunities permit and needs arise, individuals develop observational skills in terms of the behaviour of others, become expert at attributing meaning and understanding to others for their action, are able to weight and locate information relevant to a particular action, and so on. Individuals do not need to experience behaviour directly in order to master a particular rule-set – cognitive process and empathy are powerful enough to facilitate such learning.

Elaborating on these basic ideas, Harré et al. (1985) suggest that the individual develops a matrix of social relevant knowledge. Through this matrix, the individual develops a detailed understanding of distinctive social situations which they fully recognize. For each of these situations 'there is a set of rules or rule-like beliefs' (Harré et al., 1985, p. 88) which the individual has so as to be able to act appropriately in these situations. But these actions are more complex than mere behavioural responses to a recognized stimulus: not only does a person have to do the right thing, but they have to appear to be the right persona when doing so – presentation of the action can be as important as the action itself. In addition, according to Harré et al., the individual also requires a reference point in a group, organization or situation which provides feedback as to the appropriateness of their response. In so far as there are different rule-sets for different categories of persons (managers vs subordinates, men vs women, new workers vs 'old hands', volunteers vs compulsory workers, etc.), so their social psychologies will differ, though their information processing mechanisms may be identical. Through these forms of social learning, individuals learn the rules of social situations and become competent actors within them.

Social learning theory, however, does not make clear just how individuals acquire their tacit knowledge of the rules of social action – as outlined, it only offers a description of how the rules, once acquired, are invoked under appropriate circumstances. Much developmental work is needed to elaborate rule acquisition processes, especially in the context of organizations. It is also the case that social learning theory offers yet weak explanations of how rules are broken and how rules are changed. None the less, social learning theories are increasingly important in understanding socialization processes.

Psychoanalytic theories for understanding socialization have their origins in the organismic theory of person–environment fit. From this framework, the actions of an individual are manifestations of their latent traits and the latent power of their emotional make-up. Indeed, classical Freudian interpretations of the social behaviour of adults revolve around re-enactments in organizations of prior experiences, especially experiences of successful behaviour within the family. Classical psychoanalytic theory, as several commentators have suggested, provides a poor basis for understanding organizational behaviour (see Bennis, 1966). However, Erikson (1959) has elaborated a stage learning model of social development which involves three levels of analysis:

1 The organization of the human body and its development through various stages of physical maturation, growth and decline.
2 The organization of life-experience through ego-synthesis.
3 The social organization of the individual in society.

One variant of the psychoanalytic frame is transactional analysis (TA: Berne, 1961, 1964). This popularization of some key ideas from within psychoanalysis (both Freudian and Jungian) has increased the extent to which some aspects of psychoanalytic thinking have been applied to organizations. For example, the idea of ego states and 'senses of self in the social world' (known in TA as transactional modes and life position) have become devices for understanding the way in which people interact both generally (via life positions) and specifically (via transactional mode), and these have been used to analyse conversations and events within organizations (Albano, 1974). 'Game analysis', in which the hidden games of personal relationships are examined from within a transactional analysis frame, has also been used as a basis for looking at organizational behaviour (James and Savary, 1977). However, this thinking frame has produced few analytic results which enhance our knowledge of the process of socialization.

The most valuable contribution to the understanding of organizational socialization using psychoanalytic constructs, apart from that made by Freud himself, occurs as a result of the contributions of E.H. Erikson (1975). In suggesting that the way in which a person constructs meaning in their social world is a function of developmental stages and tasks, Erikson suggests that the process of socialization is an interdependent process involving the organization of experience through ego synthesis, physical development and the social organization of experience through social structure (structuration). Motivation for action is produced as a consequence of the individual seeking to reconcile these three forces (self, development and society) within themselves. This in turn has encouraged both sociologists and psychologists to develop an understanding of social development and socialization which places emphasis on this inner tension (see especially the work of Berger *et al.*, 1974; Goffman, 1961; Flugel, 1945).

Developmental theory, or more accurately *cognitive* developmental theory, gives emphasis to the stages of the development of cognition and related information processing and perceptual skills. One way of looking at this conception of socialization is to see it as one of constant adaptation during which the individual's understanding and skills become increasingly refined. Further, as the individual's understanding and skills become refined, he or she is better able to shape their environment, such that the exchange process between the person and their environment increasingly facilitates the further development of the person. A key construct here is that of equilibration (Piaget, 1950). It refers to the balance at any one time between personal and social structures – the balance is not equal, however, because the personal structures are paramount in defining social structures and processes for any given individual.

The cognitive development approach to understanding socialization minimizes the importance of concrete social experience and living conditions in shaping personal development and learning (Seiler, 1980). It also makes assumptions about normative development which take inadequate account of adaptive failure, of social pressure and deviance. More poignant, these approaches ignore gender as a factor in socialization processes (a subject examined in more depth in Chapter 4). However, recent models of adaptive coping (e.g. Howard, 1984) do seek to give greater emphasis to the nature of social experience (especially interpersonal experiences) as a basis for the development of social learning and socialization.

Ecological theories of socialization owe much to the cognitive developmental and systems model of socialization. Assuming that the environment in which an individual is placed is constantly developing as also is the individual, this model assumes that both the environment and the person are engaged in mutually adaptive processes that lead to the creation of what might be referred to as a maximal person–environment fit, i.e. adjustment is reciprocal (Bronfenbrenner, 1979). In this dynamic model, individual seek to make rule-sense of a changing environment, which in turn has rules. As the person experiences a greater variety of environments (new work settings, new locations, new countries, etc.) or is vicariously exposed to these environments, they elaborate or refine rules. As environments change, so does the way the person applies the rules he or she has developed. Though individuals in the same environment may understand their social roles and selves differently, this is a consequence of their different experiences of that and other environments and their individual differences in personal experience.

Socialization, relationships and adaptability

The ecological approach of Bronfenbrenner is commensurate with the model introduced in Chapter 2. The individual has to relate to others in the organization through a process of negotiating implicit and explicit rules of communication and relationships. In addition, the individual has to come to terms and develop rules that relate to the tasks of the organization (its social purposes), and in doing so has to recognize that organizational tasks are dynamic and subject to change. Thus, the individual will develop self-rules about adaptability. In developing these adaptability rules, individuals will recognize that their own rules are mediated by the rules and assumptions of others. Thus individuals perpetually negotiate meaning for themselves in relation both to others and to the organization. This process is iterative – the individual constantly processes their external and internal realities to make sense of their rule-set. Social action results from the attempt of an individual to act on the rules they have formed through this iterative process: action tests rule-sets and assumptions. It is only by regarding socialization processes in this way that some synthesis of the psychological models just outlined can be achieved. (Hurrelman, 1988). We call this the ecological-adaptive model.

The ecological-adaptive model does not assume that the individual develops a single rule-set in order to act in the social world. Apter (1982), for example, suggests a 'many worlds' model of motivation in which the individual relates to the environment in a variety of ways depending upon changing and dynamic features of their personality. At one time they may be conforming, planning-oriented and see their tasks in terms of achieving some extrinsic goals; at another time, they may be negativistic, sensation seeking and intrinsically motivated. As the structure of their motives switch and change, so does the way they experience their social environment. While individuals behave in an internally consistent way for some of the time, they can also be regarded as inconsistent in that they will spend some time in a state opposite to their 'normal' state.

Furthermore, there is *no* assumption in the ecological-adaptive model that the individual is seeking to conform to felt environmental pressures. Indeed, some organizations seek to encourage deviance so as to facilitate the permanent challenge to the organization itself – artistic communities are one example. Change within an organization sometimes occurs as a result of some deviance, e.g. new churches or sects are often established as a reaction of a minority group to a majority group within a particular religious community. The question of how deviant a person or group can be before they are isolated within the organization depends on the nature of the deviance and the structure and adaptability of the organization.

Key socialization features of the workplace

According to Marsden and Duff (1975), being employed creates certain rules about the structure of work experience. They suggest that work provides structure, pattern and shape to time and experience. For most people, work activities define the period of time we call a week, defines leisure in relation to non-leisure activities, defines holidays as opposed to work periods, gives economic meaning to the experience of illness and defines expectations for living standards. For a large number of workers – the majority according to Marsden's (1982) more recent account – the impact of these features of the workplace are essentially within the control of management (and, to some extent, are legally regulated): workers are powerless to shape or reshape these 'framing' rules. In work environments which are closed shops or highly unionized and regulated by collective agreements, the only power any individual has is to influence the bargaining process.

Just as the patterning of experience through the management of time serves to structure and shape experience and action in a work setting for the majority of workers, so the arrangement of power and authority within the workplace affects the extent to which individuals feel empowered or powerless as workers to make or influence work rules. For example, the extent to which an individual is permitted within working hours by both the nature of their work and the arrangement of supervision to forge relationships with others and to be adaptable is a function of power and authority in the organization.

The nature of organizational power and authority is the central subject of a great deal of organizational sociology (for a review, see Reed, 1985). What has often been missed, at least prior to Dawe's (1979) penetrating analysis, is the paradoxical attitude held by many workers towards power and authority: a great many workers are ambiguous to the power and authority exercised within their organizations. They have found ways of working within the framework of a 'truce' between themselves and those with 'authority'. If power and authority pose problems for workers who are seeking empowerment and a greater degree of social democracy in the workplace (Selznick, 1949), then the surprising feature of modern industrial societies is the relative absence of worker conflict and the decline of cooperative and democratic workers-controlled organizations. The very absence of conflicts and alternatives which are widely adopted suggests that individuals and groups have found a way of coming to terms (of 'trucing') with the way in which work is organized.

The truce between workers and the 'rules' within which they are required to work is not fixed and static, but is continually negotiated as a part of the ecological-adaptive process briefly described above: the worker engages in a conversation (Abrams, 1982; Dawe, 1979) through which he or she processes the rules of the organization and establishes a relationship within them (the truce), which assuages personal, moral and emotional issues with which the worker confronts those rules for him or herself.

Truces can take many forms. Reynolds (1976), writing about the operation of a truce between pupils and staff in a number of schools in a working-class former mining community, suggests that in a school in which the truce is strong, pupils are not punished for infringements of social rules (e.g. rules about smoking, chewing gum, wearing jewellery, drinking under age in a local pub, fighting in the street, not wearing uniforms, etc.) and are rewarded for the primary purposes of the organization (i.e. school work) rather than their adherence to social (and power-related) rules. Where such a truce does not exist or has broken down, pupils are punished for all and any infringement of social rules, with a concomitant reduction in academic performance. The key issue, according to Reynolds, is the acknowledgement by both sides in a truce of the primacy of task over rules, the need to recognize that all engaged in an organization have autonomy requirements and the importance of appearances.

In the context of the school, some pupils test the truce by certain kinds of rule-test behaviour (e.g. swearing in class, sexually explicit behaviour in play areas, etc.) and find that there are limits to the truce. They also find that these limits are regulated by both teachers and other pupils. Deviance as a means of testing rules and truces is not an unusual phenomena; indeed, it is to be expected (Pearson, 1975). What such actions achieve is a restatement both of the rules and a new beginning for the conversation between those with authority and those who are expected to obey the rules about the truce. Rule-testing is thus part of the process dynamic of truce maintenance.

From both the sociological and psychological point of view, the process of achieving and negotiating a truce within an organization (or part of the organization) does much to reconcile some competing themes in our understanding of organizational action. First, it establishes that all workers have some role to play in the construction of organizations. While some have more powerful parts than others, the way in which workers interpret and re-interpret rules and engage in truce conversations both among themselves and with others provides for an active role for all workers and for activity within the organization. Secondly, the fact of a truce permits the examination of practice – the difference between the formal organization and the organization in action. That is, using the idea of a truce as a framework for looking at the operation of rules permits the engagement of what might be termed social practice sociology (Harris, 1980). In particular, it permits the study of formal rules, rule behaviour, the attitude of the community towards rules, rules as sources of power and influence, the negation of rules through truce-like agreement (explicit or implicit), the symbolic and material resources utilized to maintain and interpret a truce, and the way in which appearances are maintained. Thirdly, the use of this rule-truce framework permits the study of both inter- and intra-organizational differences.

Just staying with this last point for one moment, Burns (1981, p. 3) has suggested that organizations are in fact complex clusters of communities:

> In practice, working organizations seem to be assemblies of relationships and activities which operate in accordance with several quite different sets of principles and presumptions – different rationales. They are, to use Levi-Strauss's useful word 'bricolages', composed out of secondhand bits and pieces of rather general notions of how to go about things, each having its own semblance of logic and its own semblance of legitimacy.

This implies that rules may be interpreted and experienced differently within different communities and that each community within an organization may have developed its own set of truce terms in relation to both rules and the power-control system that most affects them. That is, the nature of the relationships and adaptability within one community may differ significantly from that of another. What shapes these communities, according to Burns, is the tension and dialectic between the 'collaborative system' (what we have referred to as the truce) and the 'managerial structure' of the organization (the desire to manage and control through the exercise of power and authority).

By seeing organizations as rule-sets, primarily in terms of relationships and adaptability, it is possible to redefine the construct of power within an organization. While many have seen the construction of 'power' within an organization as a choice between a structuralist position (in which power is the collective property of social relationships and individuals are merely conduits for the exercise of social and political power implicit in the social situation) and an actionist position (in which power resides in the individuals' social position within the organization and rests heavily on their ability to exercise authority in interpersonal situations), there is now a third way of viewing power. Within the rule framework we have outlined here, power resides in the ability of all in the organization to engage in rule definition and truce formation. While the primary task of the organization remains important, the exercise of power concerns the means by which the primary task is achieved while maintaining appearances and recognizing that all engaged in the primary task have autonomy needs.

Learning the truce

Given this analysis, building as it does on that provided in Chapter 2, the question remains: 'How does an individual become aware of the implicit and explicit features of the truce within that part of the organization in which they will spend the greatest amount of time?'

A part of the answer to this lies in what Burns said: individuals use second-hand bits and pieces and general notions in shaping their actions in the workplace. Many of these 'bits and pieces' are tested and established in interactive settings (Gecas, 1981) and less often by indirect means (e.g. reading, training, storytelling). Some of these notions are derived from experiences in schooling and the family and from images of work derived from films, television, literature and journalistic accounts. Other notions are derived from positive comparison with the actions of peers and reference group members (Urry, 1972). This is one part of the answer to the question.

Secondly, the question returns us to the way in which the ecological-adaptive model of socialization introduced here works in practice. As a person enters an organization, they face decisions about which group or subgroup within their allocated community to join – they face decisions about relationship patterns. They will engage in a variety of activities which 'test' the relationship patterns that exist and enter into patterns of interaction which are seen by others as well as themselves as forming alliances and allegiances (Palazzoli et al., 1986). These alliances and allegiances may change depending upon issues, circumstances and the stage of development reached by the individual in the process of 'becoming' an organizational member – they are dynamic relationships, rather than static. In addition, these alliances and allegiances will not only differ in terms of the cast of characters, but also in terms of intensity or strength. What might be an alliance or coalition of convenience for one issue may be an alliance of substance and intransigence on another issue, permitting little (if any) adaptability when challenged or threatened by others.

Using the model introduced in Chapter 2, it is possible to look at the patterns of relationship and the strength of these patterns in terms of the 16 cells, and examine the nature of that relationship in terms of adaptability, both in terms of the subgroup characterized by these features *and* the relationship of this group to those who exercise power and authority in relation to it.

A third feature of the process of socialization concerns the process of enculturation – a process by which the individual comes to recognize the meaning of myths, metaphors and symbols while at the same time acquiring an ability to use the language of the organization and, by so doing, reflect upon its values. This process is critical to individuals becoming effective organizational members (Van Maanen, 1976). It is through this process that individuals develop their own rule-system of knowledge and beliefs about the organization and their part in it and an understanding of the meaning of this rule-system for their own development or containment. Notice the two levels of enculturation envisaged here: (1) the individual develops a rule-set which permits effective functioning in the organization, and (2) the individual has beliefs and values which place this rule-set in context – what might be referred to as the meta-contextualizing of rules. Describing these two levels, Harré *et al.* (1985) point out that one is very much concerned with action and appearances (level a) while the other is concerned with the personal meaning of these actions and appearances (level b). A person may appear inconsistent (and frequently does so according to Harré *et al.*, 1985, and Apter, 1982), but is seen to seek consistency at a higher level of experience (level b).

An individual engages in enculturation (also a dynamic process in which the individual is continually engaged throughout their organizational life) by means of a variety of processes, actions and endeavours. Van Maanen (1983) has identified seven pairs of strategies used to facilitate enculturation: (1) formal/informal; (2) individual/collective; (3) sequential/non-sequential; (4) fixed/variable; (5) tournament/contest; (6) serial/disjunctive; and (7) investiture/divestiture. Each of these pairs provides a frame for analysing the socialization processes within specific organizations. Some organizations are more active, explicit and coercive than others in promoting enculturation. Examples of such direct attempts of enculturation are found in the armed services (Ott, 1989; see also Stouffer *et al.*, 1949), police forces (Ott, 1989; see also Hazer and Alvarez, 1981; Van Maanen, 1975) and the US Forest Service (see Kaufman, 1960). Other organizations (e.g. private sector corporations, school systems, not-for-profit organizations) are not as direct in their attempts to achieve like-minded actions from their staff, but none the less employ strategies which seek to achieve this.

A fourth feature of the process of socialization occurs at moments of high anxiety or challenge – moments of truth – at which the belief systems and rules are thrown into high profile and need to be acted on in order to solve a problem, reduce anxiety, meet the challenge or achieve some combination of each of these three features. At such moments, individuals engage in what psychologists call 'active coping', defined as 'a person's attempts to manage (i.e. master, tolerate, reduce, minimize, etc.) internal and environmental demands and conflicts which exceeds his current resources' (Murgatroyd and Woolfe, 1982, p. 24). Often these demands exceed current resources (e.g. knowledge, skills, referral options, etc.) because the rules which are supposed to operate in such situations are not appropriate or no longer apply: the individual is required to improvise the rules or to create new rules. Doing so can make the person vulnerable within the organization.

We know little about coping in the workplace. The major coping studies have concerned personally significant life-events (especially the psychological effects of family and personal situations), only a small number of which relate to the work environment. While these studies provide some insights into coping and adaptability at a general level, they also make clear that the way in which individuals often cope with their personal life is different from the way in which they would cope with stress, anxiety, threat or challenge in the workplace (Folkman and Lazarus, 1980; Pearlin and Schooler, 1978).

In the work setting, the moments of truth that call up coping resources are often characterized by three constraining features.

1 An *incompleteness of information*: an individual or group are asked to act without access to all the facts and with little time to gather them.
2 An *inability to predict consequences with any degree of certainty*: while some aspects of consequences can be assessed, others remain in doubt, especially in the long term.
3 The *difficulty of formulating a criteria or value by which a rational choice between competing alternatives can be chosen*: not only is the situation imbued with uncertainty, there are no clear ways for assessing the alternatives.

In weighing choices of action, individuals give consideration to the current rules and their appropriateness, the consequences of improvising new rules or new interpretations of the existing rules, the utility of action for self and significant others, and the likely consequences in terms of approval or disapproval from others.

George (1976) has studied the process of reconciling these competing forces in the arena of political decision making with respect to US foreign policy in the late 1960s and early 1970s. He notes the importance of the personality of the senior officer associated with making a particular decision (style and appearance seem to be as important as substance in forming policy), and the extent to which a group within the organization are willing to suspend protocol and make porous boundaries which are otherwise impervious (i.e. suspend the rules, become more adaptable and change the basis of relationships so as to deal with one issue or complex of issues). His analysis of the Cuban missile crisis of October 1962 (and that provided by Sorensen, 1963, and Abel, 1966) is insightful in terms of the dynamics of the adaptive process. Accounts of business turnarounds, such as that at Chrysler (Gordon, 1985), are also revealing of this same process.

A fifth feature of the process of socialization is the need for the individual to experience and perhaps reconcile competing views of the organization and its culture from different communities within it. While they may be engaged in alliances and coalitions which cross community boundaries within the organization, these alliances and coalitions are unlikely to embrace the whole organization. There will be other communities holding views different from that with which the individual is familiar by different degrees. This 'many worlds' view of organizational culture seeks to indicate a further aspect of the dynamic of organizational life: it is rarely possible to understand the organization holistically, but individuals sometimes seek to do so. Equally, because there are 'many worlds' within one organization, the dialectic between the competing views of the organization (however marginally or substantially different these views may be) provide it with a cultural dynamic in which the individual is immersed, whether or not they wish to be.

Some individuals will seek to minimize the tension that they themselves may experience in living in this environment by creating contact-rules which define the frequency and nature of their relationships with individuals belonging to other communities within the organization. Others enjoy the 'many worlds' and move between them with ease, often acting as messengers between different communities within the organization and as agents of truce. Yet others seek to manipulate the dialectic in order to create situations which test the rules or the truce between communities. This complex view of organizational culture as both fractured and dynamic reflects the way in which organizations are experienced by many members (Gregory, 1983; Krefting and Frost, 1985; Lawrence and Lorsch, 1967b; Savage, 1982), even relatively modest-sized organizations. Those who are both disengaged and rigid may not see organizations culturally as anything but monolithic, which provides some explanation in itself why even small organizations may have many worlds within them.

A sixth feature of the socialization process concerns the need for the individual to reconcile competing images of themselves within the organization held by both themselves and others. As was suggested earlier, individuals may not act consistently in terms of their motivation for action. According to Apter (1982), individuals change from one motivational state to its opposite with some regularity. At one time they may be conforming and at another time they may be negativistic, even with the same people discussing the same topic. What changes is the way they experience the situation they are in. Individuals will seek to both understand and maximize the advantages to them of these reversals of motives, while seeking to minimize any negative consequences.

There are other tensions within the person which they will also seek to come to terms with. One critical tension is between the need for self-expression and autonomy on the one hand and the need to labour as a means of securing income on the other. While some individuals in organizations are able to combine self-expression and earning (at least for some of the time), most are not able to do so. This tension can be a source of significant frustration, and provides an insight into the impact of work-organization and work rules upon the personality development of the individual (Donzelot, 1981; Seve, 1978). It can be argued that the selling of an individual's labour power (knowledge, skills and understanding as well as physical powers) defines the exchange value and transaction costs between that person's wage needs and autonomy needs (Leonard, 1984). Because work occupies such a large proportion of waking time (approximately 35–40% for the average worker), we spend a great deal of time preparing for work (Sevé refers to this as the reproduction of labour power in social and leisure relations), which in turn inhibits and restricts the development of potentialities in the individual. The realization that work and preparing for work inhibit self-development can be a source of significant tension and distress for the individual: this has been at the heart of several feminist psychologies of personality development (explored more fully in Chapter 4).

While seeking to cope with changes of mood and mode within themselves, they are also seeking to adapt and cope with the way in which they are seen by others in the organization. For not all will view the same action or statement from the same person in the same way, especially those from different communities within the organization. This is more than having to come to terms with being 'labelled' as representative or indicative of the position of a particular subgroup: it is about accepting and recognizing that each individual is seen to exemplify multiple values and rule-sets within the organization, depending upon the position from which they are viewed – what the individual has to come to terms with is the impact of this realization upon their image of self.

A final feature of enculturation is the mastery of the technical tasks and unique procedures and language associated with their organization. Most organizations have developed unique procedures, processes and accompanying language in order to facilitate the achievement of the central tasks of the organization. Even experienced workers in an industry will need to learn the particular ways of doing things and referring to things when moving from one company to another. Even more technical learning takes place in moving from one country to another in terms of the way things are done. While this is a part of the enculturation process, it is a particular process and deserves to be highlighted.

Learning the truce involves the individual in seeking to master these seven features of socialization – bits and pieces, alliances and allegiances, enculturation, moments of truth, understanding and working with the 'many worlds' within the organization, self-reconciliation and technical enculturation. It also involves the individual in understanding the explicit and implicit rules associated with each of these socialization processes and making them a part of his or her work identity. Socialization is a process, not an outcome; a journey, not a destination; it takes time. What the person is doing is building a multidimensional rule-matrix for themselves which permits and supports effective functioning in the organization. As the rules change, the organization develops and people move out and into the organization, the rule-matrix has to be modified and adjusted to take these developments into account. The rule-matrix is itself dynamic, as these seven aspects of socialization are often in tension with each other and provide the individual and internalized challenges about their understanding of the organization and appropriate action.

Not all workers actively engage in the process of socialization in an intense way.

Many will seek the 'least-cost' (in terms of emotions and cognition) route to 'fitting in' and 'getting the job done' (Sandler, 1982). Others will take a differentiated approach and will work at some aspects of the seven processes just outlined, and pay less attention to others. Yet others will seek constantly to reconcile all seven features. Individual differences in the formation of the rule-matrix are not only to be expected, but to be seen as a key feature of the diversity of organizational life. From a rules perspective, the question is, what is the extent and nature of the rule-matrix in respect to these seven features which the person has developed?

Conclusion

In this chapter we have examined the nature of socialization processes in terms of rule-matrix formation within the framework of ecological-adaptability. In doing so we have again emphasized the central importance of cohesion (or relationship quality) and adaptability (see Chapter 2) and the dynamic and fluid nature of rules for action. The issue of gender as a basis for rule-matrix development and action will be examined in detail in Chapter 4.

Sex and the single organization: gender rules

Introduction

> Many organizations are dominated by gender-related values that bias organizational life in favour of one sex over another. Thus . . . organizations often segment opportunity structures and job markets in ways that enable men to achieve positions of prestige and power more easily than women, and often operate in ways that produce gender-related biases in the way organizational reality is created and sustained on a day-to-day basis. This is most obvious in situations of open discrimination and various forms of sexual harassment, but often pervades the culture of an organization in a way that is much less visible (Morgan, 1986, p. 178).

We do not need to live in an Orwellian nightmare to feel the intrusion of the organizational world; from the cradle to the grave organizations penetrate into the very essence of our lives. And those organizations, as Morgan above suggests, are far from neutral. Organizations play a vital role in the processes and outcomes of the gendering of persons. Gender is a cultural phenomenon, and organization – itself a cultural phenomenon (Denhardt, 1981) – is a central part of the cultural landscape. Organizations influence the development of gender in a number of direct and indirect ways. The language and roles of organizational life actively intrude into early childhood and may play a more direct influence in cases where children are involved in some forms of organizational life, e.g. church or playschool. Direct organizational experience comes very early into our lives in the form of school and then, often, a range of organized activities (e.g. boy scouts, girl guides). By the time we enter the workforce we have a fairly well-developed sense of organization, the broad rules that involve being an organizational member, and the expected relationship of men and women to these broad organizational rules.

Mastering the master rules*

Imagine that at an early age you are told that you will be going out into a world in which, in order to be successful, you will need to learn a series of ongoing rules. But, there is one caveat – in order to go out into the world you are required to wear a preselected pair of glasses. For some people the glasses will be blue-tinted but will not otherwise affect their vision. For other people the glasses will be pink-tinted but, in addition, will affect the ability of the retina to view the world the 'right way up'. The choice of glasses is predetermined on the basis of eye colouring – those with green eyes will receive the blue glasses, whereas those with brown eyes will receive the pink glasses. Those with the blue glasses will have to get used to coming to terms with ongoing rules through a blue haze. Those with the pink glasses will not only have to come to terms with ongoing rules as viewed through a pink haze but will have to make sense of those rules from the distorted perspective of an upside-down world.

As far fetched as this story seems, it strongly resembles what we actually do with real people in life. On the basis of genetalia we assign children a gender – or framework of master rules – through which they make sense of a whole series of other rules:

> Every Canadian child learn's society's rules of correspondence between sex and gender, as they pertain to self, others, and relations between self and others. The fundamentals of gender socialization are mastered surprisingly early. Preparatory gender learning begins in the first weeks and months of life (Mackie, 1987, pp. 115–16).

Marlene Mackie is referring to Canada, but she could just as well have been talking about the situation in any of the other major Western nations (Spender and Sarah, 1980; Oakley, 1981; Block, 1984).

The birth of a child is one of those events in which a whole series of gender rules is reconstructed and regenerated. Through phrases such as 'do you want a boy or a girl?', we remind the expectant parents and ourselves that there are different rule strategies to be engaged depending upon which biological features the child exhibits. At the most mundane level, we conform to a colour-coding rule in which we assign blue to 'boy' children and pink to 'girl' children. A series of other mundane rules follow: we provide the child with a gender-specific forename; we direct a series of pronouns (he/she, his/hers) and descriptors (e.g. little boy/little girl) at the child; we provide the child with gender-specific grooming (e.g. long hair for girls) and dress (dresses *vs* trousers); and we too often provide the child with toys that indicate gender assumptions (e.g. dolls *vs* tanks).

These and many other mundane rules present the child with a more or less stable framework through which they can begin to gain a sense of self and understand the world and their place within it:

* The use of the term *master* is a deliberate attempt to capture the cultural dominance of men over women (see Mills, 1988, p. 6).

The development of social representations of gender affords the child access to a centrally important and significant explanatory frame of reference. This system provides children with the means of interpreting actions and events according to the cultural rule system in which they live, as well as allowing them to participate in their culture by acting, thinking and feeling in ways that are comprehensible to themselves and others. In short, social representations of gender provide an important shared frame of reference which makes possible the exchange of differentiated signifiers between people; social representations of gender correspond to a semiotic code which allows children to participate in social life by providing an explanatory framework for the interpretation of their own and others' actions, thoughts and feelings (Duveen and Lloyd, 1986, p. 222).

Through the *looking-glass self* (Cooley, 1902) children come, literally, to see themselves as others see them. Others, in particular the primary care-givers, approach child rearing not only 'equipped with gender stereotypes and gender role attitudes', but with a concern with sex-appropriate behaviour (Mackie, 1984). At birth infant girls and boys are likely to be viewed differently, e.g. with girls viewed by their parents as smaller and softer and boys viewed as bigger and stronger (Rubin *et al.*, 1974). Parents develop and build upon these early images. The way a young child of around 6 months is handled and spoken to by its mother, for example, is likely to differ depending upon whether the child is a girl or a boy (Smith and Lloyd, 1978; Duveen and Lloyd, 1986). Similarly, in regard to play, studies of mothers' reactions to the gross motor movements of children indicate that they are more likely to encourage the activity of boys but to attempt to calm the activities of girls (Maccoby and Jacklin, 1974; Duveen and Lloyd, 1986). Fathers, similarly, reveal gender typing in their child-care practices. Here is one example from Garvey (1984, p. 195):

Girl (26 months)	**Girl's father**
(*playing with her teddy bear*)	
Teddy's a man.	What are you?
You're a boy.	Yeah, What are you?
A menace.	Yeah, a menace. Apart from that, are you a boy or a girl?
Boy. [*Laughs*]	Are you? What's Trevor?
	[*referring to the younger male sibling*]
A girl. [*Laughs*]	You're silly.

Referring to the example, Catherine Garvey informs us that 'playful misapplication of gender categorization becomes quite common around the age of three' (pp. 195–6). What is also interesting is the way in which the father is concerned – however playfully – to ensure that the child is sure of her gender.

In terms of ontological security, gender is surely a crucial, if not *the* crucial element:

Simply by being human, a strong need emerges before too long to make sense of its cognitive environment. Therefore, the child is an active agent in its own gender development. . . . In a sense, the self-motivated child socializes itself (Mackie, 1987, p. 124).

The child's own development of a gendered self is reinforced through a series of social interactions with adults who are concerned to reinforce their own sense of gendered self. The child develops a sense of self in a world rich in symbolism. Through language development, the child begins to learn the rules of gender labelling. At the beginning, the child's self-identification with a gender label may be no more complicated than accepting their own name' (Sherif, 1982). Eventually, they learn to distinguish the sex of other children on the basis of their names. As children grow they hear various labels being attached differently to the behaviour of boys and girls, e.g. what a *big, strong* boy; what a *pretty, little* girl.

Around the age of 2 or so, as children move from the 'preparatory stage' (Mead, 1934) of development to the 'play stage', they begin to acquire greater linguistic and role-taking abilities. In the process:

> The gender schema – the meaning of girl/boy as an organizing concept – becomes more sophisticated. Moreover, this cognitive development is accompanied by enhanced competence in gender expression . . . and, consequently, increased sex differences in behaviour (Mackie, 1987, p. 128).

EARLY ORGANIZATIONAL EXPERIENCES

Perhaps the earliest organizational symbolism that intrudes into the lives of many children is the different roles that their parents can be seen to play. Fathers, more often, are seen as 'going out to work', whereas mothers are viewed as 'staying at home'. These are powerful symbols that attach gender labels to paid work *per se*, to types of work, and to location within the wider society. By middle childhood, children tend to associate occupations with gender (Duveen and Lloyd, 1986, p. 227). The different domestic roles and expressive styles of fathers and mothers also help to instil important gender rules that can affect the child's eventual organizational destiny. In traditional households, for example, the child may learn to view cooking and cleaning as female tasks and more 'technical' tasks (e.g. household repairs) as man's work; the child may also learn to associate assertiveness with masculinity and demureness with femininity. As these become rules or expectations, they influence not only the person's occupational choices but their ability to do certain jobs; males tend to find it easier than females to undertake 'technical' work (Cockburn, 1985).

Kindergarten and elementary school are early organizational experiences that reinforce gender differences and help to shape future paid work-related destinations. Stephen Richer's (1979) study of Ottawa kindergarten classes provides a telling example to how teachers emphasize gender. He found that teachers found it convenient to line children up according to gender and to use gender as a motivator (e.g. 'the girls are ready, the boys are not'; 'who can do it the fastest, the boys or the girls?': quoted in Mackie, 1987, p. 133):

> During coordination exercises, commands were given by gender: 'Boys put your fingers

on your nose; girls, put your hands on your laps; boys, touch your toes.' When someone slipped up here, the teacher's astonishment sometimes took this form: 'Are you a girl? I thought all along you were a boy' (Richer, 1979, quoted in Mackie, 1987, p. 133).

In an Australian study of primary schools, Terry Evans (1988) provides examples of how teachers can help to develop the notion of sexuality in children:

> Dave Stone, a younger teacher at Linfield, played upon heterosexuality in his relationship with the girls. . . . He frequently used terms such as 'gorgeous', 'beautiful' and 'darling' when teaching the girls. Mostly the girls appreciated these references and he seemed to enjoy being the focus of female attention. Such exchanges serve to construct the importance of masculinity and femininity to the children; they are also a foundation for, and an expectation of, future heterosexuality (Evans, 1988, p. 108).

Evans goes on to provide another example, this time of the activities of a female teacher, Mary Thompson:

> When a child knocks on her classroom door during a lesson . . . the child is greeted with the words, 'Come in if you're good looking.' The child slides back the door to be confronted by the children and teacher gazing at him or her. Mary Thompson then asks the class, 'Is he/she good looking?' The class respond with mixed yells of 'yes' and 'no' (Evans, ibid.).

Evans comments that the behaviour of Stone and Thompson, although intended as harmless fun, is 'predicted on romantic, heterosexual relationships; relationships which are the foundation of traditional Western family formation and which lead to the deep gender divisions of adult life' (Evans, 1988, p. 108).

Notions of femininity and masculinity permeate school activities and the preparation of children for adulthood. Assertiveness, introduced in the home environment as a sign of masculinity (Duveen and Lloyd, 1986), is further refined in the school environment. Boys are expected to behave in an assertive manner, whereas girls are expected to be passive. This is reflected in such things as school activities. Girls tend to engage in play activity, whereas boys tend to become involved in games (Richer, 1984). The difference contains potentially enormous consequences for later entry into organizational life. In playing competitive games, boys become familiar with complex notions of rules and rule negotiation, roles and role taking, teamwork and leadership – in short, 'a learning environment for the cultivation of skills later demanded by bureaucratic work organizations' (Mackie, 1987, p. 137). Girls, on the other hand, 'prefer turn-taking activities, where each girl skips or bounces a ball'; consequently, they are frequently engaged in watching what it going on. Female play is more often individual, dyadic or confined to small groups, it is quieter and more restricted in body movement, and it is more likely to be carried on indoors (Mackie, 1987, p. 135). The general outcome appears to be that:

> Boys emerge from the Game Stage with the ability to take the role of the generalized other, to comprehend the abstractions of social relationships. Girls, on the other hand, have become more and more proficient in taking the role of significant others (Mackie, 1987, p. 137).

In short, boys are more prepared for the 'public' world of work and girls are more prepared for the 'domestic' world of the home. This fact is, of course, reinforced in a number of more explicit ways (Spender and Sarah, 1980). Again Evans (1988) provides a useful example. His descriptions of the activities of a particular female teacher reveals a number of points where gender lessons are reinforced, in this case unwittingly by the teacher who is particularly anxious to encourage sexual equality in her pupils. The teacher, Marily Carmody, teaches in a context of male authority, the principal and deputy principal both being male. On the particular day under discussion, she arrived late due to car problems. Describing her difficulties to the children she tells them that she 'had to telephone for an "RACV man" to fix it'. She then gets the class prepared for a television programme concerning people who work at sea. The maritime work, as depicted in the television programme, is 'replete with images of strength, toughness, bravery and excitement' (Evans, 1988, p. 98); there are no women in the programme.

It is not surprising that various studies of boys and girls report that children tend to mirror adult stereotyping of certain occupations according to gender – with men being seen as the dominant public figures and women the dominant private figures (Duveen and Lloyd, 1986, p. 227).

Before they leave primary school, many children have developed a pretty good sense of the working gender rules of organizational life:

> I reckon women should stick to the housework. . . . So the Dads get the money and the women don't have to get the money. They can just stay at home and get the Dad's money (Carl, Australian primary schooler, quoted in Evans, 1988, p. 103).

Evans (1988) provides a number of examples:

Tanya (grade 3) speaking about women as panel beaters:

> The men would have to go over it again. The women might scratch it and not paint it properly. They probably could do it, but the men could do it better (Evans, 1988, p. 102).

Leila, Tanya's friend, speaking on the building trade:

> If a girl came and did building with the boys she would be crazy. It's a man's job. Girls can't lift fifteen bricks at once, boys could (Evans, ibid.).

Matthew, speaking on female opportunities:

> Ladies, they don't have a good wide choice of jobs as men do (Evans, p. 103).

Pearson (1985, p. 329) cites similar evidence from the USA:

> Children as young as three years old recognize that jobs are sex-typed. When children between the ages of three and six were asked the traditional question, 'What do you want to be when you grow up?', the boys tended to choose adventure careers, including police work, sports areas, etc; while the girls selected quieter careers, such as nursing. Seventy per cent of the boys and 73% of the girls chose stereotypical careers for themselves. In addition, 14% of the children felt that it was not proper for men to feed babies; 20% felt that it was not proper for men to pour coffee for seated women; and 49% felt that it was not proper for women to be repair people.

Despite the relative stability of the symbolism of gender rules throughout childhood, adolescence brings new pressures to the individual and, one might add, new possibilities:

> The question 'Who am I?' takes on special urgency in adolescence. Pubescent changes (a body growth rate equal to that of early childhood and the new addition of genital maturity) disturb the sense of self established in childhood. The adolescents' task is to reestablish identity: to refine 'a sense of who they are and what makes them different from everybody else' (Santrock, 1984:425). Gender identity, an understanding of oneself as a sexually and socially mature male or female, is a fundamental component of this refined identity (Mackie, 1987, p. 147).

Unfortunately, such attempts at an understanding of self all too often take place in the context of a school system in which traditional sexist attitudes are predominant. Young men and women are encouraged, trained and directed towards sex-typed occupations (Spender and Sarah, 1980; Pearson, 1985; Griffin, 1985). Here Christine Griffin (CG) interviews two young women about their experiences with school careers officers (CO):

> *CG*:   Did the careers officer give you any information on what you wanted to do, the ambulance driving?
>
> *Sue*:   No, what they told me, I already knew from the school. They told me to stay on in school and do a secretarial course [laugh]. The CO was trying to put me off the idea of the ambulance service because he said it's mostly all men, but I'm not worried [laugh].
>
> (Moorcroft, white fifth former)
>
> *CG*:   Have you ever thought of jobs like engineering, mechanics, that sort of thing?
>
> *Lorna*: I thought of mechanics [laugh]. You have to train for years, if you do it wrong you're out.
>
> *CG*:   Have you seen the careers officer?
>
> *Lorna*: Yes but they said they don't think I'd got much chance because there's lots of boys going for the job but I'd rather do mechanics anyway [laugh].
>
> (Moorcroft, Afro-Caribbean fifth former)

By and large, young women are prepared throughout the school system to be 'feminine', and when they come to search for their femininity – to clarify their identities – they are overwhelmed with images of domesticity; of love, marriage, motherhood, etc. Work images, particularly those associated with technical and skilled work, sit uneasy with traditional views of womanhood.

Likewise, young men are prepared to leave school as 'men'. As these young men search for their identities through the lens of masculinity, they will often find that they are expected to be life-long workers, to be anti-feminine (e.g. not to show emotion, to be successful and outdo others in countless ways), to be aggressive, to be sexually active and forceful (e.g. to be the initiator of sexual activity) and to be self-reliant (e.g. tough, cool, in control: Doyle, 1985, p. 91). This preparation advantages males over females in a number of ways but it also creates a web of rules (of masculinity) that influence the way male activity is constrained and male identity constructed within and by organizations, experiences that are not wholly positive (Willis, 1977). The problem with mastering the rules of gender is that very few of us get it right and, hence, suffer the consequences of somehow feeling that we are incomplete. For girls, like those quoted above, there may be the dilemma of wanting to do certain kinds of male-associated work while retaining some image of femininity. For those boy unable to fully conform to the ideal rules of masculinity, life can be embarrassing and cruel:

> I tried to believe my parents when they told me I was a boy, but I could find no objective proof for such an assertion. Each morning during the summer, as I cuddled up in the quiet of a corner with a book, my mother would push me out the back door and into the yard. And, throughout the day . . . I thought of the girls sitting in the shade of porches, playing with their dolls, toy refrigerators and stoves.
>
> There was the life, I thought! No constant pressure to prove oneself. No necessity always to be competing. While I humiliated myself on football and baseball fields, the girls stood on the sidelines laughing at me, because they didn't have to do anything except be girls (Julius Lester, reflecting on his childhood, 1976, pp. 270–71).

Even those boys that do manage to 'live up to' the expectation of manhood can find the rules hard to maintain. Here is an excerpt from the life of actor Kirk Douglas and his reflections of masculinity and its consequences. He tells the story of how, at the age of 7, he attempted to assert his masculinity over his older sister Kay:

> As we left the store, Kay and I would play a terrible game of 'who's going to pick up the meat?' First, there would be an argument about who was going to carry the meat. I insisted that she carry it, she insisted that I carry it. The package of meat would drop to the sidewalk and we'd both walk away. It was a game of nerves: who was going to break first and go back and pick up the meat? . . . We'd walk along, each waiting for the other to break. I ran back.
>
> It was my attempt, even at that young age, to try to assert what I suppose is male chauvinism. My father was rarely around to help me, and here I was trying to assert myself over all my sisters by making Kay pick up the meat. I wanted to feel like a man: I could go out and get the meat, but the woman should carry it. A man is supposed to be strong, to be active, he must do things. He must provide and protect the womenfolk. What a lot of shit that is. All the movements now are encouraging women to be stronger. I'd like to be in a movement for men to be weaker. The right to be weak, to be passive, the right to do nothing. Why do men always have to be strong? We're not, and we know it. Why do we force ourselves to play those roles and why do men and women force those roles on each other (Douglas, 1988, pp. 12–13).

In the workplace, masculinity in the form of machoism often serves to mask the difficulty and danger of manual tasks (Willis, 1979). Upon entering manual-type jobs, young men can often find that to 'fit in', to be 'one of the boys', they need to display a toughness and bravado towards the work that discourages them from complaining about such things as safety conditions and the physically exacting nature of the job (Davies, 1989).

Gender rules at work

The pervasiveness of gender rules throughout the education system has been refined over time, accompanying and reflecting sexist organizational developments generally. The interrelationship between organizational development and gender rules has helped to create a sense of reality in which the 'organizational world' – the world of work – appears to confirm sexist ideas acquired at school. For those leaving school the workplace confronts them with a myriad of gender rules, often conveyed in vivid imagery. The association of organizational power and maleness, for instance, is constantly made evident in a vast number of ways. The fact that the ownership and control of most private companies, throughout the Western industrial world, is in the hands of men (Bilton *et al.*, 1983; LaSota, 1985; Hisrich and Brush, 1986) is witnessed through such things as media focus and reports on rich and powerful men, pulp biographies of corporate executives (e.g. Iacocca: Iacocca with Novak, 1984; Sculley: Sculley with Byrne, 1987) and local knowledge of major owners and executives. Likewise, the 'masculine' character of organizational power throughout the public domain is made clear through images of male-dominated governments, civil services, judiciary and police forces (Spencer and Podmore, 1987b); male-dominated armed forces (Isaksson, 1988); male-dominated universities (Tancred-Sheriff, 1987); a male-dominated medical profession (Lawrence, 1987); and a male-dominated media (Crean, 1987). Through a myriad of images we are confronted with the understanding that 'it's a man's world' and that within that world it is men who are the leaders, the managers, the executives; it is men who are the professionals; it is men who are skilled and technically minded; and it is men who are scientific.

Images of females differ markedly from that of males. The powerful imagery of the male organizational world provides the major lens through which females are viewed, serving at one level to suggest the absence of women from positions of importance and, thus, at another level, to cast images of women at work in a contradictory light. We are constantly reminded that females have a more tenuous relationship to work than males. As we saw from the previous section, young women (and young men for that matter) are directed to sex-typed jobs and too often receive pressure to resist even the notion of considering work that is perceived as the traditional preserve of men (or of women). Most images of females at work tend to reflect (and thus reinforce) women's location within a narrow range of occupations (Peitchinis, 1989) – occupations that more often than not mirror the kind of domestic role that women are expected to conform to (e.g. serving, caring, cooking, etc.). Images of those women who have managed to break the mould are rarely presented in a positive and straightforward manner. Female executives rarely hit the headlines and even then the focus is generally on the media's perceived shortcomings or failures of those women, e.g. Mary Cunningham's departure from Bendix,* and the arrest of Leona Helmsley.†

---

* Sexual innuendo and jealousy forced Mary Cunningham to resign as chief executive of Bendix (see Cunningham with Schumer, 1984).
† Leona Helmsley, the owner of a large US hotel chain, was found guilty in late 1989 of tax evasion.

The dominant image of females is one of domesticity. They are presented as periphery to the world of work (Feldberg and Glenn, 1979). Even where women do make it into the higher echelons of corporate life or into non-traditional areas of work, the remarkableness of such achievements serve to remind us tht it *is* a man's world; the attainment of individual women being viewed against a measure of how far into the male domain they have successfully ventured.

As young men and women enter the organizational world, they do so in the shadow of a series of understandings about the nature of men and women, their relative worth and their differing relationship to paid work. Those understandings come to play an important role in the construction of organizational reality. These 'extraorganizational rules' (Clegg, 1981) help to shape entry into and expectations within organizations.

Gender rules at work, as we shall discuss later, vary according to the type of organization involved, its history, its location, the people involved, etc. But many of the rules are a variation upon a number of more central gender rules.

MEN IN A MAN'S WORLD: CREATING AND SUSTAINING ORGANIZATIONAL MASCULINITY

The general 'it's a man's world' rule is expressed in different ways and forms depending upon different organizational settings. For example, the expectation that males conform to some rule of toughness may be expressed as aggressive competitiveness among the higher echelons of the corporate world, as cold unemotionalism within the office world, and as machismo among blue collar workers. Different workplaces, occupations and organizational locations highlight different aspects of supposed masculine traits, e.g. male protectiveness and police work, aggressiveness and military service, strength and steel-making, leadership and management, skill and engineering. Stuart Clegg (1981) has suggested that the very way in which different forms of organizational masculinity are shaped leads to different forms of rules of control. For the unskilled worker, the work process is controlled through the expression of machismo. The worker, not wanting to appear 'soft', views 'difficult, uncomfortable or dangerous working conditions' not directly as 'employer-imposed hazards ... but as challenges to masculine prowess' (Livingstone and Luxton, 1989). In the case of assembly line workers, control is also achieved through the technology itself, i.e. through the conveyor belt the work rate is determined. For the skilled worker, control is often achieved through encouragement of male pride in technical knowledge. This form of control has its limits, however, given that knowledge also bestows power; hence some employers have been concerned to increase workplace control through the process of deskilling (Braverman, 1974). In regard to office workers, organizations often seek to control the work process through a process of incorporation, i.e. seeking to 'involve' the employees through such projects as company outings, sports and social clubs, company images. In recent years, the popularity of the notion of 'corporate culture' can be related to organizational searches for new ways to involve employees in the company (Lee and Lawrence, 1985).

For those in the process of becoming young men, school and community served as the all important introduction to gender rules but paid work stands before them as the finishing school. Here they learn to be 'men'! The pervasive nature of gender rules ensures that resistance to some of those rules can lead to a failure to 'fit in' at work, and characterization as something less than a 'real' man. On the shop floor, joking is often used to remind people of the masculinity expectations of the workplace's culture. The major forms of joking centre around three rules of sexuality: (1) the ideal, typical – real – man syndrome, (2) definitions of males as not-female; and (3) the normalacy of heterosexuality. Here a male steelworker describes what it takes to do his job: 'You got to be tough and you got to be willing to take risks. You got to be strong. It takes a real man to work here' (Livingstone and Luxton, 1989, p. 252). Within the workplace of that steelworker, the work itself is characterized 'as feminine and to be conquered': 'It's a real bitch', 'give her hell':

> Similarly, malfunctioning machinery is called by derogatory terms for women – bitch, slut – which often have explicit sexual connotations. Disliked bosses are similarly described by terms which cast aspersion either on their masculinity and sexual ability – wimp, cream puff, dick – or identify them with negative female terms – bitch (Livingstone and Luxton, 1989, p. 253).

Similar expressions are recorded throughout studies of male workshop culture (Willis, 1979; Collinson, 1988; Davies, 1989). Alongside jokes, other aspects of the workplace culture remind people about the culturally expected rules of sexuality. Pictures of nude women, sexually suggestive horseplay, and bragging about sexual activity all form part of the cultural context within which male self-identity is formed:

> Each worker, over time, establishes a strong self-identity inthe shop. . . . The self-definition includes such things as his manner and type of dress, morning ritual of arrival, dressing, having coffee, checking his machine, etc. It also includes his identity as a (skilled worker) – the level of skills and capabilities he asserts. . .
> The use of jokes to deny an asserted self-identity is a major theme. . . . The individual's position in the hierarchies of sexual prowess, physical strength, intelligence, or skilled (worker) is a basis for much of the mimicry (Boland and Hoffman, 1982, pp. 376–7).

The stark use of sexuality in the shop-floor environment can be contrasted with the organizational life of the office and professional workers. Here – in the world of bureaucracy – expectations of masculinity have been shaped around notions of rationality. A male entering this area of work for the first time soon comes to learn that the rules of this particular game involve appearing to be detached, logical, unemotional and absorbed in the work process. In this world, the hidden gender rules stress that such things as sexuality have little apparent place. The male bureaucrat and professional derive their sense of 'manhood' from milieux that associate rational behaviour with masculinity. Interestingly, conformity to the rules of bureaucratic behaviour serves a double function in the definition of self-identities – serving to lend to the male bureaucrat and air of superiority in contrast to, on the one hand, supposedly less rational blue collar counterparts (Stearns, 1979) and, on the other, supposedly irrational females. The added power of the hidden aspects of gender rules is that they often stand for something else, e.g. being detached is valued at one level as a male trait but at another level as a necessary professional act; being logical is at one and the same time a sign of masculinity and of scientific behaviour. The hidden rules become subsumed under a myriad of formal, written rules – turning bureaucracy into a male discourse and a system for attaining defined ends at one and the same time (Ferguson, 1984). Hence males whose behaviour appears to fall short of the ideal-typical rationality are in danger not only of being characterized as effeminate but also as unstable, unreliable and unprofessional.

The duality of masculinity and rationality contained within bureaucracy is both complementary and contradictory. At one level, bureaucratic behaviour denies sexuality, insisting on the 'desexualization of the organization' (Burrell, 1984), while at another level it confirms male dominance. Thus, bureaucratic environments often consist of series of images of denials of sexuality alongside open displays of sexuality:

> While I was working in marketing the men in the office began to put pornography up on the walls. First there were Page 3 type pin-ups and then the sort of pictures you get in porn mags. In one they even used a pin-up as a dart board and used to throw the darts in her tits. I told them that I didn't like it but it wasn't until I realized that I wasn't getting anywhere that I decided to complain to Personnel. They wrote a memo asking for all the 'girlie' pictures as they called them to be taken down (female market researcher, quoted in Root, 1984, p. 89).

Entering the world of management and/or the executive levels of the corporate world, males find that they are expected to exhibit male-associated characteristics of toughness, competitiveness, aggressiveness and control (Stearns, 1979). These concepts make up part of our understandings of management – a concept that is riddled with notions of masculinity (Brener et al., 1989). The world of the organizational leader is replete with masculine-associated images. John Sculley's book on his corporate experiences, for example, is full of descriptions of organizational conflict and references to 'Boot Camp' and to 'Cola Wars'. Iacocca, likewise, describes his corporate experiences in terms of masculine images of 'The Showdown', 'Aboard a Sinking Ship', 'Trial by Fire', 'Public Man, Public Office', 'A Bittersweet Victory'. In Robert Lacey's (1986) account of the Ford company, we get a graphic account, complete with male metaphors, of corporate life:

> Lee Iacocca's paranoia went into overdrive in the latter months of 1977. Telling Marian Heiskell a story about how once, by accident, he had bumped his head on a car door, he informed her that, at the moment the accident happened, he had assumed he had been shot.
>
> On the other hand, there certainly was somebody persecuting Lee Iacocca in the mid-1970s, and it was a pretty big somebody at that. Henry Ford II wanted to drive his

president right out of the Ford Motor Company, and Iacocca's accusation . . . that his employer was engaged in 'salami-slicing' – cutting off one part of his body after another until Iacocca would finally be driven to admit defeat – is not that far from the truth. . . . It did not prove so easy, however, as Lee Iacocca fought back . . . Guerrilla warfare escalated to open confrontation as 1977 advanced. . . . 'It was hell,' remembers Tony Feaheny, then vice-president in charge of engineering. 'There were Iacocca's men and Caldwell's men. They would come to you separately, trying to advance their own projects, trying to get ammunition'. . .

It was open war, and Lee Iacocca had no illusions as to who his real enemy was. He could skirmish with Philip Caldwell as long as he liked, but if he wanted to come out the serious and ultimate victor, he would have to set his sights higher than that. Lee Iacocca would have to take on Henry Ford II himself (Lacey, 1986, p. 646–7).

Another strongly gendered characteristic of executive life is the expectation that family life comes second to the organization; often executives devote most of their waking life to company activities:

I think my family life has suffered. My children were really raised by my wife because I was working eighteen hours a day, and when I wasn't working I spent time with other people in the organization. I was devoted to this place seven days a week (a retired CEO, quoted in Aird *et al.*, 1988, p. 102).

Interestingly, that CEO had been in charge of the same company that the steelworker quoted at the beginning of this section was employed at! There are at least two gender rules implicit within the form of commitment expected of executives: (1) that men, as opposed to women, are expected to spend their whole working lives in paid work, and (2) that, more likely than not, this dedication to organizational duty will be achieved with the aid of a wife (Kanter, 1977).

One's spouse is key. It is the essential factor in the whole thing because the person is part of team. We have meetings and conferences where you are expected to bring your spouse with you. She plays a role in trying to build a team spirit, and goes out of her way to meet the wives of others and also the other people in the business (Edward Crawford, CEO of Canada Life, quoted in Aird *et al.*, 1988, p. 102).

Once again the heterosexual rule is implicit in such sentiments. And corporate leaders do tend to act if that heterosexuality rule appears to be being breached. In 1987, for example, the Canadian airline Wardair attempted to prevent one of their male attendants from wearing an earring. The company argued that it would be bad for business because passengers would associate the earring with homosexuality and, through that, AIDS.

It is hardly surprising that, through words and deeds, new executives, managers and employees alike are expected to conform to the image of dedication to work, the competitive spirit, and a 'healthy' dose of heterosexuality. Even the metaphors that managers use to motivate employees are usually laden with male-associated team sports or military images (Riley, 1983).

Alongside organizational experiences at work there are a vast array of clubs, pubs and other organized activities which help to sustain certain images of masculinity.

From pubs and bars for working men, through service clubs such as Rotary, Kinsmen and Lions for professional men, to Men's Clubs for the rich and powerful, a variety of organized activities and venues offer males the opportunity to escape family responsibilities, to share and develop male cameraderie, and to develop important work-related networks (Rogers, 1988). While a number of men may resist the draw of such activities, others may feel

> obliged to join in the system whether they like it or not. One man admitted: 'My reason for drinking beer is to appear tough. I heartily detest the stuff but what would my pals say if I refused. They would call me a cissy' (Rogers, 1988, p. 27).

The rules of gender conformity is socially pervasive and often hard to avoid if not resist!

When women enter

For males, gender socialization at work can be a long and difficult road, particularly for those who are not inclined to be tough, competitive, aggressive, non-emotional or macho. Things are particularly difficult for homosexual males who are often required to conform to dominant heterosexual values. But for females, the workplace too often presents them with a hostile, or at best contradictory, environment in which narrow, restrictive and discriminatory images of women are fostered.

The two most pervasive rules that women encounter are Rule 1: It's a man's world; and Rule 2: It's a man's work. Rule 1 serves to inhibit females from consideration of entering the world of paid work in any permanent sense. Rule 2 serves to discourage females from considering employment in a whole range of jobs, industries, occupations and professions.

Rule 1 is enacted through such phrases as 'a woman's *place* is in the home'; through statements such as that by a large US cinema chain, which in the 1980s advertised its part-time job opportunities as 'suitable for moms'; through corporate brochures which highlight male employees; and through organizational symbols such as logos (Large, 1988) and names, e.g. longshore*men*, railway*men*, fire*men*, the Work*men's* Compensation Board, The Independent Order of Odd*fellows* (Meissner, 1986).

Often enough a female does not have to be told about Rule 1; she has only to look around. Take the Canadian town of Yellowknife for example. The capital of the North West Territories, Yellowknife is famous for such things as mining, bush plane aviation and oil exploration. It is very much a 'man's town' as its history books make clear:

> A lot of stories are told about Yellowknife's early years . . . [but] most of those early prospectors, miners, pilots, police and administrators and *the women who cooked and washed clothes and sometimes even prospected with the men* were too busy to write about their lives (Jackson, 1984, p. 5: our emphasis).

Historic accounts of Yellowknife, however accurate, indicate that men played leading roles across a range of activities – politics, exploration, aviation, local government office, and so on – while women were confined to a few:

> By 1939, there were many women in town. They worked as waitresses, nurses, and drivers of the water taxis. . . . There was a women lawyer and a woman teacher (Jackson, 1984, p. 8).

The existence of a woman lawyer is one of a small handful of exceptions, but even then domestic associations manage to creep in. In regard to the 'NWT's first female prospector', Vicky Lepine, we are informed that:

> Once in town, she washed clothes during the day and dishes at night at the Wildcat [cafe]. In the summer of 1938 she went out prospecting in the bush, staked her claims, and sold them for $3,500.
>
>   She bowled over the writers who came to visit the town in 1938: 'She is the best man in the bush, the best friend, the best chum. Where there is heavy work, she is the most capable, the hardest working, the most helpful. . .' (Jackson, 1984, p. 8).

Even the town's only female Member of Parliament is explained away in terms of the 'Evita syndrome', i.e. explaining a women's achievements in terms of her husband's position:

> Few people who cross the Mackenzie river . . . on the 'Merv Hardie' ferry know that Mr. Hardie was a Member of Parliament for the North West Territories for three terms. After Mr. Hardie died in 1961, his wife, Isabel, was elected Member of Parliament *in his place* (Jackson, 1984, p. 20: our emphasis).

A similar story can be told in regard to many of the small towns and cities throughout the industrial West (Fig. 4.1). In the large cities the situation, although much more complex, none the less gives a strong impression of male dominance of organizational life.

The power of this rule (Rule 1) is witnessed in the fact that it is conveyed as historical fact, a situation that has existed since time immemorial. Yet the real history of female workplace activity is far more complex. Women's presence within the workforce has fluctuated over time. Women have alternately been heavily involved in paid work and repulsed from the workplace depending upon the needs of employers, the fears of male employees, the relative strength of female organizations, and dominant social values (Strumingher, 1979; Ryan, 1979; French, 1985).

This rule takes its toll on some women's sense of self in the world:

> I stayed at the hospital for two years until I got married. My husband made enough money as a carpenter that I didn't have to work outside of the home. We had three boys so I had plenty to keep me busy in the house (quoted in Schroedel, 1985, p. 102).

For those women who none the less attempt to overlook or bypass the rule, someone usually steps in to remind them of its significance:

Fig. 4.1 Gender opportunities in a northern Canadian town.

POLITICS

types of office	# of female office holders	comment
M.P. (Federal)	0	Only two female office holders
M.L.A. (Provincial)	0	–
Reeve (County)	0	–
County Manager	0	–
County Councillors (×8)	1	–
Mayor (Town)	0	–
Municipal Manager (Town)	0	–
Town Councillors (× 6)	1	–

LAW

types of office	# of female office holders	comment
Lawyers (5)	1	Only 1 female in any branch of the law.
RCMP Sgt	0	–
RCMP officers (5)	0	–

BUSINESS

# of business (# unkown ownership)	# solely/co-owned by females	comment
181 (12)	21/21	Approx 26% of businesses involve female owners, of which half involve joint ownership usually with husbands.

TYPES OF FEMALE BUSINESS(#)

type of bus(#)	type of bus(#)	comment
Flowers and Fashion (8)	Hairstyling and Beauty (7)	The majority (64%) of female businesses involve traditional female-associated activities and symbols, e.g., cleaning, beauty and diet, fashion and flowers, preparing and serving food. Wholly male-owned businesses reflect a more diverse range of activities.

Fig. 4.1 *continued*

type of bus (#)	type of bus (#)	comment
Cleaning (3)	Hotels and Restaurants (4)	–
Financial and Career Consulting (4)	Arts and Crafts (2)	–
Farming stores (3)	Oilfield and Garage related (4)	–
Construction and Hardware (3)	Diet (1)	–
Confectionary (1)	Health (1)	–

EDUCATION

types of office	# female office holders	comment
President (University)	0	Only 3 females in positions of authority – all in the University, and only 1 at a senior level.
Vice President (Univ. ×3)	0	–
Governing Cncl Chair (Univ)	0	–
Other University Managers (10)	3	–
High School Principal	0	–
Elementary School Principal	0	–
Superintendant of Schools	0	–

RELIGION

type of office held	# female office holders	comment
Rev (United Church)	0	There are no female pastors in this community.
Pastor (Church of God)	0	–
Pastor (United Pentecostal Church)	0	–
Rev. (Christian Fellowship)	0	–
Father (Ukranian Greek Orthodox Church)	0	–
Pastor (Evangelical Lutheran Church)	0	–
Pastor (Missionary Church)	0	–
Rev. (Anglican Church)	0	–
Pastor (Church of Jesus Christ of Latter Day)	0	–
Pastor (Alliance Church)	0	–
Deacon (Ukranian Catholic Church)	0	–

Fig. 4.1   *continued*

SPORTS

# clubs	*# female office holders*	*comment*
14	7	Women hold 50% of the leading positions – being responsible for such sports as gymnastics, the horse club, minor ball, badminton and curling. Men take the lead in hockey, curling, fast ball.

SOCIAL & COMMUNITY CLUBS

# of clubs (of which leader is unknown)		*comment*
65 (14)	25	Women play leading roles in just under 50% of the clubs. Leadership and membership tends to be concentrated in such clubs as auxiliary branches of male clubs (i.e., the kinettes, the lionesses, the Royal Canadian Legion Ladies Auxiliary) and in such activities as dance (4 clubs), community care and childhood services (6), arts and crafts (2).

HEALTH

type of office held	*# female office holders*	*comment*
Medical Officer of Health	0	Of 26 leading positions in the health system only 6 (24%) are females and 2 of them occupy traditional female-associated positions (i.e., nursing)
Health Unit (CEO)	0	Female CEO was removed by the Health Unit Board.
Snr. Public Health Inspector	0	–
Public Health Inspector (×2)	0	–
Hospital Chair	0	–
Hospital Administrator	0	–
Director of Nursing	1	–

Fig. 4.1 *continued*

types of office	# female office holders	comment
Hospital Chief of Staff	0	–
Extendicare Administrator	0	–
Extendicare Director of Nursing	1	–
Medical Health Clinic Manager	1	–
General Practitioners (×5)	0	–
Veterinarians (×2)	0	–
Chiropodist	0	–
Dentist (×2)	0	–
Pharmacists (×4)	3	–

> My dad works over at Bangor in the ammunition depot, so I asked him what it would be like working with all men. The only thing he told me was if I was gonna work with a lot of men, that I would have to *listen* to swear words and some of the obscene things, but still *act* like a lady, or I'd never fit in (female truck assembly line worker, quoted in Schroedel, 1985, p. 92).

Failure to heed Rule 1 can sometimes lead to marital stress:

> I mean my husband left me. He was very jealous of my working with a lot of men and used to follow me to work (female truck assembly line worker, quoted in Schroedel, 1985, p. 96).

> My first husband did not want me to go to trade school. He felt like maybe I was going out with somebody there. He accused me of having physical relationships with men (female electrician, quoted in Schroedel, 1985, p. 191).

Rule 2 signals that if women do enter the public sphere of organizational life, then their activities should be restricted to work that is in line with their 'female qualities'. Again, a woman does not have to be told what work opportunities exist for her. She learns to associate certain organizations/professions with men (e.g. mining, engineering, Rotarians) and others with women (e.g. nursing, cleaning, elementary school teaching, day-care board). Attempting to cross the line into areas not usually considered 'women's work' can be difficult, because men are often the organizational 'gatekeepers', manning both the physical (e.g. security) and occupational (e.g. recruitment) barriers. Recruiters are most likely to employ those who resemble their own characteristics – usually white, middle-class, male (Abella, 1984; Silverman and Jones, 1974; Dubeck, 1979). But when she crosses the line and attempts to enter 'non-traditional' work, she is often forceably reminded of Rule 2:

> I had a lot of fears about being a woman with so many men. The scariest thing was the sense of being alone. It was real obvious to me . . . that the men weren't overjoyed about my being there. . . . For a long time I wasn't allowed to do certain types of jobs. I had to fight hard for that. Some of the men would take the tools out of my hands (female pipefitter, quoted in Schroedel, 1985, p. 20).

The situation is hardly less different for middle-class as opposed to working-class women:

> . . . [the law] is a career based to some extent on competition and hustling and hitting people on the head and so on. Old fashioned people like me tend to think that's more the masculine rather than the feminine role (male barrister, quoted in Spencer and Podmore, 1987a, p. 115).

Within the context of the broad rules (1 and 2), there operate a series of interconnecting rules, rules that are at times complementary and at times contradictory. Underlying Rule 1, as we have seen, there are rules about male behaviour, about masculinity. There are also rules about femininity. Women may be expected to be 'motherly', 'wifely', 'sisterly', 'sexy', 'daughterly', and so on. How any woman is classified and expected to behave will, of course, depend upon a combination of organizational rule features.

Some organizations, for example, put a premium upon assumptions of female domesticity. The medical profession is a case in point. Nursing – with its emphasis upon care and nurturance – has been developed as a specifically female vocation, and in the process discouraging females from other areas of medical practice (Ehrenreich and English, 1973). In case we ever miss the point, the domestic rule is embodied in the very naming of nursing categories, i.e. sister, matron. Those women who become doctors often find that they are channelled into certain specialisms associated with the 'female function', i.e. gynaecology and obstetrics, family planning, psychiatric problems and paediatrics (Lawrence, 1987).

Other organizations put a premium on sexuality. The airline industry seems to illustrate this point best. Since the inception of airline attendants, sexuality has been used to sell air travel (Nielson, 1982). Attendants, until recently, we almost exclusively female. The air hostesses, as they were called, were generally recruited for their looks and were trained in the art of grooming, serving and smiling (Hochschild, 1983). The selling of sexuality remains a serious problem within the airline industry. Whereas some of the established airlines have modified their practices in the recruitment of airline attendants, some of the newer airlines still insist upon attempting to control their employees' sexuality. Wardair, for example, was the subject of a Canadian Human Rights Commission case in the late 1980s. The company was accused of recruiting only apparently attractive, slim and young women and then laying down a set of written and informal rules that dictated the way these young women were to look and even the kind of underwear they were expected to wear. Similarly, Singapore Airlines make extensive use of sexuality throughout its advertising, and most likely its recruiting, practices:

> The airline has an ideal image of a stewardess. So, I would say that discrimination begins even before the applicants are selected. . . . Women are usually discriminated against their age, weight, height, outward appearance and marital status. Usually the airline prefers women between the age of 18 and 25, single, slim, attractive, tall and between a certain weight. As for the guys, they do not need to have all these qualities (interview with former male airline steward of SIA).

Expectations of women as domestic in nature or as sexual objects is rife throughout organizational life and can be witnesed through such things as male attitudes of protectiveness and paternalism; sexist male talk, joking and innuendo; symbolism in the form of graffiti, 'nude calendars', and pin-ups; and sexual harassment. Sexuality, in one way or another, serves to sustain negative images of females; to control female employee behaviour; to put females 'in their place', i.e. at the bottom layers of organizational hierarchy; and to encourage and excuse sexual harassment.

More than any other aspect of gender-rule behaviour, sexuality is intricately bound up with a sense of identity and that's what makes it the most invidious, most pervasive and most destructive aspect of organizational life. In the following example, we can see the multi-layered form that the sexuality rule takes. In the excerpt below, a female plumber describes her attempts to fit into a male environment:

> [When] this new supervisor arrived [every] joke he told was either racist or sexist. I don't remember a lot of them, but one that stuck in my mind was, 'My wife didn't mind that I was bringing home scalps, but not ones with holes in them.' Something on that order – pretty gross. It really infuriated me – the idea of scalping a woman – a woman's cunt, as he called it. . .
>
> Another time . . . I was under a sink undoing a nut with a basin wrench. . . . He said, 'Get off your cunt and go get that.' I was shocked. . . . Finally, I started screaming, 'You fucking asshole!' But I didn't feel any better. He just smirked like he'd gotten what he wanted. It's so fun to get women fired up. What really hurt me was this guy standing around that I had been working with and felt really good about, and he didn't say a damn thing. . . . None of the other men would have said something like that to me, but with him they felt like they had to stick up for another guy. . .
>
> The union hasn't been much better. . . . One time I ripped some porno of a wall, a poster-size crotch shot of a woman, and the apprenticeship coordinator said I should have called him in, but that I had to understand I was in a man's trade, and that the men shouldn't have to live by my rules. . .
>
> The last thing that happened was that there's a Rigid'Tool calender. . . . They show women in sleazy bathing suits looking like they're almost fucking tools, and these calendars appeared in our apprentice classrooms. . . . So for three nights a week, three hours a night, you're supposed to look at the front of the class at the blackbord with that calendar on it (quoted in Schroedel, 1985, pp. 59–61).

The harsh, constant, graphic and violent nature of the sexist reality that that female plumber had to endure is regrettably not unusual (Martin, 1987; Kramer, 1989; Gutek, 1985; Hearn and Parkin, 1987). The day-to-day outcomes of the activation of the sexuality rule lead to reinforcement of female feelings of insecurity and inadequacy (Gutek, 1985), fear and depression (Hearn and Parkin, 1987), anger, hurt and pain (Schroedel, 1985), stress (Cooper and Davidson, 1982), and other psychological disturbances, (Busfield, 1989) and guilt:

> 'Susan' was a 19-year-old former intern in 1979 when she contacted Crommelin about finding a job. He took her to dinner, then insisted on stopping at his apartment. When

she accompanied him inside, she says, he immediately knocked her down and raped her. Ashamed and confused, she let him drive her home (quoted in Kramer, 1989, p. 50).

Thus, even at the point of rape, some women can come to feel that it is they who are somehow guilty.

For homosexual women they are caught between double rules of *hetero*sexuality. Here a female sailor poignantly describes how organizational rules can create a sense of reality that has a profound effect on the self:

Nine times out of ten there was a lot of competition among the women for the men's attention. If a man appeared to get along with or like another woman, the first woman would flirt with him, try to be more attractive and make sexual inferences. . . . The whole situation was very difficult for me for many reasons. Until I came out I had a terribly hard time dealing with my own conscience because I was not being honest about my sexuality, and that was difficult because I had been an active, functioning homosexual for a while. It was hard for me. . . . There was nobody to reinforce my visions of what was going on. I felt very alone. These people were functioning in a very different reality than I was. There was nobody there to tell me that I was okay, that I wasn't sick, and that I wasn't strange. You know, I didn't see any happy homosexuals around me, and therefore it was difficult for me to maintain any kind of positive self-image (quoted in Schroedel, 1985, pp. 85–6).

The strength of organizationally generated negative images of female sexuality is likely due to the link between organizational processes and the generation of male identity. Masculinity, as we have already seen, is built into the way certain jobs and occupations are understood. Thus, when those understandings are challenged male identity is also likely to be challenged:

Society recognizes construction workers as being very macho and virile. When a woman comes along who's five foot three and a hundred and twenty pounds and can get in there and do their type of work, it's a blow to their ego, a real shock. So the men are threatened by it (female carpenter, quoted in Schroedel, 1985, p. 38).

[When] a woman comes on a job that can work, get something done as fast and efficiently, as well, as they can, it really affects them. Somehow if a woman can do it, it ain't that masculine, not that tough (female pipefitter, quoted in Schroedel, 1985, pp. 20–21).

Such problems are not isolated to a few men. In the late 1980s, a poll in Canada claimed that a combination of factors that included 'the advance of women through the workplace' appeared to be 'undermining the self confidence of Canadian men' (Fiber, 1986).

While sexuality rules question the very being of females, technical and bureaucratic rules question their competence and abilities. Children, as we have already seen, are taught to believe that it is men who have the competency to fix things, operate and maintain machinery, that *skill* is a male quality:

I probably had some fears about being qualified, about being able to do thing as well as a guy, since you've been told all your life that guys are better at fixing things (female plumber, quoted in Shroedel, 1985, p. 55).

Alongside that teaching there has been history of socialization in which females have been discouraged from involvement in anything 'technical' (Cockburn, 1985):

> Some women just don't have the brute strength to [be a machinist], but I think the biggest *dis*advantage is from the moment they're born. Somebody's gonna raise them to be a 'woman' – not to get their hands dirty, not to go out with Daddy and his hammer and nails. She's not gonna develop the mental skill or agility. I know I have that problem with hand–eye coordination. . . . I think if I had been taught when I was a little girl that it was okay for little girls to play baseball, I would have developed that hand–eye coordination. There are other things that men take for granted. Boys, when they are growing up, learn how to fix their cars, learn what a feeler gauge is or how to set spark plugs, how to understand mechanical levers. Women don't have that advantage, no matter how much training they get (female machinist, quoted in Schroedel, 1985, p. 131).

Within the confines of the bureaucratic workplace competency is judged in terms of such things as logic and rationality and, as these are features attributed to males, it is hard for many women to be seen as fully having such qualities. Male professionals who display logic and reason are more likely to be viewed as competent than females who exhibit the same characteristics. Either those characteristics will be overlooked where a female is involved or they will be attributed to some fault in the woman's character (Spencer and Podmore, 1987b). This has consequences for promotion and leadership – making it less likely for a female to be promoted to the higher ranks of management (Harriman, 1985).

Together, various gender rules cohere in the construction of organizational cultures in which women are more or less discriminated against, and come to view themselves and be viewed as more or less positive (Mills, 1988a). The 'more or less' in each case will depend upon the nature of the organizational culture involved.

Discourse, confusion and resistance

So far we have concentrated on the powerful impact of largely negative gender rules. There is little doubt that such negative rules play a dominant part in the lives of most women and men and, as such, along with the needs of simplicity, they have received our full attention. However, it should be clear that gender rules are never simply received, nor are they unilinear, or completely one-sided. We do not all face the same range of gender rules; some people experience a far greater exposure to negative rules than others do; people resist some rules and accept others.

Growing up, a child's experience of sexist attitudes may be mediated through the anti-sexism of her or his parents, through activity in organizations which attempt to discourage anti-sexist behaviour, and through their own reflexive thinking and refusal to be pigeon-holed.

How very different will have been the experiences of a child exposed to a church organization in which women and homosexual males have been ordained as opposed to that of a child who has been exposed to a traditional church organization. Or take, for example, experiences in the Girl Scouts. American Girl Scouts in the period up to the 1980s were encouraged to learn cake baking and other cooking skills, sewing, and a range of other activities that mirrored the domestic roles they were expected to occupy. Girl Scouts of the 1980s, on the other hand were taught to be aware of sexist attitudes:

> The handbook for girls aged six to eleven, for example, [included] a game in which scouts clip from magazines pictures representing 'men's work', 'women's work', and 'both' – or at least, the handbook corrects itself, 'what some photographer or artist showed as these kinds of work'. What do you think – are they right? Ask yourselves, 'Who says so?'.
>
> Girl Scouts now read just about every activity in vocational terms. Motherhood is considered a 'career' choice – listed in the new Girl Scout book *Careers to Explore*, right along with Gas Station Attendant and President of the United States. And . . . in the same book, six-to-eleven-year-olds are invited to diagram their career potential: listing a favourite toy, for example, as well as who uses it and what job it helps to prepare for (Flick, 1983).

Throughout social life, children will be confronted by a series of gender rules experienced through a number of social institutions and practices (e.g. the law, the political system, the church, the family, the education system and the media). But those rules will likely not be experienced as a monolithic system. Each set of rules will be 'located in and structured by a particular *discursive field*', i.e. competing ways of giving meaning to the world and of organizing social institutions and processes (Weedon, 1987). Within any given discursive field, not all discourse will carry equal weight or power and thus some rules will come over more clearly or authoritatively than others but, non the less, competing rules may be heard. If we take our church example it can be seen that traditional understandings of gender will predominate, but the alternate rules about the role of women and the character of homosexuality will also find a place in the rule experiences of members. The law provides another useful example. Children of the 1980s and 1990s come to learn that certain forms of sexist behaviour are unlawful (e.g. sexual harassment) and that there is legislation and legal bodies concerned to promote such things as equal pay, equal opportunities and to discourage sex discrimination. They may also come to learn, however, that the legal pronouncements, practices and institutions predominantly express more traditional sexist practices. Lord Denning, for example, in a 1977 British Court of Appeal case argued, in relation to an action brought under the Sex Discrimination Act, that it would be:

> Very wrong if the statute . . . were to obliterate the differences between men and women or to obliterate all the chivalry and courtesy which we expected mankind to give womankind, or that courts must hold that all the elemental differences of sex must be disregarded in the interpretation of an Act of Parliament (quoted in Khan and Mills, 1988).

Even where such attitudes are not expressed, the outcomes can trivialize the problem. Often equity programmes have little legislative teeth or will-power to back them up (Tancred-Sheriff, 1988). Damages for sexual discrimination can be small. In the UK, for example, industrial tribunals are bound to award meagre sums for 'injury to feelings' in sex discrimination cases (Khan and Mills, 1989). The whole issue of sexual harassment is fraught with legal and organizational inaction, confusion, and leniency (Mills, 1988a; Khan and Mills, 1990). The newspapers throughout Europe and North America are sadly full of stories of the sexist behaviour, remarks and sentencing of male judges (e.g. York, 1989), lawyers (Spencer and Podmore, 1987a) and police officers (Martin, 1987).

Faced with a variety of gender rule experiences it is not surprising that children question 'the way things are'. The school system itself, of course, consists of competing discourses. Alongside the dominant sexist values, there are a number of competing understandings that offer different views of reality – this may be due to the efforts of a particularly enlightened headteacher, group of parents, trade union group or a feminist group. The alternative voices may not win out but it is likely that they will at least muddy the waters a bit, raising questions about the legitimacy of certain rules. The fact that children have to be reminded constantly of the rules (e.g. about preparation for 'men's work' or for 'women's work') is testimony to the fact that they are continually questioned and probed. Thus, when children come to enter the world of work, they likely do so with a sense of the traditional 'way that things are' but also with a sense of questioning or of unease that things might be other than how they are.

Each organizational reality will itself more or less confirm traditional gender rules depending upon the nature of the organization (e.g. steelmaking *vs* civil service), its location (e.g. Yellowknife *vs* Ottawa), the tasks to be undertaken (e.g. engineering *vs* computing skills), the legal constraints that it works under (e.g. mining *vs* atomic energy), the character of the workforce (e.g. homogeneous, traditional working class *vs* heterogeneous workforce), and the management (e.g. authoritarian *vs* participatory) and type of people involved (e.g. placid *vs* questioning). None of the examples are meant to signify better or worse situations but, rather, likely differences in experiences and competing discourses. Steelmaking, for instance, has always been traditionally male employment – being located in homogeneous working-class areas, drawing upon traditionally male-associated skills, managed by traditional authoritarian managers, and involving people who, seeing in the work a sense of masculinity, left aspects of their employment unquestioned. When females enter this industry, they usually find traditional rules – both at work and in the community – being raised in a forceful manner. However, it may well be that the sharpness of the situation, coupled with the fact of female presence in the steel mills, leads to a more open acceptance of a need to rethink the rules:

> My wife works in a factory . . . I had a woman on my crew. I don't think she made any difference. I think it's *natural*. I think what we've done in the last 40 years is unnatural, in the fact that it was an all-male environment. Steel making is not, doesn't require a great amount of brawn. It's pretty well a push-button business now (male steelworker commenting on the entry of females into the industry, quoted in Livingstone and Luxton, 1989, p. 264).

In the civil service, by way of contrast, employment tends to be sited in a cosmopolitan centre, drawing upon a heterogeneous workforce, undertaking a number of tasks not traditionally or clearly male associated, and with a workforce that is both placid (due to its bureaucratic environment) and questioning (due to its relatively high levels of education). Yet the evidence suggests that in such environments sexist rules – cloaked in rationalizations – become subtle but none the less pervasive (Walters, 1987). In the British higher civil service, for example, there exists a stress upon such things as rationality and meritocracy, which are viewed 'in universal terms and from which gender-based qualities or experiences are judged to be absent'. In effect, while appearing to support equality of opportunity, this set of rules affords competency to those most able to conform to their expectations while ignoring the fact that males are better placed to conform. Hence many women share the following experience:

> I, like many others . . . was keen to continue working after the birth of my first child but doing less hours than I had done. The department was not interested – there is a widespread dislike of such arrangements at all levels (female civil servant, quoted in Walters, 1987, p. 25).

In terms of location, research indicates that some organizational operations draw upon and reinforce traditional gender rules (Mills, 1989a). In southern US mills towns, for example, textile companies often build their organizational control on traditional patriarchal familial forms, employing whole families to work in the mill, in each case, under the supervision of the male head (Blauner, 1967). Interestingly, *Savvy* magazine devoted an issue to the question of location. Of 10 major US cities they rate Seattle 'the best city for women' and Atlanta the worst. Seattle gained points for the fact that 'women's share of managerial and executive jobs stands at 43.6%; that Washington State has an equal rights amendment; that women's share of state legislature ranks 4th in the US; that state and city contracts guarantee pay equity; and that state law guarantees maternity leave'. For Atlanta it is only noted that 'women's share of managerial and executive jobs stands at 37.2% and that a woman is the mayor of suburban Marietta' (*Savvy* Magazine, 1988).

Organizational tasks reveal the same kind of problems that we discussed above in relation to organizational character. Certain tasks, such as engineering, have traditionally been associated with males and thus have been closed to females. Other, newer tasks, such as computing, are less gender-typed, although it has become clear that even here certain-higher level work has become much more the domain of males (Kramarae, 1988). The ambiguity, none the less, provides the grounds of a contested terrain. In some organizations, an ambiguity of the gendered nature of tasks can raise a number of questions about the validity and viability of gender rules. The whole field of women-in-management provides a prime example. Managerial tasks have traditionally been viewed as male-associated, drawing specifically from masculine traits. Where females occupy positions of authority and power it provides examples of competing discourses and thus competing understandings of gender rules (Agocs, 1989). Sylvia Rhys (1988) provides a different kind of example. In her study of nursing in the British health system, she argues that the modern nurse (traditionally female) is expected to combine the female-associated trait of 'caring' with the male-associated trait of 'mastery' in that the nurse is expected to 'look after patients within a bureaucratically administered context'.

Legal constraints intervene in organizations in different ways and hence their potential to influence gender dynamics varies. For example, in Canada, the Employment Equity Act requires that companies doing a certain amount of contract work with the Federal Government establish equity hiring targets and practices. One might expect that within such companies there would be some moves towards employment equity and, hence, the strengthening of the equity discourse within those companies. Companies that are not affected by this kind of legislation might be less inclined to take any steps (Agocs, 1989). The law can also intervene in more negative ways. Until recently, legislation actually prevented females from working in some industries and sectors, e.g. mine working. Even where prohibitive legislation has been lifted it can leave a legacy or residue of feeling within the organization. Patriarchal feelings of protectiveness and safety concerns for females do not simply evaporate in the face of legislative changes. US miners, for example, may come to accept that women can do the job without losing a sense that it is not right – on safety grounds – for them to work in the industry. In a different way, as the movie *Silkwood* suggests, the secrecy of the atomic energy industry can mitigate against women (and men), questioning the work – even to the point where conditions are life-threatening.

As far as employment equity programmes go, management can play a central role. A 1984 Canadian Royal Commission on employment equity found that Crown corporations which were more successful in initiating coherent and consistent employment equity programmes were those in which senior management had made a clear commitment to such changes (Abella, 1984). *Savvy* magazine has reported on the effects of management upon opportunities for female employees. Highlighting 'The Best Companies for Women' the magazine argued that certain managers made a considerable difference. The Payless Cashways company, for example, was rated highly:

> it would be hard to find another group of enthusiastic women who are as convinced that 'the sky's the limit' when asked how far they can go at their company. And these are women selling lumber, screwdrivers, faucets, plumbing fixtures and fertilizers. . . .
>
> David Stanley, CEO, came to Payless in 1980 and shook the cobwebs out of a chain that was run by men who had spent most of their working lives selling building materials. One way he's made an impact is by hiring smart, sassy women. A former anchorwoman on the evening news now handles sales promotions. And Susan Stanton, who formerly ran the country jails in Kansas City, is the senior vice president for administration and corporate planning. She is also an officer of the company, as are Linda French, general counsel and secretary, and Jean Warren, assistant treasurer (Dusky and Zeitz, 1988).

Barbara Garson (1979), a decade earlier, made similar points about contrasting organizational locations.

And then there are the ordinary people who make up organizations, those who are required to follow and carry out the rules. Far too often men and women accept gender rules as 'normal' and thus acceptable. Far too often the force of the gendered reality in which they exist compels people to comply, to avoid 'making waves'. But from time to time people question gender rules, they find alternative ways, they ignore what they don't like, and they resist. Sometimes action is individual:

> [In] general the guys were really good . . . [they] never gave me the feeling that I was taking the job from a man or food from his family's mouth. If I needed help, I didn't have to ask, if they saw me struggling, they'd come right over to help (female truck assembly line worker, quoted in Schroedel, 1985, p. 92).

And sometimes it is collective, like the men of the Duarte (California) Rotary Club who, in 1977, took the unusual step of admitting female members. Or the General Faculties Council of the University of Lethbridge (Alberta, Canada) who, in 1989, adopted an institution-wide 'non-sexist language' policy.

Sometimes action takes the form of the development of alternative subcultures. In a tobacco factory studied by Pollert (1981), female workers developed a shop-floor culture of their own which flew in the face of the prevalent rules which presented a view of women as individualized, objects of sexual gratification, things to be controlled. The female shop-floor culture, on the other hand, encouraged the women to work together and help each other out, to break some of the more formal rules of control and collectively to resist – through joking and verbal abuse – the sexist remarks and actions of male employees. Similarly, Lamphere's (1985) study of a Rhode Island apparel factory found that the development of a women's culture on the shop floor helped the women workers to resist some of the harsher elements of sexism. Such actions, as both Pollert and Lamphere observe are, however, only partial forms of resistance and may also generate adaptation and consent.

Supportive action against sexism is, of course, often sought through membership of feminist groups outside of the organization and, increasingly, within the organization. For example, in Schroedel's (1985) account of women in non-traditional jobs, a female carpenter describes how she belongs 'to a group called Women in the Trades' in order to feel supported, to gain sympathy and understanding and 'to share the feelings of accomplishment'.

Finally, resistance within organizations can sometimes be dramatic:

> Finally one day . . . this young man who had been hassling me ever since I started, was standing around with the other guys looking at a dirty magazine. . . . They were all giggling and brought it over to me. I said, 'I've had enough of this shit', and pulled the centerfold out of the magazine and burnt it up with a cigarette lighter. That kind of stopped then, and as new people would come in they would get the story, so I didn't have to deal with a lot of that afterwards (female pipefitter, quoted in Schroedel, 1985, p. 20).

Sometimes it can be in the form of legal action:

> In Los Angeles, supermarket checker Hallie Edwards walked into a storeroom and found a manager exposing himself and groping for her breasts. . . . In Cambridge, Mass., college freshman Helene Sahadi York went to her Harvard professor's office looking for research help. She found an instructor determined to kiss her. In New York, typist Doreen Romano's boss offered her a raise if she would sleep with him. When she refused he fired her. In each case the women did not ignore the incident. Edwards and Romano won out-of-court money settlements; York's professor received a university reprimand. 'Men are learning that women are not going to take this kind of behaviour', says Romano's lawyer (Newhall *et al.*, 1982, p. 345).

Sometimes it can take the form of organizational action. For example, the then newly formed Northern Canadian Rotary Club, was prepared in 1988 to risk its charter to admit women members. Throughout 1989, various Canadian women's university teams abandoned male club names such as the Lancerettes, the Robins or the Lady Rams: the University of Windsor women's team dropped the 'ettes' from their team name to become Lancers like the men; women at Carleton University, Ottawa dropped the name Robins in favour of sharing the male team name – the Ravens; and the Ryerson Polytechnic, Toronto women's teams dropped the prefix 'Lady' and became Rams like the men. And sometimes action takes the form of strikes, demonstrations and widespread political action.

The outcomes of various actions – passive or questioning – contexts and processes results in a series of competing discourses out of which certain gender rules come to dominate and mark one organizational culture out from another. Most organizational cultures are marked by sexist rules but they are rules that constantly need to be maintained in the face of challenge and questioning. Gender rules, as with any other set of rules, are outcomes rather than fixed, immutable entities.

— 5 —

Institutionalization and change

Introduction

All human activity is subject to habitualization. Any action that is repeated frequently becomes cast into a pattern, which can then be reproduced with an economy of effort and which, *ipso facto*, is apprehended by its performer *as* that pattern. Habitualization further implies that the action in question may be performed again in the future in the same manner and with the same economical effort . . .

Habitualized actions, of course, retain their meaningful character for the individual although the meanings involved become embedded as routines in the general stock of knowledge . . .

Institutionalization occurs whenever there is a reciprocal typification of habitualized actions by types of actors . . . . Reciprocal typifications of actions are built up in the course of a shared history. They cannot be created instantaneously. Institutions always have a history, of which they are the products. . . . Institutions also, by the very fact of their existence, control human conduct by setting up predefined patterns of conduct, which channel it in one direction as against the many other directions that would theoretically be possible (Berger and Luckmann, 1984, pp. 70–72).

Tradition heal thyself (graffiti on an Edmonton wall, Alberta, 1989).

This chapter is about the relationship between institutionalization and change. The organizational literature is rich in accounts of organizational construction and development. It is equally rich in accounts of change. What is lacking is accounts that attempt to relate the two features of organization in a direct and explicit fashion: the work of Hinings and Greenwood (1989) is a rare exception. Just as sure as change is a regular feature of organization, so too is institutionalization; you cannot have one without the other.

THE RULES OF CHANGE

Change refers to perceived and felt differences, that a situation is made or somehow becomes different. Within the management and organizational literature, this broad use of the concept is evidenced through references to numerous factors, influences or pressures that organizations face: new technology (Morgan, 1988); takeovers and mergers (Sales and Mirvis, 1984); executive succession (Gilmore, 1988); power struggles (Medina, 1982); market fluctuations (Peters, 1989); and changing employee attitudes and expectations (Dyer, 1984). The view that changes of this type and magnitude have implications for organizations has given rise to a body of literature specifically focused upon *organizational change*. Within that literature, *organizational* change tends to have a specific meaning, usually referring to the need for a restructuring of the organization's rules of control, i.e. the literature is not so much interested in advising which markets to enter or what technology to adopt, as in suggesting ways to adapt the organization to facilitate new market strategies or the introduction of new technology. This has given rise to a number of *rules* for change, with organizational/management theorists competing to have their rules enacted.

The central and unifying rule throughout the literature is that change is an inevitable feature of organizational life. Daft (1986, 291) goes so far as to argue that 'change, not stability is the natural order of things'. Thus, organizational leaders are encouraged to prepare themselves to master (Martel, 1986), implement (Lippitt *et al.*, 1985), manage McLennan, 1989) or ride the waves (Morgan, 1988) of change.

There are a number of assumptions that are implicit within this rule. In varying degree it is suggested throughout the literature that change is irresistible, that it is desirable, that it can be dealt with, and that issues of change should be addressed to those in charge of organizations.

The managers of change

By focusing upon managers the organizational change literature addresses a specific set of control issues, viz. how to alter organizational practices in line with the perceptions and change strategies of those in charge. This helps to lay the basis and set the tone for the other assumptions. It helps us to ignore such questions as whether change is in the best interests of other organizational members, and/or non-organizational members. The takeover of Wardair, for example, resulted in a considerable number of redundancies throughout the company and has raised concern among Wardair customers that service standards will drop, and among passengers generally that a weakened competition (Canada has once again only two major airlines) will lead to fare increases.

Irresistibility

Much of the literature assumes that change is an objective phenomenon that organizational managers need to plan for or react to (Legge, 1984). The underlying assumptions here are largely related to the issue of who change is addressed to. It is assumed, for example, that a failure to adapt to change can lead to such things as a lack of competitiveness, organizational inertia, a failure to grow, organizational contraction and death, and a threat to the power and position of the controllers themselves. On the contrary, there is the suggestion that the effective management of change can in itself enhance organizational power through the subsequent success of the organization. But change is a matter of degree and by underlining a *need* for change strategies we are creating a rule that ignores such questions as whether, or to what extent, change can be ignored. To use another movie example, *Witness* reminded audiences that there are some organizations which have chosen to ignore change. The so-called Pennsylvania Dutch communities in the USA have chosen to ignore many of the changes of the twentieth century. In a similar way, many of the Hutterite communities throughout Canada, while accepting some technological changes, retain the basic dress and way of life of more than a century ago. Indeed, one need not look further than the Catholic Church to find many examples of a resistance to change that is embodied within that organization's value system.

Desirability

As has already been shown, organizational change is felt to be necessary either to fend off potential disaster or to achieve the aims of growth and development. The presentation of change as desirable, however, tends to mask one or two crucial questions. For instance, who – if anyone – is changing the organization likely to benefit? In the Wardair and GEC cases discussed above, not all parties to the organization can be said to have benefited. How much change is desirable? In some industries and organizations the pace of change is relatively slow and that slowness of pace may well be an important feature of the organization's survival. To take the case of the Catholic Church, for example, its slowness of pace probably helps to sustain its philosophy, image, and a necessary sacredness of its institutions. Interestingly, in other areas of organizational and management theory, it has clearly been established that many organizations faced with relatively certain and non-complex environments do not necessarily need to face up to the question of change in quite the same way as organizations that operate within dynamic organizations (Burns and Stalker, 1961; Ouchi, 1980).

Charles Handy (1983) indicates that the very features that help to structure an organization's culture may determine the extent to which they need to react to change. The 'power culture', for example, is one based upon resource power and built around a strong central figure. Handy cites smaller entrepreneurial companies, robber baron companies of the nineteenth century, trading companies, finance companies and some trade unions as examples:

> This organization works on precedent, on anticipating the wishes and decisions of the central power sources. There are few rules and procedures, little bureaucracy. . . . These cultures . . . have the ability to move quickly and can react well to threat or danger. Whether they do move in the right direction will, however, depend on the person or persons in the centre; for the quality of these individuals is of paramount importance in those organizations and the succession issue is the key to their continued success (Handy, 1983, pp. 178–9).

This can be contrasted to the 'role culture' which, to all intents and purposes, is

Handy's name for bureaucratic organization. The strength of the role culture is the ability to act and process rationally and uniformly:

> The role organization will be found where economies of scale are more important than flexibility or where technical expertise and depth of specialization are more important than product innovation or product cost (Lee and Lawrence, 1985, p. 118).

Adaptability

The idea that managers can somehow be reactive if not proactive contains a number of interesting assumptions. Again this assumes that change is a fact, an object, a thing to be confronted. But, as John Child (1972) has effectively argued, change relies to a considerable extent on the *perceptions* of key decision makers. If management do not perceive the occurrence of change, then, within certain limits, change will not be a problem for that organization. For example, with the rapid development of computerization, a number of company leaders were concerned not to be left out in the cold. They purchased expensive systems which, in many cases, did not alleviate organizational problems but added new costs. Those managers could have chosen to ignore the current computerization trends (at least in the initial stages) without cost to the organization.

On the other hand, management perceptions can be the cause of change. It may be that a group of managers come to the conclusion that the company could do better if it was reorganized. The perception of a need for change can occur without the existence of any significant external pressures.

Even where external pressures are felt or perceived to be a problem for the organization, it is not clear that they can be addressed at all, let alone addressed effectively. In the context of an economic slump, for example, some organizations may be able to take advantage of the change while many others may not. In terms of political change, the Communist government of Poland, for example, appeared totally unable to adapt. It felt that the only way to meet the challenge was by ending its monopoly of power. In terms of market forces it has been suggested by some theorists that certain changes may be beyond the ability of the organization to deal with – that changes in consumer behaviour may lead to an organization being 'selected out' (i.e. closed) of the market (Hannan and Freeman, 1977; Aldrich, 1979). These assumptions constrain us not to ignore the role of perceptions in change and the complex relationship between organizational reality and societal change.

Institutionalization and change

The concepts *change* and *organizational change* are often confused within the literature with the result that change is counterposed to stability. Martel, for example, begins his book on mastering change by informing us that:

> We live in a world of change, yet we act on the basis of continuity. Change is unfamiliar; it disturbs us. We ignore it, we avoid it; often we try to resist it. Continuity, on the other hand, is familiar, it provides safety and security . . .
> The new approach is to recognize that change is natural and to be expected, and that continuity is unnatural and to be suspected (Martel, 1986, p. 11).

This statement has several weaknesses. First, as we have argued above, it is problematic in its uncritical fostering of a belief in the inevitability and desirability of change. Secondly, it fails to recognize that substituting a focus on order with a focus on change amounts to substituting one institutionalized rule with another. Thirdly, the intent of such statements is to encourage the development of organizational structures that are more capable of responding to change, i.e. to counterpose one form of continuity with another! In other words, in dealing with change *per se* we do not, as Martel does, need to focus upon the contrast between institutionalization and change but rather upon the specific character of the institutional rules.

Despite a tendency to conflate change and organizational change, much of the related literature is primarily concerned with questions of organizational structure and restructuring. Focus is upon devising (or altering) structures that assist organizations to be more flexible in 'the face of change'. Change strategies can include restructuring to encourage greater employee commitment, more flexible working practices, improved motivation, and so on. This can involve structural redesign, including job rotation, job enlargement, job enrichment, quality circles, autonomous work groups and a lessoning of formal rules and procedures. Or it can involve human process techniques, including sensitivity training, survey feedback, process consultation, team building and intergroup development (Robbins, 1988). It can also involve such things as retraining schemes or the recruitment of specialists within the organization, and the development of such things as interorganizational networks (Palmer, 1983) and political connections to monitor an increasingly complex environment. Organizational change, then, has as its central focus the problem of control.

In order to understand organizational change, we need to focus upon organizational processes of control, seeking to understand how rules come to be arrived at, how they influence future outcomes, and the role played by those in charge of organizations in the process of change and of organizational change.

Stuart Clegg's (1981) focus upon rules of control provides us with a useful focus for the analysis of the relationship between organization and change. Clegg's method of organizational analysis involves at least three central factors: first, that rules of control are a key dynamic in the life of organizations; secondly, that organizations need to be understood as unique entities – developing out of specific combinations of rules in particular historic contexts; and, thirdly, that organizational rules and their impact upon specific organizations need to be understood in a broader macro context of social change in which events in one place will have an impact upon events in other places.

Organizational control

Organizations may be distinguished from other social arrangements by their 'preoccupation with controlled performance' (Buchanan and Huczynski, 1985,

p. 454). This is best explained through discussion of how organizations come into being. Organizations are established by a particular person (e.g. Mary Kay Ash) or group of persons (e.g. the Bolsheviks) to achieve a certain end or ends. People are hired or recruited to help in the achievement of those ends. People's activities are structured around those ends. Those in charge of the organization are concerned to ensure that everyone works towards the achievement of those ends.

Organizational control arises out of a number of factors:

Ownership

Organizations begin from a sense of ownership – founding members having invested various combinations of time, money and ideas. A sense of ownership encourages in its founders a desire to ensure that *their* ideas are strived for.

When Henry Ford and his associates established the Ford Motor Company it was to achieve a combination of goals that included car production, profits and the realization of an engineering dream. Those hired to work for the company were *means* to those ends, and thus their activities had to be co-ordinated in a controlled way. But the history of the Ford Motor Company was to be one of constant purges, firings, humiliations and conflict as Henry Ford dealt with those he believed were challenging *his* vision of the company and its operation. Ford's humiliation of others included his own son, Edsel, whose attempts to introduce a new type of car were literally smashed before his eyes (Lacey, 1986). Likewise, when a group of Marxist leaders established the Bolshevik Party, they set out to recruit only those who could be counted on to struggle for a particular vision of revolutionary change and in a particular organizational fashion. The Bolshevik Party was characterized by a series of organizational arrangements that were not only perceived as means to an end, but as *the* means to the end of socialist revolution. Those characteristics included the notion that the party needed to be an élite body of professional revolutionaries; that membership of the party be restricted to those who not only accepted the party's programme and paid its dues but who also accepted regular work in one of the party organizations; that membership be concentrated upon the working class (Rothstein, 1950); and that organizational decision making be resolved through a process of 'democratic-centralism' i.e. in principle the notion is that once decisions have been collectively arrived at all parties are bound by those decisions until the next agreed upon decision-making period.

The history of communist parties, from the Bolsheviks onwards, has been one of struggle around those organizational arrangements; struggle, which until recently, usually resulted in the expulsion, imprisonment or death of the challengers.

Organization

Organizations arise out of a need to draw upon the activities of a number of people – most organizations rely on the employment or recruitment of a number of people to undertake various aspects of the defined goals. People are usually employed on the basis of a particular activity that they can perform and this serves to arrange their activities in a distinct pattern of working relationships or division of labour. By entering into organizational arrangements, participants become more or less locked into, i.e. controlled by, those arrangements. In other words, how we relate and how we relate to during organizational hours will be significantly determined by the organization we find ourselves in and our location within that organization. Let us give an example from our own experience. One of us (AJM) was previously a railway guard on London's underground railway. As an employee of the underground, Albert's main experience of fellow working people was, naturally enough, of railway workers. As a guard, his main working relationships were with fellow guards and with train drivers. He had less to do with booking clerks and platform staff.

Task

The employment of someone to undertake certain activities usually involves the assignment of specific jobs with defined tasks. The task itself will generally serve to control the type of activity that the person will usually engage in during organizational hours. Hence as a railway guard, Albert Mills was expected to be stationed in the last car of an assigned train, to operate the doors at specific times, and to ensure the safety of passengers during the train's operation. Those activities restricted his ability to engage in a number of other personal or organizational activities.

Co-ordination

Allied to task definition and the organizational division of labour is the question of co-ordination. Various tasks are related to other tasks and this controls activity, e.g. at Athabasca University the work of editors is directly related to the development of course materials by faculty members. This determines who the editors need to work with in order to carry out their tasks.

Operational processes

The nature of the tasks and the way they are co-ordinated will depend to a large extent upon the way the operational, or production, process has been thought out and the type of 'tools' required to do the tasks involved. The simplest example is that of the conveyor belt in many automobile industries. At one level, the belt represents someone's (designer, engineer) idea of how to produce automobiles in a most efficient manner. At another level, the belt represents someone's (owner, director, shareholders) decision to employ that form of production. The automobile worker is thus controlled in at least two major ways: (1) the pace of their work is controlled by the pace of the machine, and (2) the way they produce cars is controlled by a predetermined choice of production method.

Conflicts of interest

Most organizational arrangements arise in part out of a recognition, fear or concern that people will not strive, or strive hard enough, to achieve organizational ends if they are left to their own devices.

The issue of control is heightened within organizations by the fact that those who seek membership or employment do so for a variety of ends that do not necessarily coincide with the ends, or interpretation of ends, of those in charge of the organization. People take jobs for all kinds of reasons (economic necessity, social pressure, status, authority, power), and once they are in a place of work they often develop a new set of goals (good working conditions, promotion, health and safety concerns). Likewise, those who seek to join what Etzioni (1961) calls *normative* organizations (e.g. trade unions, political parties), do so for a variety of reasons not necessarily connected with the defined central organizational aims. People join political parties for all sorts of reasons, including social pressure (e.g. joining the German National Socialist Party in the late 1930s), an interest in becoming a parliamentarian (e.g. joining the German Social Democratic Party in the first decade of the twentieth century), social status (e.g. joining the Socialist Unity Party in the post-war German Democratic Republic), or to take over the direction of the party (e.g. Trotskyite 'enteryism' into the British Labour Party).

The extent to which individual goals are viewed as conflicting with those of the organization will depend upon a number of factors not least of which is the attitude of those in charge of the organization. For example, if organizational commitment is deemed to be important and the willingness to work unending hours is taken as a sign of that commitment, then time off for child-care responsibilities may be seen as a conflict of interest. If, on the other hand, flexible work arrangements are deemed to be important, then time off for the care of children may not be viewed as contradictory to the organization's operations. In a 101 ways actual and perceived conflicts of interest generate a series of direct control mechanisms – time clocks, piece work rates, membership renewal drives, performance appraisals, the employment of supervisors, etc.

Command structure
Nearly all organizations have different classes of member, with people officially ranked in terms of authority and power. Authority structures signal who is allowed to make decisions and who is not, what type/level of decisions can be made and by whom, who can communicate with whom, and who has to take orders from whom. This has at least three dimensions of control: (1) the range of decision making that a person can take is restricted; (2) a person's activities are directly or implicitly controlled by a designated superior; and (3) a person's potential for obtaining resources is channelled in a particular flow, i.e. up or along a specified chain of command.

Psychological needs
Control needs are not simply structural outcomes but reside within the psychological make-up of the people involved. Most, if not all, people seem to have some desire to gain a measure of control over their lives. People strive for some measure of autonomy and they also strive for some degree of certainty in their lives. There are of course extremes in the degrees of control for which people strive –

ranging from a complete desire to be controlled through to a pathological desire to control everything – and this would not be interesting if it were not for the fact that such personality types have too often come to exemplify certain organizations throughout history e.g. the National Socialist Party of Germany, the Moonies.

Strivings for control, autonomy and a reduction of uncertainty mark the activities of organizations. There are those who satisfy some psychological need to control the activities of others (e.g. Sgt 'Fatso' Judson in *From Here To Eternity*); there are those who cannot stand to have their authority questioned (e.g. Henry Ford); there are those who seek to reduce control over their working lives (e.g. active trade unionists); and there are those who seek a controlled environment for reasons of (ontological) security and safety. Ed Lawler (1976) suggests three reasons why people would want to be controlled:

1 Control mechanisms can provide feedback on performance.
2 Control processes provide people with structure, definition of methods and an indication of how their performance will be measured.
3 Control provides comfort to those people who appear to depend upon a tightly ordered reality (i.e. authoritarian personalities). A desire to reduce uncertainty appears to be a factor that affects people at all levels of the organization, from those who wish to 'understand' what they are doing through to management who seek predictability in their ability to plan.

Sexuality
As we discussed at length in Chapter 4, sexuality is intimately linked to power and control. Through the process of socialization, images of masculinity and femininity are constructed but in such a way that they stand in opposition to one another, e.g. male = strong, female = weak (Glennon, 1983). The social construction of gender is built around a number of implied and explicit power differentials, differentials that are not only reproduced within organizations but, all too often, are enhanced by organizations. This sets up at least four control dynamics. First, there is a tendency of various males to reproduce what they see as the traditional power relationships of men over women. Male managers often use sexuality as a control strategy over female employees (Eldridge and Crombie, 1974; Davies, 1989), or for attempting to gain the upper hand over female managers (Cunningham and Schumer, 1984). In similar ways, other male employees often attempt to control the activities of female co-workers through references to sexuality (Livingstone and Luxton, 1989). Secondly, there is a tendency among some male employees to resist what they view as illegitimate control by female managers, i.e. men who do not like being told what to do by a woman (Spencer and Podmore, 1987a). Thirdly, there are a number of female employees who resist what they perceive as control through sexuality. Fourthly, there are a number of females who seek to overcome sexist notions that inhibit their ability to manage or to become managers.

Race and ethnicity

Racism – fostered and perpetuated through centuries of colonial domination and kept alive through the dynamics of social inequity – all too regrettably retains a certain vitality in modern society (Manley, 1975; Khan and Mills, 1989). Racism is often reproduced through organizational divisions of labour in which whites supervise and manage people of colour, and through informal processes in which whites attempt to control non-white co-workers and subordinates on the basis of colour. As with sexuality, racism leads to a number of control dynamics within organizations (Khan, 1984; Parmar, 1984; Abella, 1984; Iles and Auluck, 1989; Miller, 1986; Bell, 1989).

Control and change

Organizational control and change are integrally related; change generates, and is generated by, issues of control. For example, the automobile company chief that finds that production is being held up by steel supplies may seek to reduce future uncertainty by establishing control over steel production. The urge to control in this case leads to change. Within the steel-making plant taken over by the automobile company, we might expect changes in the way production is controlled. In this case, change leads to new forms of control; indeed, it can be argued that change and new forms of control are indistinguishable in this case.

Within an organization, the introduction of, say, new technology will be experienced as new forms of control. Computerization, for example, has introduced a myriad of different organizational requirements. The activity of some employees is now no longer flexible in terms of geographical location within the organization; work needs to be done at a particular computer terminal and cannot usually be done at home unless the employee has a home-based computer and access to the mainframe.

Cultural rules

The dynamics of control arise out of the activities of a number of people who are variously concerned to develop, maintain, enforce, interpret, apply and resist control mechanisms and demands. In the event and over time this leads to the establishment of a series of rules within an organization. These rules and the process through which they are enacted, followed and resisted come to characterize what we might call an organization's culture. That is, each organization will be composed of a different configuration of rules that, along with the people who enact, follow and resist those rules, characterize that organization's culture (Mills, 1988b). The development of any given organizational culture will have profound implications for future organizational change. Hence the need to understand organizational change in the context of the dynamics of organizational institutionalization. The two are inseparable.

Clegg (1981), as indicated in Chapter 1, suggests that there are six strategic areas of control that cohere into organizational rules – *extra-organizational, social regulative, state, reproduction, technological* and *strategic* rules; rules that provide the building bricks of an organization and which set the tone for change.

EXTRA-ORGANIZATIONAL RULES

Our discussion of gender rules in Chapter 4 illustrated the myriad of ways that understandings about the character and relative social worth of men and women permeate organizations. We saw how those understandings can become solidified into sets of informal rules about who should be allowed to enter any particular organization, who should be allowed to undertake certain tasks, who was to be deemed capable of undertaking certain tasks and of occupying positions of authority and how certain tasks should be undertaken (e.g. 'in a ladylike fashion', 'in a manly way'). We also saw how those understandings are reflected in the more formal rules of organizations in regard to such things as differential recruitment, training, promotion and wage rates for men over women.

Extra-organizational rules can also refer to understandings based on notions of race and ethnicity. The character of any given set of extra-organizational rules within an organization will depend upon a number of factors. At the broadest level it will depend upon dominant social rules. Apartheid, for example, is a collection of racist understandings that cohere in a network of rules which serve to exclude non-whites, not only from a range of social activities, but from the concept of dignified social life itself. Thus, in South Africa, we are not surprised to find that racism is a major distinguishing feature of organizational life throughout most organizations. Racism is, of course, not a unique feature of South African society. Most other societies provide their own peculiar examples. Ella Bell (1989) indicates how social understandings reflected in myths and stories can have an effect upon the respective aspirations and recruitment of black and white women to positions of management in the USA. Bell argues that stories such 'the Snow Queen' help to encourage white females to develop characteristics of strength, aloofness, calculability, and so on, that will assist them to be perceived as potential managers. Myths about the black 'Mammy', on the other hand, help to encourage black females to see themselves as nurturant, caring, subservient and powerless – characteristics that hinder the ability of black women to be seen as potential managers.

Racism in the USA – as was so vividly displayed during the civil rights struggles of the 1960s – varies across states and regions. Thus, we might expect to find that regional differences in social attitudes to race and to racism are reflected in different organizational realities. Here is an example of how traditional southern values and practices were translated into organizational realities in the tobacco industry of Durham, North Carolina in the 1920s and 1930s:

> Historically, black labor of both females and males has been critical to the tobacco manufacturing industry. As cigarette manufacture became mechanized blacks were hired as stemmers, sorters, hangers, and pullers. These 'dirty' jobs were seen as an

extension of field labor and therefore as 'Negro work' for which whites would not compete (Jones, 1987, p. 323).

Jones goes on to describe how local white attitudes to 'race' are reflected in, and exacerbated by, the tobacco companies:

> Race restricted the black population to segregated neighborhoods and also determined the kinds of jobs black females could get. Black female tobacco workers also faced discrimination as poor people and as females. Although class and sex restraints punctuated the lives of white female tobacco workers, their impact was reinforced by management policies. Although white females' wages were a fraction of white males' and inadequate to support a family, black females' wages were even lower. According to some black female tobacco workers, the wage inequity led many white women to consider black women inferior. This in turn led to an atmosphere of mistrust between black and white females. Management strengthened racial and class inequities in hiring practices, working conditions, and spatial organization of the factory, and therefore impeded the formation of gender bonds among working-class women (Jones, 1987, pp. 324–5).

Black and white women were segregated within the factories, with black women doing the 'dirtier jobs'.

Even within broad societal or regional contexts, differences in the peculiar mix of people will lead to differences within organizations. Rotary International (RI) provides several examples. RI does not discriminate on the grounds of race; however, as late as 1982, the Birmingham, Alabama club limited membership to 'any white male person of good moral character' – a court order ended that practice (Rogers, 1988). In another case, despite the fact that RI did discriminate on the grounds of sex in 1977, the Rotary Club of Duarte, California admitted three women into its membership. This resulted in RI revoking the Duarte club's charter and was followed by a lengthy legal battle, ending in a 1987 California Supreme Court ruling which ruled that RI's 'men only' rules were unlawful. In a similar case in Canada, the all-male membership of a rotary club in a small Northern town voted unanimously in 1987 to admit female members. The decision was remarkable given the male character of the town (see Fig. 4.1). Most members were willing to risk the loss of the club's charter in order to redress what they saw as unacceptably discriminatory rules. Events overtook the club, and in November 1988 RI ruled that rotary clubs within Canada could admit females into their membership; the local club in question immediately recruited two female members. From the other direction, a number of rotary clubs in the heart of supposedly liberal Massachusetts are still, in the late 1980s, resisting female membership, and one of the Edmonton, Alberta clubs was still debating whether to admit women in the 1990s.

TECHNICAL RULES

Any given production process will naturally reflect the organization's particular goals – conveyor belts are found in automobile manufacturers rather than hairdressing salons; printing presses are found in newspaper companies rather than coal mines. But production processes are developed out of broad technological contexts. Once Henry Ford had introduced the notion of conveyor-belt production, for example, it was very difficult for new car makers to produce automobiles in any other way. The conveyor belt and car production became synonymous. This only recently began to change in the late 1960s, with Volvo's decision to 'change the rules' and produce cars by way of autonomous work groups (Weir, 1976).

Technical rules do not simply refer to physical items such as plant and machinery, but to the techniques and organization of production. In other words, to produce goods or a service requires such things as the use of physical apparatus (e.g. tools, instruments, machines, appliances, gadgets, weapons), and the organized or co-ordinated (e.g. departmentalization, divisionalization, bureaucratization, team) application of techniques (e.g. skills, methods, procedures, routines) (Buchanan and Huczynski, 1985, p. 212).

Different eras, societies and geographic locations are characterized by different technological contexts, i.e. dominant technical rules that influence organizational development. Ursella Franklin (1989) has usefully characterized this process as one in which the technological context provides the web within and out of which organizations pattern their specific technical rules. For Karl Marx, the web can be viewed as a *mode of production*. Marx viewed human history as a series of radically different modes of production – slavery, feudalism, capitalism, socialism – rooted in distinct patterns of ownership and organization ('relations of production') and of tools ('means of production'). Prior to capitalism, for instance, production was generally on a small scale, carried on in a number of cottages (literally a cottage industry) or on the land, utilizing relatively simple tools (hand looms, hoes, etc.), generally undertaken by family groups, and geared to more or less immediate consumption (or 'use value'). Ownership and control in this feudalist mode of production was in the hands of the landowners and rested on mainly traditional ties and bonds. As feudalism gave way to capitalism, new ways of production developed. The key form of ownership could now be characterized as ownership of the means of production. New inventions (e.g. the steam engine, the spinning jenny) opened up the possibility of vastly increased production, possibilities that were seen as being facilitated by moving production out of the cottages and into factories. Production as well as employment was now governed by market forces. The new mode of production created new patterns of control. Now deprived of the means of survival, workers were forced to seek employment in the new factories. No longer in their own homes, workers came under the direct control of a new breed of supervisors and overseers, and the physical control of the factories themselves. Further control was experienced through the development and co-ordination of specific techniques for carrying out production.

Michel Foucault and Alvin Toffler, in very different ways, have detailed how the dominant technical rules of early capitalism influenced the spread and development of each new organization. Foucault argues that 'control over the body' has come to dominate modern thinking and is intricately bound up with the development of organizational practices:

> This political investment of the body is bound up, in accordance with complex reciprocal relations, with its economic use; it is largely as a force of production that the body is invested with relations of power and domination; but, on the other hand, its constitution as labour power is possible only if it is caught up in a system of subjection . . . ; the body becomes a useful force only if it is both a productive body and a subjected body (Foucault, 1979, p. 26).

It is Foucault's contention that in the machine age the metaphor of machine was extended to the human body and allowed people to view the body as something to be used, to be controlled, towards productive ends. This way of understanding the body, this 'discourse', became reflected in a variety of methods of control. According to Foucault, discipline, focusing upon the minute control of the body, came to characterize all organizations: 'prisons resemble factories, schools, barracks, hospitals, which all resemble prisons' (Foucault, 1979, p. 288). Hence as capitalism developed, so did a dominant form of production that strongly influenced the way that individual organizations developed.

Similarly, Alvin Toffler (1981), referring to capitalism as the 'Second Wave', details how the principles of organization, and techniques of production come to be adopted across a range of organizations:

> In one Second Wave country after another, social inventors, believing the factory to be the most advanced and efficient agency for production, tried to embody its principles in other organizations as well. Schools, hospitals, prisons, government bureaucracies, and other organizations took on many of the characteristics of the factory – its division of labour, its hierarchical structure, its metallic impersonality (Toffler, 1981, p. 45).

Not even the art of making music is immune:

> The orchestra even mirrored certain features of the factory in its internal structure. At first the sympathy orchestra was leaderless, or the leadership was casually passed around among the players. Later the players, exactly like workers in a factory or bureaucratic office, were divided into departments (instrumental sections), each contributing to the overall output (the music), each coordinated from above by a manager (the conductor) or even, eventually, a straw boss farther down the management hierarchy (the first violinist or the section head) . . . . The music factory had been born (Toffler, 1981, p. 46).

Toffler argues that we are now in a new, *Third Wave*, epoch in which decentralization is a major feature of the way we conceptualize and organize social life. In this current wave – which has been underway for three or four decades now – we are encouraged to think of new ways of organizing:

> The corporation – like most other organizations – will also undergo drastic restructuring as the ground rules of Third Wave civilization come into play. Instead of a society synchronized to the tempo of the assembly line, a Third Wave society will

move to flexible rhythms and schedules. Instead of the mass society's extreme standardization of behaviour, ideas, language, and life styles, Third Wave society will be built on segmentation and diversity. Instead of a society that concentrates population flows, and other features of life, Third Wave society will disperse and de-concentrate. Instead of opting for maximum scale on the 'bigger is better' principle, Third wave society will understand the meaning of 'appropriate scale'. Instead of a highly centralized society, Third Wave society will recognize the value of much decentralized decision-making (Toffler, 1981, p. 365).

Whatever the validity of Toffler's predictions – and our two examples below indicate that 'Second Wave' thinking is still with us – the point stands that in different eras we can detect definite technological trends and that those trends have a tremendous influence upon organizational thinking and development. That is not, however, to support some notion of technological determinism. Particular ways of organizing are outcomes of ideas, practices and struggles at a given point in time. Historical periods are dominated not only by styles of organizing but the struggles of those who wish to maintain that style (e.g. Charles I of England, the Kerensky Government of 1918 Russia, the Polish Communist Party of the late 1980s) and by those who seek to establish alternatives (e.g. Oliver Cromwell, the Bolshevik Party, *Solidarity*). And within certain technological eras, we find those who establish distinctive alternative ways of producing and organizing; for example, the Anabaptists in the time of Sir Thomas More (cf. More, 1969), Robert Owen's model factory at New Lanark (cf. Thomson, 1980) and the 1970s British workers' cooperatives (cf. Mills, 1974). Within the broad context of a technological era, choices are made. As John Child (1972) has expressed it, those in charge of organizations in large part decide what goals they are going to pursue, what environments or markets they will attempt to operate within, and what method of production they will employ. The Wardair company provides a number of useful examples.

Max Ward initially began a small one-plane operation in Yellowknife (in the Canadian North West Territories) in the late 1940s. Naturally, his decision to found an airline company meant that his operation centred around an aeroplane – a Fox Moth:

> young Ward, operating single-handed from dawn until dusk, hauled prospectors and supplies into the mining exploration camps that were springing up in the area. In addition to flying the Fox Moth, he maintained it, cleaned it, loaded it, and ran the business all by himself (Sutherland, 1978, quoted in Melady, 1989, pp.130–31).

The central forms of technical rules depended upon the characteristics of the plane itself and self-discipline. Ward's early company, the Polaris Charter Company, did not last long, but he was back 4 years later with a new company, Wardair Limited. Wardair Limited started life with four aeroplanes, still operating out of Yellowknife. Eventually Ward decided to get into the charter business, and by 1976 Wardair had established itself as Canada's largest international charter airline – this time operating out of Edmonton. Ward had changed his operation and the base of his operations. In the process, his company had developed from one centred around aeroplanes to one that involved a range of technologies and technical rules. Pilots, flight attendants, mechanics, cleaners, booking clerks, all had to be hired, co-ordinated, controlled. Finally, Ward decided to get into the scheduled airline business. That decision did not simply involve a change of market but critical choices concerning the employment of technology. With the routes involved and the scale of operation, Ward needed not only to make careful decisions about the type of planes to buy but also what kind of computerized system to employ. The computerization alone was to cost Ward something in the order of C$100 million, and by Ward's own estimates it would take at least 2 year's to adapt the company to the new systems. By the end of those 2 years, the company was financially overstretched and Wardair was brought out by PWA.

The introduction of vastly different technologies over the years turned Wardair into an organization that became increasingly characterized by systems of technical control in which technical rules grew more and more sophisticated and Ward was forced to employ increasing numbers of specialists (e.g. one of his last advertised appointments was for someone to head a Management Information Systems Department).

The technology chosen by any given organization will have very different implications for the way organizational life is experienced. In the manufacture of automobiles, for example, the employees' experience of technical rules will be very different depending upon whether they are working in a largely automated, robotic plant (Fiat), in autonomous working groups (Volvo) or on a conveyor belt (Ford).

Technical rules will differ depending upon whether the activities of employees are loosely or highly interdependent (Thompson 1967), loosely or tightly coupled (Perrow, 1984), geared to environmental certainty or uncertainty (Burns and Stalker, 1961), or based upon unit, mass or process forms of production (Woodward, 1958). If, for example, the production process of a group of organizational members is sequentially linked (e.g. continuous process production work), then technical rules will be felt through such factors as group work pressures, with the output of one group becoming the input of the next group. Less pressure of this kind may be felt where, as in a department store, the activities of the employees are not directly interrelated. In situations of relative environmental uncertainty, employees (e.g. as in the microcomputer business) may be less likely to experience tight or rigid technical control given that the organization needs them to be free to take relatively quick decisions in the face of rapidly changing and complex market conditions. The nature of some industries (e.g. nuclear power) have led those in charge of associated organizations to design tightly controlled technical environments. Charles Perrow (1984) argues that this has led to situations of 'tightly coupled' systems in which a problem in one part can put serious strain on the other parts. Perrow is also instructive on how meta-technical rules come to influence organizational design at the level of individual nuclear power stations. Perrow details how private utilities came to develop nuclear reactors in the context of US government pressure, a situation of 'undue haste' which has resulted in the development of a 'particularly complex and tightly coupled design' (Perrow, 1984, p. 39). Perrow goes on:

> Even if there were a technological breakthrough and a much safer design were available, it is very unlikely that one would be built in the United States in the next decade or two. . . . A new design would not attract much interest in the financial community; utilities generally find themselves with excess capacity because the rise in demand for electricity . . . has steadily dropped since 1974. . . . Further, it would take over ten years to design and build a new facility, even if it were significantly less complex than those we have now. Thus, we will have to live with the plants we have, safe or not; new, dramatically safer ones do not appear to be in the offing, and probably will not be built for a long time to come (Perrow, 1984, pp. 39–40)

The movies *The China Syndrome* and *Silkwood* depict how tightly coupled, tightly controlled technical rules impact those who have to work within them. In real life, the Chernobyl and Three Mile Island disasters were in fact disasters of system design – systems accidents as Perrow calls them. Finally, in terms of direct, supervisory control, the nature of the technology can obviate the necessity of having large numbers of supervisors; the ratio of supervisors to subordinates is likely to be less in mass production systems where a large part of the control is designed into the machinery (Woodward, 1958).

SOCIAL REGULATIVE RULES

In the late 1840s, Marx and Engels depicted the nature of work relations under capitalism as one of naked control:

> The bourgeoisie . . . has pitilessly torn asunder the motley feudal ties that bound man to his 'natural superiors', and has left remaining no other nexus between man and man than naked self-interest, than callous 'cash payment'. It had drowned the most heavenly ecstacies of religious fervour, of chivalrous enthusiasm, of philistine sentimentalism, in the icy water of egotistical calculation. . . . In one word, for exploitation, veiled by religious and political illusions, it has substituted naked, shameless, direct, brutal exploitation (Marx and Engels, 1967, p. 82).

Indeed, it must have seemed to many at that time that this was so. Yet, particularly as we approach the twenty-first century, it now seems evident that organizational control is rarely so naked, so callous, so clearly brutal. Organizational control is often subtle, implicit, sometimes rewarding, and not altogether unwelcome. As we discussed above, organizational control can provide some people with much needed clarity and direction, it can provide a framework of integration and co-ordination, and it can assist the process of goal attainment. But in order for those things to be valued, organizational control also needs to draw upon deeper psychological processes and needs.

In the early years of the twentieth century, the rapidly industrializing USA projected the image of a harsh, cold working environment for the industrial working class. The work of Frederick Taylor did little to dispel that view. Taylor's ideas about how best to manage the modern factory confirmed Marx's predictions about the development of capitalist relations of production. Taylor argued that greater productivity and organizational efficiency could be achieved through a combination of (1) the 'scientific' redesign of tasks, that (2) involved a reduced reliance on the employees' need to think (control would be through the task design itself), and (3) incentive schemes that linked pay to rates of productivity (Taylor, 1911). This was indeed an approach to management which emphasized 'naked self-interest' and 'egotistical calculation'!

Despite the fact that Taylor was discredited in his own time (Rose, 1975), many of the basic ideas of Taylorism and of scientific management have remained popular to this day. Harry Braverman (1974) has detailed the unending application of scientific management throughout factories and offices and the resultant 'deskilling' of labour.

None the less, this kind of approach has not proven successful with all workplaces across time and space. Widespread industrial unrest, rightly or wrongly associated with attempts to introduce Taylorist ideas, led to the establishment of a US House of Representatives Committee to look into scientific management. In 1911, Taylor himself was called before the committee to answer charges that his theories were encouraging labour unrest (Rose, 1975; Morgan, 1986). It had been recognized that in some situations the *appearance* of naked self-interest may not act as an effective form of control, nor encourage the desired increases in productivity.

Organizational control had to be sought along other avenues. Following Taylor, management theory began to be developed out of the concerns of employers to get answers to their organizational problems. In one such notable attempt – the Hawthorne Studies – enquiry ranged through ergonomic studies of seating and lighting, through anthropological studies of group dynamics, to clinical studies of the relationship between personality and organization; the tone had been set for the future development of management and organization theory.

The Hawthorne Studies developed out of a concern by the General Electric Company with a number of organizational problems (i.e. productivity, absenteeism, motivation) at their Hawthorne works in Chicago in the early 1920s. The various studies that make up the Hawthorne Studies involved, at different stages, engineers, anthropologists, psychologists and business professors, and were conducted over a period of nearly 15 years. What the Hawthorne Studies gave rise to was a number of clues as to how employee needs might be meshed with organizational demands. In particular, it was suggested that the organization should develop ways to build employee commitment through group dynamics. One of the study's major findings was that employees appear to form informal work groups from which they derive satisfaction and a measure of control over the work process. It was noted, however, that while informal groups play an integrative function, they may do so in a way that is counterproductive, i.e. they may restrict output through the development of informal goals that are 'lower' than formally stated goals. Elton Mayo, one of the leading researchers involved in the studies, argued that management had to find ways of encouraging informal group development while retaining control over output. Mayo, drawing upon the work of Emile Durkheim, believed that in the modern world, work organizations were replacing traditional forms (e.g. the church, family, community) of social integration, that the modern workplace – with its division of labour and its requirements of time, commitment, interdependence and economic necessity – could provide the structure so needed to fill people's lives with meaning. This seemed particularly relevant to Mayo in the face of a workforce at the Chicago works that largely consisted of new immigrant workers 'in need of some mechanism of social integration'. Mayo, this time drawing inspiration from Vilfedo Pareto, also believed that people were propelled by irrational impulses and were in need of control. Hence the modern factory provides both the mechanism of social integration and of control if only it can encourage the development of informal work groups under the leadership of officially designated supervisors or leaders.

The Hawthorne Studies also suggested that employees enter organizations with deep-seated psychological problems, which are often manifested in forms of anti-organizational behaviour. This idea seems to have come from Mayo, who was heavily influenced by the work of Freud. Mayo was the first management theorist to suggest a link between organizational practices and psychological well-being, albeit in a profoundly one-sided way that left the negative impact of the organization out of his account. The Hawthorne researchers actually devised a programme for the (compulsory) provision of psychoanalytical counselling to all employees by trained company counsellors.

In the six decades since the Hawthorne Studies, management theory and practice have gone in a number of directions. Various schemes have been devised for improving the workplace and the output of the workforce – job enrichment, redesign, rotation; autonomous work groups, quality circles; T-groups, management training; employee participation, involvement, worker directors; quality of working life schemes; and so on. Many of these schemes have arisen out of management theory but, as Peters and Waterman (1982) state, industry is replete with numerous ways of attempting to incorporate, integrate and motivate employees – from social clubs, to beer busts, to 'employee of the month' awards, to picnics and office parties. Here is one of many examples:

General Motors finance staffer: – Look, I've been in a foundry, there's no way those guys are going to sing songs like the Japanese or the Tupperware ladies.
Second person (from the Midwest): – Caterpillar makes top-drawer equipment. Those people are UAW workers. They don't fool around with hoopla.
Third person (also from the Midwest): – I was transferred to Peoria. I didn't work for Cat. But every year they put on a 'machine day'. All the Cat people and their families go out to the proving grounds and get free beer and sandwiches. Last year's theme was 'Cowboys and Indians'. All the machines were dressed up in costumes and given names. Then the machines engaged in contests, devouring hills and stuff like that. Everybody lapped it up.
Second GMer: – You should see South Gate. The plant manager really enjoys whooping it up. The place became a smorgasbord of signs: 'Beat Japan', and the like. Why, they even enticed some Hell's Angels types into singing 'God Bless America' at a recent rally (quoted in Peters and Waterman, 1982, p. 263).

In numerous ways, employees find themselves enmeshed in a number of rules designed to regulate the social arrangements of production and organizational processes.

At the level of the individual organization, which social regulative rules are in force will depend upon a number of factors that include:

1 Which theory of management is currently in vogue (e.g. Human Relations in the 1960s, Organizational Culture in the 1980s).
2 Which type of technology is being employed, i.e. does the technology control the work process or is there a need for alternatives?
3 What is the prevailing economic situation, i.e. is a situation of high unemployment, for example, acting as a broad form of organizational control?
4 What is the composition and character of the workforce, e.g. are they unionized/militant and does this make it more difficult to control them? Are they highly professionalized and require less direct forms of control?
5 What is the character and aims of management involved, e.g. do they feel under pressure? Are they ruthlessly determined to achieve nothiong less than a certain level of profitability?
6 What are the environmental circumstances, e.g. is the organization operating in a more or less stable environment?
7 What is the dominant socio-legal value system, e.g. is it morally, socially or legally acceptable to treat employees in certain ways?

To quote Clegg and Dunkerley (1980, p. 516):

> Ramsay (1977a) has observed how one social-regulative class of intervention sponsored by the state, that of reforms calling for participation, has been a cyclical occurrence, varying with the fortunes of the world economy. At times of full employment and high wages, calls for 'participation' have generally increased. The development of Mayoite strategies during the Second World War may be noted in this context. The rise and fall of the fortunes of work humanization practices similarly have followed this pattern.

In Britain in the mid-1970s, government legislation to introduce 'worker participation' schemes throughout industry came at the end of a 5-year period of high unemployment, unprecedented industrial and political strikes, and a widespread number of worker 'sit-ins', 'work-ins' and 'worker cooperatives'. This was a dramatic switch from 5 years earlier, when government legislation was primarily designed to curtail rank-and-file trade unionism (Mills, 1982).

REPRODUCTION RULES

In many ways and in many instances social regulative rules can be found to be deliberately designed to achieve a manipulative end. Richard Daft, for example, explains how top management can manipulate organizational culture to their ends:

> The underlying value system of the organization cannot be managed in the traditional

way. Techniques top managers use to convey the appropriate values and beliefs are rites and ceremonies, stories, symbols, and slogans. Executives often need to learn ceremonial skills, and how to use speech, writing, and gestures to influence company values. Symbols, stories, and ceremonies are techniques to manage organizational culture, which is hard to shape by conventional means (Daft, 1986, p. 487).

Yet, by and large, the strength of social regulative rules more often lies in the fact that they are *not* simply and deliberately constructed in order to manipulate. Their vitality, as with other forms of rule, are to be uncovered within dominant modes of discourse. A discourse involves several elements – leadership, ideas/ideology, practices, personality – that in dynamic combination serve to *reproduce* the status quo.

How is it that when faced with a system of control people more often than not accept and obey orders, 'go with the flow', attempt to fit-in, and so on? Amitai Etzioni (1961), in attempting to answer the question of why people comply, argues that there are three central possibilities – *coercive* (threats of punishment of some kind), *utilitarian* (exposure to financial rewards and sanctions) or *normative* (appeal to a person's values and convictions). Which form of compliance is dominant will, according to Etzioni, depend upon the type of goal that the organization is pursuing. Thus, *coercive* compliance is more likely in organizations that pursue *order* (e.g. prisons, concentration camps), *utilitarian* compliance is more likely where organizations pursue *economic goals (e.g. industrial and commercial businesses)*, and *normative* compliance is more likely in organizations that pursue *culture* goals (e.g. churches, political parties, educational organizations).

Etzioni's approach is useful in indicating how rules of compliance can affect organizations in different ways, depending upon the goals of those in charge. But there is a problem of oversimplification in that compliance with non-*culture* goals is reduced to narrow calculative ends.

In the work of Max Weber we find a comprehensive attempt to understand the relationship between obedience, organizational practice and social understandings. In discussing the relationship between *The Protestant Ethic and the Spirit of Capitalism*, for instance, Weber links the development of the new capitalist economic organizations with the rise of Protestantism. Protestantism – Calvinism in particular – with its emphasis upon frugality, hard work, investment and evidence of prosperousness as a sign of heavenly destination was, according to Weber, ideally suited to the needs of an emergent capitalism. The new breed of Calvinist entrepreneurs in many ways set the tone, or 'rules of the game', for successful business practice in the early days of capitalist development.

The protestant ethic of 'hard work' was one of the first cardinal rules of capitalist industry and it is likely that it was neither fully imposed nor followed out of naked self-interest or fear, gaining much of its vigour from the fact that it was a value strongly linked to religious beliefs (Weber, 1976). In *The Theory of Social and Economic Organization* (1969), Weber develops further the relationship between social understandings and organizational reality. Here Weber details the intricate relationships between the spread of 'scientific thought' throughout modes of thinking (from science, to politics, to religion, and so on) and the development of bureaucratic organizations. It is Weber's contention that the growing dominance of bureaucracy can be found in the growing dominance of a rational-legal way of thinking. For Weber, bureaucratic organization succeeds in that it reflects the rational, calculative expectations of its members. This is not a narrow calculative thinking, as witnessed in Etzioni's scheme, but a way of understanding – a worldview that is based upon rational-legal thought (Weber, 1947). Hence people obey orders, accept authority, when and where they believe that authority to be *legitimate*. That is not to say that they have to agree with the person handing out the orders nor believe that the orders are sensible. Obedience comes from a belief in the legitimacy of the position and an understanding that the system is 'fair'. Within that context it is possible to argue that people may *also* obey out of narrow calculative ends. But bureaucracy – the spread of bureaucracy – is not simply built out of a rational-legal world view; bureaucratic organization, in turn, helps to reinforce that world view.

Marxists, in seeking to understand the problem of obedience, have focussed their attention upon the role of *ideology* and specifically the role of the capitalist in the development of controlling ideas. In *The German Ideology*, for example, Marx and Engels (1976, p. 59) wrote that 'The ideas of the ruling class are in every epoch the ruling ideas, i.e., the class which is the ruling *material* force of society is at the same time its ruling intellectual force.' This argument has often crudely been interpreted to mean that the capitalist class *invents* ideas to sustain their own rule, that *ideology* can be equated with a manufactured set of ideas designed to distort reality to the ends of one class over another. Indeed, there are examples of such practices to be found within liberal capitalist and fascist states, but it is highly unlikely that they could be sustained. Ideas that do not accord with the experiences of a people are bound to come unstuck. Proof of this contention can be found, ironically, in the demise of the East European communist parties in 1989.

Ideology, to be viable, must match the interests and experiences of a large number of people even if a section of those people stand to gain more than the rest. Antonio Gramsci recognized this fact in attempting to understand the viability of capitalist thinking in post-First World War Italy. For Gramsci, capitalism has developed into a cultural system in which people come to understand themselves and reality through a powerful set of ideas that are reinforced through a network of intellectual leadership. That intellectual leadership consists of a number of people who are drawn from the owning and controlling groups in society and from those who come to identify their interests with the status quo (i.e. supervisors, managers). Within industry, those in charge, building upon existing cultural values, provide a kind of cultural or *hegemonic* leadership to employees, i.e. people obey because, up to a point, it conforms to their cultural expectations. Therborn explains it thus:

1 Ideological formation tells individuals *what exists*, who they are, how the world is, how they are related to that world. In this manner, people are allocated different kinds and amounts of identity, trust and everyday knowledge. The visibility of modes

of life, the actual relationship of performance to reward, the existence, extent and character of exploitation and power are all structured in class-specific models of ideological formation.

2 Ideology tells *what is possible*, providing varying types and quantities of self-confidence and ambition, and different levels of aspiration.

3 Ideology tells *what is right* and wrong, good and bad, thereby determining not only conceptions of legitimacy of power, but also work-ethics, notions of leisure, and views of inter-personal relationships, from comradeship to sexual love (Therborn, 1978, quoted in Clegg and Durkerley, 1980, p. 409).

Within the broad framework of ideological reproduction, management theory has been viewed as playing an important role in regard to the maintenance of the organizational patterns of ownership and control (Clegg and Dunkerley, 1980). As we argued above, the development of modern management practices and theory have developed hand in hand. Scientific management developed out of management concerns and in turn has come to have an important influence over management practices (Braverman, 1974). The development of theories of management, in a world of organizational concerns, has led to the development of schools of management, of business, of administration, of organizational analysis. Nowadays, one would be hard pressed to find a manager in a medium-sized to large business organization who has not undergone some form of 'management training'. The power of management theory is reflected throughout organizations as rules of management. In a recent management class of one of the authors, a group of practising managers was asked to design an 'ideal organization'. One group came up with an outline for a golf club. The club was described as having 10 employees and as being divided into five departments each with its own manager. Given the opportunity to invent a totally different kind of organization, these managers found themselves unable to escape traditional management thinking. They invented a highly bureaucratized golf club!

The relationship between management theory and management practice is very much like the relationship between Hollywood and reality, where art imitates life only to be accepted as a substitute for reality. Hearn and Parkin (1983) have indicated how the discrimination of women in organizations has come to be reflected and strengthened through management theory. Here is another example. In 1979, Rosabeth Moss Kanter wrote an article in the *Harvard Business Review* which argued that effective management is one which *empowers* employees. This article cut across conventional wisdom, which at that time was focusing upon training managers to develop a combination of task and people skills and to recognize when/how to apply one set of skills over the other. By the early 1980s, Professor John Kotter of the Harvard Business School was teaching a related course on Power and Influence. Slowly but surely, this approach began to take hold among leading executives of a number of US companies – empowerment had become the new rule of management thinking. By 1989, *Fortune* was reporting on the widespread nature of this trend:

Listen to the new gospel of executive power: 'The more you have, the less you should use,' says Reuben Mark, CEO of Colgate Palmolive. 'You consolidate and build power by empowering others.' Mark expresses an increasingly common view. Virtually all the chief executives polled by FORTUNE . . . says they share power more than they did five years ago, and more than the CEO before them (Stewart, 1989).

At the individual organization level, the kind of reproduction rules in use will vary according to the existence, extent and type of management training that managers have undergone; the economic climate; the type of employees to be managed; the thinking of the top executives; and the type of goals and technology involved.

STATE RULES

All organizations operate to some degree or another under legal constraints, and within the broad context of government policy and action. In the latter case, organizational operations will be affected by government policies (e.g. entry into the European Economic Community; membership of GATT; the Canada–US Free Trade Deal) that change the rules of doing business. Entry into the EEC, for example, meant many changes for British companies. Tariffs were lifted on the exchange of goods between EEC countries and this meant easier access for British goods into those countries. On the other hand, it also meant increased competition as British companies had to face the advent of easier access for non-British EEC goods into the UK. That particular policy decision led to British involvement and adherence to EEC regulations and standards that eventually altered many of the production practices of UK companies.

A similar situation was evolving in Norther America towards the end of the 1980s. The Free Trade Deal led to a far greater flexibility of access for US companies into Canada and vice versa. As a result of the deal, joint US–Canadian bodies have been established to adjudicate on standards and disputes, and this is beginning to affect the way certain North American companies have to think about their operations.

In the Soviet Union, the advent of *glasnost* had led to greater levels of decentralization and autonomy for many Soviet business organizations. This had led to the exploration of a number of joint ventures with foreign companies. In the German Democratic Republic, Hungary, Poland and the USSR, dramatic changes in governmental policy have led to changes in the way newspapers are able to operate.

In terms of legal enactments, organizations face a broad set of demands. Contracts of agreement, minimum wages, the employment of minors, occupational health and safety requirements are some of the many examples of legal rules that impinge upon the way an organization is run.

Many laws are universal throughout a legal jurisdiction, e.g. child labour laws, but some laws, governmental policies and codes of conduct will affect different organizations in different ways. Sexual harassment laws, for example, may have much less of an impact upon a single gender organization than on one in which both men and women are involved (to date most cases in Canada, the UK and the USA involve charges of harassment of women by men). Smoking bans in the late 1980s tended to be more widespread throughout public rather than private business organizations. National security is much more of an issue in nuclear power stations, defence-related industries and the armed forces, while health regulations are more likely to be an issue in restaurants and hospitals. The US–Canada Free Trade Deal was welcomed by the Alberta gas industry which hopes to benefit from greater access to US markets but it was opposed by the Ontario wine industry which perceived US access to its markets as a threat.

STRATEGIC RULES

Clegg and Dunkerley (1980, p. 533) define strategic rules as 'an intervention in the spheres of both production and circulation', in contrast to social regulative and technical rules which 'are an intervention only in the production of commodities, and not their circulation'. Many business organizations when faced with rising costs and decreasing profitability will seek either to change their production methods and/or to control the market itself. The development of monopolies and of multinational corporations are major organizational attempts to gain strategic control over various markets. Typically, multinational companies have gained greater strategic control by founding operations in Third World countries:

> These enterprises are there precisely because of the reduced cost of the labour process, the possibility of multi-factor supply for core production (in the USA, etc), and the frequently observed phenomenon of transfer pricing. . . . In terms of their control of the labour process, what is not assured by wages which in the local context are considered to be high wages, coupled with a large reserve army of the unemployed, can frequently be assured by the policies of the domestic state. This assured quantity is the existence of a compliant work force asserting no power (Clegg and Dunkerley, 1980, pp. 534–5).

These kinds of strategic rules are evidenced in the highly developed states as well. In the 1970s, the Chrysler Corporation, using the threat of a massive pull out of its operations, were to pressure the British Government into providing the company with financial assistance. In that same decade, various companies moved out of Britain and into Spain to take advantage of cheaper labour, less restrictive company laws, anti-trade union laws and greater financial incentives (Mills, 1982).

Within the highly industrial nations, takeovers and mergers provide ways of gaining strategic advantage over the market. In Canada, Pacific Western Airlines merged with Canadian Pacific to become Canadian Airlines International. This made them the second largest airline in the country, after Air Canada, and gave them considerable strategic advantage over the market than previously. In the late 1980s, however, a third airline, Wardair, entered the market and offered fierce competition. In mid-1989, the PWA Corporation acquired Wardair in order to ensure its strategic position.

Strategic rules more or less afford an organization a measure of control over its operating environment and will depend upon such things as the size of the company (financial holdings), its competitive position (monopoly, oligopoly, cartel), its location (in underdeveloped nations, in the less developed sectors of an industrial nation), and its importance in relation to a specific economy (a company town, the main employer in an underdeveloped region). Strategic rules can and will affect employee control within the organization. Mills (1988a), for example, has indicated how powerful organizations (*vis-à-vis* the local economy) can take advantage of patriarchal family structures to achieve cheap labour and ready-made systems of control. Clegg and Dunkerley (1980, p. 534) argue that 'in low-wage, less developed social formations . . . hegemonic forms of domination will recede in importance', i.e. control is more likely to rest on the threat of unemployment and the possibility of starvation and arrest.

ACCOUNTING RULES

An important area that is not considered by Clegg it that of *accounting rules*. Broadly, this area centres around judgements about profits and loss, costs and prices, savings and investments – judgements that guide the decisions of managers as to where to invest, what to charge, how to be more profitable, when and where to cut losses, etc.

Marxists have long argued that the development of capitalism is conditioned by fundamental movements and their impact upon the average 'rate of profit' (Mandel, 1975; Rowthorn, 1976). This sets the context in which decisions are made and, as we have seen over this century, we have been faced with periods of depression, recession and booms. Without going into too much depth here, it can be argued that the depression of 1929 was in large part caused by adherence to a set of rules. Stock market speculation is a classic case of judgements made according to a set of underlying rules. When key stockholders began to react in a certain way, others followed suit and sold, and the resultant stock market crash was handled by a government and businesses that, in turn, were locked into an inappropriate conventional wisdom:

> People often speak as if the 1929 Crash made the Great Depression of the Thirties inevitable. It did not. It took policymakers, embracing one wrong choice after another, to lock the world into that gloomy fate (Magnet, 1987).

The logic of the day – the rules of accounting – told President Hoover to attempt to balance the federal budget, to tighten the money supply, to introduce and strengthen protectionist trade barriers. They were the wrong rules, and it took a sort of neo-Keynesian logic on the part of the federal government to put the ailing economy into reverse; that, and the threat of war!

Within broad economic contexts, accounting rules influence the way that organizations are structured and take decisions. One broad set of rules concerns the choice between optimizing or satisficing. Depending upon a number of factors, including economic climate, specific market conditions, competition and the decision makers involved, organizations may decide to attempt to optimize or sacrifice their levels of profitability. The choice will most probably have dramatic implications for the company involved. The case of the GEC-EE company in the UK provides a useful example. When the new company came into being as a result of a merger in 1968, it was the largest employer in the UK private sector of industry. By the end of its first year, its pre-tax profits stood at £49 million and were to reach £77 million for the year 1972. Much of the new company's increased profitability was due to the efforts and profit maximizing philosophy of the managing director, Arnold Weinstock. The *Sunday Times* newspaper noted that:

> When Arnold Weinstock entered G.E.C. his prime task was to weed out waste. Getting to grips with this has involved making every manager in the group acutely conscious of fractions of a penny, and personal responsibility for profit has been raised to virtually unparalleled peaks (quoted in Mills, 1982, p. 309).

As far as Arnold Weinstock was concerned, 'if it doesn't pay, it doesn't stay'. A key problem for the workforce lay in the interpretation and rigidity of 'waste' and 'profitability'. Weinstock's concept was geared to desired rates of profit and whole factories (or sections) were closed down where they were not realizing the right margin of profit, and if the capital could be more profitably re-employed elsewhere. This policy led to a large number of lay-offs and closures including those factories that were profitable but were not profitable enough (Mills, 1982).

A totally different example, that of cost accounting, provides another area where we can see how accounting rules impact upon organizational development. The way in which a company undertakes cost accounting can have significant consequences. According to Harvard accounting professor Robert S. Kaplan, 'Many U.S. companies don't know where they are making money and where they are losing' (quoted in Worthy, 1987). Many executives in the USA are making decisions based upon 'hopelessly obsolete' accounting practices:

> Over the past two decades most corporations have thoroughly revamped their manufacturing processes, notably by replacing people with machines. Yet the typical accounting system still focuses on labor costs, so the magnitude of the errors in cost estimates has gotten worse (Worthy, 1987).

A typical problem involves the allocation of overhead to unit costs:

> accountants have big trouble dealing with overheads, a black hole that swallows up everything from the equipment used to fashion a product to the security guard who watches over the plant at night. How much of the purchasing agent's salary is attributable to the semiconductor chip, how much to the typewriter, how much to the hundred other products made in the same plant? What about the grease that keeps the machines humming, or the computers that make sure payment checks come out on

time? Boiled down to its simplest form, the question becomes: Which products cause which costs? (Worthy, 1987)

If, how and with what priority such accounting issues are listened to can affect a number of organizational practices. Here is one example, a case where 'cost compentency' was seen as a priority:

> At [IBM's] Lexington, Kentucky, plant . . . typewriters and computer keyboards move not from one common functional department (fabrication say) to another (assembly), but flow through their own tightly arranged production lines.
> At some IBM plants, the workers on the lines are responsible for doing their own maintenance, quality control, and other jobs that were formerly handled by central departments serving the whole plant. While the new layouts were motivated by the company's desire to speed the production cycle and reduce work-in-process inventory, the arrangement gives accounting a clearer picture of which costs are associated with which products (Worthy, 1987, pp. 52–3).

While at one level IBM's decisions may appear to be a combination of technological and accounting decisions, it is likely that their technological restructuring was itself deeply influenced by the current interest in a new Japanese accounting technique – *just-in-time* – a process that involves organizing production practices in such a way that it does not rely on large inventories. In accounting terms this saves on inventory costs and in production terms it encourages managers to think critically about the way they organize. While some US companies have learned to 'sharpen' their social regulative rules by way of 'corporate culture' developments, others have looked to Japanese accounting rules as ways of improving productivity. Yet,

> Even in this era of just-in-time inventories, many companies ignore the cost of carrying inventories when evaluating the profitability of individual products. . . . [For example] a food processing company that churned out so much inventory . . . had to lease container cars on a rail siding just to hold the stuff. The seemingly profitable product was a loser if the costs associated with the excess inventory were charged against it (Worthy, 1987, p. 48).

But the situation can go the other way; overestimating can be a problem and can negatively affect investment opportunities. For example:

> Says Lee Steel, a cost accounting expert at Touche Ross 'Suppose you think you're making an 8% margin on a product. Even though you could probably gain market share if you added capacity, you probably won't invest in that area because of the low margin. But what if your margin is really 15%?' Steele is now working with a large electronics company whose fuzzy cost system, he believes, has obscured countless investment opportunities (Worthy, 1987, p. 52).

The point in all this is not to suggest that Kaplan, Worthy, The IBM company, or Lee Steel have the right answers; rather, that whatever accounting logic is arrived at will have a crucial bearing upon organizational reality.

Institutionalization and change

As we have seen above, there are several major areas of potential rules of control, that those rules are influential in the construction and development of organizations, that organizations will be constructed in different ways depending upon their relationship to the various rules and the personnel involved, and that a given configuration of rules and personnel involved in their enactment will constitute a unique set of experiences that we will call an *organizational culture*.

How any given organizational culture is developed and maintained needs to be understood in relation to its unique history, its relationship to rule developments at the macro level, the specific history of the society in which it is located, and the specific discourse from which social reality is viewed. For example, from 1918 onwards, a number of communist parties came into being throughout the world. They were founded in the context of what they saw as the failure of social democratic parties, the success of the Bolsheviks and the Russian Revolution of 1917, the oppressive character of capitalism and the rise of fascism. In many ways, these parties were of a similar type in terms of structure and philosophy, a fact reinforced and strengthened through their membership of the Communist International, which monitored and expelled those parties that did not conform to a certain pattern or way of operation.

If we look closer we will find that each party has a unique history and location that eventually contributed to dramatic differences between parties. Some parties were founded out of splits from other parties (e.g. Bolsheviks), some out of mergers of existing parties (e.g. Communist Party of Great Britain: CPGB); some were founded in conditions of illegality (e.g. Bolsheviks), some in conditions of relative legality (e.g. CPGB); some operated under conditions of parliamentary democracy (e.g. the German Communist Party: GCP), some operated under neo-feudalist conditions (e.g. Communist Party of China); some operated within imperial nations (e.g. the CPGB), some operated under imperialist domination (e.g. the Vietnamese Communist Party); some operated under dramatically changing situations of legality (e.g. the GCP in the 1930s and 1940s; the CPUSA under McCarthyism; the Communist Party of France under the Nazi occupation), some operated under relatively stable conditions (e.g. the CPGB); some became the ruling party within society (e.g. the Communist Party of the Soviet Union: CPSU; the Socialist Unity Party in the German Democratic Republic: SED; the Polish Communist Party), some played a part in government coalitions (e.g. the CPF and the Italian communist parties immediately following the Second World War and in selected periods in the 1970s and 1980s), and some remained an opposition, non-governmental party (e.g. the CPUSA and the Communist Party of Canada); some operate in the context of a highly developed working class (e.g. CPGB, GCP), some operate in the absence of a well-established working class (e.g. the Iranian Communist Party).

INSTITUTIONALIZATION

In the course of organizational development, macro-rule *influences* will be shaped – through the interactions and perceptions of organization members – into a set of *rules*. What was once considered one of several alternatives (e.g. the possibility of selling cosmetics through department stores) will become *the* way of doing things (e.g. the Mary Kay direct sales way of selling cosmetics).

An organization's 'way of doing' things become reflected and maintained through a series of symbols (Dandridge, 1985), stories (Martin *et al.*, 1983), metaphors (Morgan, 1986), official rules and regulations (Ouchi, 1980), political action (Riley, 1983), ceremonies and rites (Peters and Waterman, 1982) and language (Evered, 1983).

Institutionalization appears to serve various purposes, i.e. to have a number of useful outcomes. For organizations, institutionalization can provide stability, regularity, certainty and control. After initial periods of socialization and training, employees are able to understand what is required of them, how certain tasks are to be undertaken, how 'things work' around the organization. This obviates the need for constant supervision and training (people know what to do), it assists the flow of information and communication (people understand 'what is going on'), it identifies recruitment needs (who will 'fit in'), and it may even lead to organizational commitment and motivation (people identify with/feel good about the organization). Institutionalization is also invaluable in helping potential clients, suppliers and other external bodies to 'know who they are dealing with'. For individuals, organizational institutionalization can assist them to know what is expected of them, to know what to do, to understand what is meant and what is going on, to 'feel a part of' the organization, to have a sense of regularity and certainty in their working relationships, to meet a demand for order and coherence (Douglas, 1986), to maintain a sense of ontological security, and to act as a 'sense making' device (Heritage, 1984). In the words of Mary Douglas (1986, p. 48):

> Past experience is encapsulated in an institution's rules so that it acts as a guide to what to expect from the future. The more fully the institutions encode expectations, the more they put uncertainty under control, with the further effect that behaviour tends to conform to the institutional matrix: if this degree of coordination is achieved, disorder and confusion disappear.

In the process of establishing an organizational culture, a way of thinking, or 'thought style' (Fleck, 1979), is established which 'sets the preconditions of any cognition, and it determines what can be counted as a reasonable question and a true or false answer' (Douglas, 1986, p. 13).

> Institutions create shadowed places in which nothing can be seen and no questions asked. They make other areas show finely discriminated detail, which is closely scrutinized and ordered. History emerges in an unintended shape as a result of practices directed to immediate, practical ends (Douglas, 1986, pp. 69–70).

Were ideas simply arrived at conspiritorially and/or imposed upon organizational members, it is hardly likely that a strong sense of institutionalization would develop:

> Any institution that is going to keep its shape needs to gain legitimacy by distinctive grounding in nature and in reason: then it affords its members a set of analogies with which to explore the world and with which to justify the naturalness and reasonableness of the instituted rules, and it can keep its identifiable continuing form (Douglas, 1986, p. 112).

At Athabasca University, for example, reference to implicit *principles* in such terms as 'open' (University) or 'distance learning' is often used to justify a number of practices (e.g. a rigid commitment to the use of 'course packages', opposition to activities thought to 'mirror' more traditional universities, an insistence that all students pass an English competency test):

> Any institution then starts to control the memory of its members; it causes them to forget experiences incompatible with its righteous image, and it brings to their minds events which sustain the view of nature that is complementary to itself. It provides the categories of their thought, sets the terms for self-knowledge, and fixes identities. All of this is not enough. It must secure the social edifice by sacralizing the principles of justice (Douglas, 1986, p.112).

At Athabasca University, the annual convocation provides one of many opportunities to cultivate the sacred purposes of the institution. Involving only a small graduating group each year, the ceremony allows each graduate to be individually introduced by way of a brief biography. The biographies tend to focus upon the 'unique' struggles that each student had in completing a degree through distance learning. The ceremony encourages those involved to contrast favourably the activities of Athabasca with more traditional universities. When, on one occasion, a key graduate speech focused upon many of the perceived problems of the university, some members of the institution moved to have all future speeches vetted: the fact that such a motion was rejected had as much to do with 'liberal' institutionalized thinking as a subconscious view that future convocations would, once again, be fully confirmatory.

Andrew Schotter (1981), drawing upon the metaphor of the computer, describes institutions as 'machines for thinking', i.e. that organizations provide conceptual frameworks that reduce the need for individuals to think through each and every problem. As we carry out our work at Athabasca University, we need not deal directly, immediately or on-goingly with questions concerning the institution's ability to bring in adequate funds or adequate supplies, which suppliers to contact, issues of copyright, university–government relations, and so on. All these issues lie elsewhere in the institution. Likewise, in arriving at policy decisions as members of the university's Academic Council, we rely on the fact that a collective of people will bring different bits of information and thinking to bear on specific questions.

This aspect of institutionalization also allows people to feel that they are not fully responsible for the activities of the organization: 'the individual tends to leave the important decisions to his [sic] institutions while busying himself with tactics and details' (Douglas, 1986, p. 111). We know this aspect of organizational life only too well – from the remonstrations of former Nazi functionaries to current encounters with minor bureaucrats who inform us that they 'don't make the rules'.

This brings us to the point that institutionalization has its negative side too. First, it must be said that we cannot presuppose that in each case factors positive to an organization have been institutionalized. Hence the organization may well have habitualized 'bad' practices. Employees may be regularly 'cutting corners'; certain departments may institutionally be unable to communicate with one another; certain managers may continually leave employees to their own devices in situations where clear direction is needed. In such cases, people may not know what is required or expected of them; co-ordination may be limited; employees may lack a sense of identity while, ironically, the organization gives off a definite but negative identity; members may feel a sense of belonging to only part of the organization; people may not know how or want to 'fit in'.

But even where there are a number of positive outcomes of institutionalization, they may contain concomitant negative features. The literature on bureaucracy is rich with examples. Robert Merton has suggested that bureaucracy can lead to a number of problems:

1 The development of depersonalized relationships (as people respond in terms of rules and roles rather than to persons).
2 An overconcern with (official) rules to the extent that rules are seen as ends in themselves.
3 Rigidity of behaviour (caused through an over-reliance upon rules and the use of categorization as a decision-making technique).

For Merton, these factors have negative consequences not only for the organization but for individual personality development (Merton, 1936, 1940). This is a theme taken up by Chris Argyris (1957), who argues that the 'mature personality' is unnecessarily constrained by the dictates of bureaucratic working. Selznick (1949) takes up the theme of divided loyalties, arguing that bureaucracies involve considerable departmentalization which encourages departmental as opposed to organizational loyalties, conflict as opposed to cooperation. Finally, Alvin Gouldner (1954), addressing the issue of motivation, argues that bureaucratic rules, by defining unacceptable behaviour, increase knowledge about minimum acceptable behaviour, i.e. encourage low levels of motivation and productivity.

Many of the features identified by Merton, Selznick, Arygis and Gouldner apply to organizations generally, as witnessed in William Foote Whyte's (1956) image of the grey flannel conformity of the *organization man* [sic], or in Rosabeth Moss Kanter's (1977) account of the 'stuck' *men and women of the corporation*. Kanter's account has the added insight of showing how the institutionalization of certain practices can lead to the exclusion or restriction of opportunities for women. Looking beyond institutionalization *within* organizations, some commentators have argued that organizational construction may, in specific circumstances, be in itself inherently negative (Illich, 1981; Mills and Chiaramonte, 1990).

CHANGE

Organizational change is integrally related to the processes of rule formation detailed above: meta-rules, specific organizational cultures, and given personalities all have a peculiar bearing upon organizational change.

Meta-rules
Throughout this chapter, we have referred to the influence of meta-rules upon organizational construction – apartheid, colonialism, segregation, anti-discrimination legislation, modes of production, scientific management, *glasnost*, rationality, just-in-time, and so on. Changes in meta-rules can have profound influences on pressure for change within organizations. To return to our example of communist parties, we have witnessed, through a whole series of different historical events and contexts, a series of changes throughout the once similar communist parties. Some parties were redesigned as 'mass' parties, opening membership up to large numbers of people rather than restricting it to cadres (e.g. post-First World War Italian Communist Party). Some parties altered their strategies to conform with the peculiar national circumstances under which they lived; in the event some parties dropped their adherence to violent revolution (e.g. the CPGB's policy of a *British Road to Socialism*; the CPF's *Socialism in the Colours of France*). Some parties dissolved themselves (e.g. the CPUSA in the 1940s; the Hungarian Communist Party in 1989). Some parties have introduced radical change while retaining power (e.g. the CPSU's *glasnost*). Some parties have militarily resisted calls for change (e.g. the Chinese Communist party of 1988–9). Some parties have handed over power (e.g. the Polish Communist Party's abdication to *Solidarity* in 1988).

In every case internal changes, influenced by a number of external rule contexts, in turn influenced changes across communist parties. In the 1970s, we witnessed the advent of *Eurocommunism* in which several major West European communist parties 'liberalized' their way of viewing social progress and, in the event, criticized several fundamental aspects of the way the CPSU (and other East European communist parties) organized their state. Noting the changes, Ernest Mandel made some telling comments about rule changes in the communist world and their potential for further change:

> The leaders of the Communist Parties of Western Europe are now defending some elementary principles of democratic liberties and human rights for the phase of construction of socialism *in their own countries*, while the Kremlin has not excommunicated them the way Tito and Mao were excommunicated. Thus, one can be an advocate of a multi-party system, genuine freedom of the press, and the real right of the workers to strike after the overthrow of capitalism without automatically being dubbed a 'frenzied anti-communist', 'agent of imperialism', or even 'Hitlerite-Trotskyist'. A question is thus immediately posed: suppose a Czechoslovak, East German, Polish, Bulgarian, Soviet (or Yugoslav!) Communist demanded application of these same principles in his or her country as well? (Mandel, 1979, p. 62).

We know how 'liberalization' demands were received in 1979. Things were different a mere decade later. The elevation of Mikhail Gorbachev to General Secretary of the Soviet Communist Party in March 1985 meant not simply a change of leader – a change of leadership style – it came to mean a fundamental change of the rules; the rules of organizing, the rules of thinking, the rules of living. *Glasnost*, as we know only too well, allowed members of other East European communist parties an alternative way of addressing their problems. They no longer had to operate within a certain set of assumptions; they could now consider other options. The discourse had changed.

Not only did a series of meta-rule changes influence thinking within communist parties, but they also influenced the way we were able to *think* about those events at the time. How we understand the development, change and even demise of some communist parties will depend to a great extent upon the discourse – or rules of thought – of the time. Our understanding of communist party developments will have been influenced by a background of growing fascism in the 1930s, by Stalinism in the 1940s and 1950s, by the Cold War in the 1960s, by anti-imperialist struggles in the 1970s, and by *glasnost* in the 1980s. These contexts of thought shape the way we view what is occurring.

At the time of writing, there are a number of meta-rule changes – some dramatic, some not so dramatic – that are clearly finding a reflection at the level of organizational change. *Glasnost*, for instance, represents tremendous change that has implications far beyond Eastern Europe. Certainly in terms of business, it is likely that *glasnost* has set the scene for the 1990s. A new discourse is opening up on the possibility and desirability of doing business with the Soviet Union and other East European nations (Kirkland, 1987).

The advent of *glasnost* will almost certainly affect such things as government policies towards trade with the East (state rules), the ability of business organizations to operate within new markets and to have a greater freedom of operation within those markets (strategic rules), and thinking about the nature of management (reproduction rules). Towards the end of 1989, US President George Bush was already considering removing barriers on a range of previously restricted high-tech items that US companies could sell to the Soviet Union; meanwhile, a number of other US companies were jumping into the new market:

> Many Westerners are likely to be put off by the enormous regulatory burdens that still accompany doing business in the Soviet Union. But a few are already jumping in. John Naylor, president of the consumer products division of Connecticut-based SSMC, hopes to sign an agreement by the end of the year to produce 50,000 Singer sewing machines a year in a factory near Minsk. . . . 'The time for American business to get into the Soviet market is now, while the changes are taking place,' says Donald Kendall, former chief executive of Pepsico and now chairman of its executive committee (Kirkland, 1987, p. 88).

By the end of 1989, American companies had indeed jumped into the Soviet market. Prominent among US companies were Chevron, RJR Nabisco, Eastman Kodak, Johnson & Johnson, and Archer Daniels Midland – organized in a consortium. Changes in these companies' intentions to trade in the USSR began, following *glasnost* and *perestroika*, which changing perceptions of the leading decision makers, perceptions of change not shared by everyone: 'for every U.S. company on the prowl in the land of the bear, hundreds are hanging back' (Kraar, 1989, p. 171).

Decisions to enter the Soviet market have brought organizational change within themselves. Now these companies have to hire people and even departments who can come to terms with the intricacies of the Soviet Union. Five major companies, as we have seen, have felt the need to establish a consortium, with all the organizational development that that involves. And operating within the USSR itself presents a number of new organizational challenges. The Ford Motor Company, for example, hopes to get a foothold in the Soviet Union, but has a number of organizational questions to resolve:

First the Soviets want to import Ford cars from West Germany – some 100,000 annually for three years – 'so that some results of perestroika would be seen on the streets of Moscow'. Ford has no trouble with that part, since the Soviets would pay in hard currency. As a second step the U.S.S.R. wants to modernize an auto factory in Gorky to assemble those cars solely for the Soviet market and later make all their components. Soviet and Ford officials [however] . . . never could agree on 'how far that integration could go' (Kraar, 1989, p. 168).

Increased trade has seen a number of Soviets becoming involved in US management training programmes (cf. Leinster, 1989). Soon Soviet organizations will be faced with new accounting rules and theories of management.

Another 'g' word that is changing organizational practices in the 1990s is 'green' – a reference to environmental concerns that are pressuring organizations to rethink their technological strategies. Environmental protectionist groups have existed for some time, but it was not until the 1980s that they began to make any broad impact upon social thinking. In West Germany, the Green Party began to receive increasing numbers of votes throughout the 1980s and this was a trend evidenced at the level of the parliament of the European Economic Community (EEC). In the 1989 elections to the EEC Parliament, a significant number of environmentalists were elected, and even in the UK the Green Party received around 20% of the vote and were placed third after the Labour and Conservative parties.

The 'green revolution', as some have termed it, has been translated into social, legal and economic pressures for change within companies:

Once thought of as little more than business-bashing cranks, the Greens have moved from the political fringe to the center. Consumers are in the forefront of the drive, combing supermarkets for ecologically friendly products. . . .

The ramifications for European industry, and all Americans doing business there, are enormous. Many companies face huge increases in capital investment and production costs. Automakers, including Ford and General Motors, will spend an extra $7 billion a year between now and 1993 to install antipollution equipment in all cars (Tully, 1989, p. 159).

The EEC has passed a series of laws that force companies to change their practices. These laws impose strict limits on emissions from new power plants and requires existing ones to meet the standards by 2003; stringent standards for water quality has forced the UK government to spend the equivalent of $35 billion to modernize their equipment; and tough new auto emission regulations have come into force:

> Pressured by the Germans and the rising power of the Greens, the EC stunned the industry by imposing U.S.-style standards on all European cars by 1993.
>
> The impact is enormous. The new standards will force automakers to equip cars with expensive three-way catalytic converters that reduce emissions of hydrocarbons, carbon monoxide, and nitrogen oxides. The cars will also need fuel-injection systems. The converters work only with injectors, which feed the engine with precisely mixed doses of gasoline. Both are standard in the U.S. But of the ten million gasoline-engine cars made last year in Europe, fewer than three million had catalytic converters and fewer than four million had fuel injection (Tully, 1989, p. 162).

In addition to the auto industry, other industries such as soft drinks and disposable packaging are coming under a number of legal constraints. Several EC countries are moving to restrict the use of plastic beverage containers: West Germany had introduced a quota system that restricts disposable packaging to 20% of the soft-drink market and 10% for beer, while Denmark has banned all disposable cans for beer, mineral water and soft drinks. Interestingly, Denmark's actions were subsequently upheld by the European Court of Justice, which held that Denmark had a right to take action on environmental grounds even where it led to a constraint upon 'free trade'. These actions hold major possibilities for the expansionist Pepsi and Coke companies:

> Coke is relying on the same 'convenience packaging' it uses in megaplants all over the world: tin and aluminium cans and plastic bottles, which are cheaper, lighter and easier to transport than glass bottles (Tully, 1989, p. 164).

The changing social values (extra-organizational rules), legislation (state rules) and policies (strategic rules) that are forcing some companies to make dramatic changes to their production processes (technical rules), are also helping some companies to expand: supermarket chains are cashing in on new 'green' products (e.g. Tesco in England; Superstore in Western Canada); certain US car companies are better prepared to change over to the new technology (e.g. GM in Europe); and the manufacturers of such things as glass bottles and auto-emissions equipment (e.g. Bosch of West Germany).

Technological change is, of course, one of the largest, most rapidly changing areas of change to confront organizations. Article after article throughout the business press centres upon the rapidly changing technological world – in every case there are large-scale implications for the workplace; how it is structured and how it might be restructured; how we communicate and how they relate to one another.

Here are just a few of the many examples. The development of the Boeing 7J7 aircraft, with 150 seats in a two-aisle arrangement is predicted to cut by half the average turnaround time for deplaning passengers (Labich, 1987). The potential impact of this new plane is on training, reduced staffing levels, and increased performance expectations of flight attendants.

Changes in the US steel industry throughout the 1980s have led to large scale closures, unemployment, radical changes in steel production methods and changes in work rules. Previously, the technology of steel making had relied upon large-scale integrated methods in which ore was turned into pig iron and then converted into steel. This large-scale operation was locked into a set of technological rules that it took a depression in the industry and widespread closures to alter. In terms of production costs and market needs, the so-called up-start mills appeared to do well in the 1980s. These mills are extremely efficient recyclers of steel. The other mills, however, needed dramatic organizational changes. A large number of closures (technical rules: 444 mills closed down in the USA in the period 1981–6), coupled with tax laws that generously assisted the steel industry (state rules), helped many of the remaining companies to retool. But other organizational changes were also demanded within those companies. For example:

> At USX the United Steelworkers resisted management's effort to contract out more work. But the union made a major concession in its current contract, agreeing the elimination of 1,346 jobs out of a total of around 20,000 (down from 75,000 five years before). The goal was to be achieved by revising work rules.
>
> The company had long felt hobbled by archaic practices dating back to an era when USX ruled a mighty oligopoly. In many plants a millwright assigned to install a machine had to await the arrival of a truck driver to move it to the site. Now the millwright drives the forklift himself. The emphasis is on broadening an individual's skills, so that much of the work force can be used interchangeably. Those displaced are generally pensioned off (Ross, 1987, pp. 97–8).

In this example we can see clearly how changing strategic rules led to changes in technological (and social regulative) rules and the way that production was organized.

Computerization is, of course, a key site of meta-change in the way we think about technology and is setting the tone for organizational changes throughout industry. Companies are employing increasing numbers of computers to replace workers. As one former employee put it:

> I started at Bethlehem Steel's Burn Harbor mill in 1977 and lost my job in 1984. I worked in the human resources department as a secretary. A computer took my place (quoted in Magnet, 1988, p. 48).

In the banking industry, cash-card machines are rapidly replacing bank tellers, and both IBM and Sears invested more than $250 million to deliver services to consumers by personal computer and thus, one must suspect, reduce the number of sales and marketing personnel.

Computerization is also changing work practices. Video-conferencing, for example, has considerable potential, e.g. it can allow a Calgary doctor to learn a surgical procedure performed elsewhere, and an Edmonton lawyer to argue a case before the Supreme Court of Canada, sitting in Ottawa – both the doctor and the lawyer can use local video-conferencing facilities. Indeed, in Alberta, the system 'is so popular that the video-conferencing facilities are "nearing saturation" at core hours' (Bartlett, 1989). The possibility of this development have not been lost on Athabasca University – video-conferencing could radically alter the rules of distance education, turning it from a primarily print-based to an electronic face-to-face process.

Ongoing technological rules at Athabasca University include the introduction of the fax machine (speeding up communication *and* expectations of the need for speed!), a computerized registration system (restructuring much of the secretaries' work towards data entry; initially reducing teaching flexibility in the requirement that classroom assignments conform to menus designed to cope with home-study materials), and the widespread use of monitors and PCs (allowing faculty members to work from home; encouraging electronic mail as a primary form of communication).

Organizational culture

As we have indicated above, an organization's culture can have a vital effect on its potential for change. The organizational change and organizational culture literature suggests that organizations should build a number of areas of flexibility into their operations to allow for change. That is easier said than done. Culture is not so easily manipulable. The culture will be determined to a certain extent by the goals (Etzioni, 1961; Handy, 1983), by the market (Burns and Stalker, 1961), by decision makers (Child, 1972), and through the actions of the various other organizational members (Mills, 1988a). An organizational culture that encourages flexibility may not be prepared for the very change that requires employees to give flexibility. Similarly, organizational members socialized to respond flexibly to a number of market changes may not necessarily be prepared to respond to far-reaching technological or structural changes within the organization. On the other hand, those organizations that are structured bureaucratically, and in which people are encouraged to be rules-minded, may none the less respond favourably to change in which people are given greater autonomy. As we have seen with events in the Eastern Bloc, certain organizational changes are rapidly occurring in situations that were previously rigidly controlled.

The key factor in understanding organizational change is to take into account the specific characteristics of any given organization and the dynamics involved in attempts to introduce change. Organizational change needs to be viewed as a political process which involves attempting to change existing rules of specific organizational cultures. The two cases below provide illustrations of the complexity of the change process.

Case I: Changing the rules at IBM

International Business Machines (IBM) is almost always cited in discussion about organizational culture, usually as an exemplar of a flexible company ready to meet the challenge of change. Peters and Waterman (1982) refer to the significance of IBM's philosophy of 'respect for the individual' in that it permeates the culture of the organization and results in the achievement of 'extraordinary results through ordinary people'. Deal and Kennedy (1982) discuss IBM's employment of maverick leaders, or 'outlaws':

> At IBM, top management created the IBM Fellows Program to free outstanding technical personnel from organizational constraints. Deciding that the company was too straightlaced, that maybe there were too many white shirts around, this bastion of conservatism through this program encouraged its outlaw heroes – just as they do most things in that highly structured company, systematically. Ads in *Newsweek* described the program by speaking about IBM's affection for 'Dreamers, Heretics, Gadflies. . . .'
>
> In all, about fifty such outlaw heroes were consciously and deliberately created as countercultural to the rest of the organization but crucial for instilling the ethic that ideas are really important, that a creative personal style can make an important difference (Deal and Kennedy, 1982, pp. 51–2).

These and numerous other examples indicate that IBM is a company that is able to meet the needs of change and is successful as a result. Indeed, IBM worked so well that others wished to learn how:

> For four years in a row, from 1983 to 1986, it was voted the world's most admired company by *Fortune*. 'Big Blue' (the name derives from the colour of its main-frame computers and the suits worn by its salesmen) has almost 60 per cent of the world's mainframe market (Hamilton, 1989, p. 44).

None the less, in recent years:

> the corporation's performance has been lacklustre, its problem not running the world, but running itself. In the early 1980s, it enjoyed sales growth of about 15 per cent – up to five percentage points ahead of the industry – and there were dreams of a $200 billion turnover by the mid-1990s. But since 1985 the company has lagged behind, managing only 6 per cent growth, compared with the industry's 9 per cent. Turnover reached $59.7 billion in 1988.
>
> For three years in succession, between 1985 and 1987, IBM's profits tumbled, an embarrassment not experienced since the Great Depression. From 1984's peak of $6.6 billion, they sank to $5.3 billion in 1987 (Hamilton, 1989, p. 44).

So what had happened? IBM's problems had quite a bit to do with the culture. To begin with, IBM had developed a set of technical rules which were designed to ensure that customers were locked-in to the company. Once an organization buys IBM equipment, they then have to rely upon IBM or IBM-compatible machines. This strategy worked well for many years and forced many a customer to stay loyal to IBM, but it was not a loyalty born out of conviction. IBM's dedication to customer service (a kind of social regulative rule) was increasingly flying in the face of the customers' technical needs (technical rules):

> Bewildered and frustrated by the proliferation of incompatible machines, buyers have spurred the movement toward 'open systems,' a universal standard that would allow

software to run on many different brands of hardware. That clearly threatens IBM and other large computer makers ... which have traditionally clung to proprietary machines and programming (Dreyfuss, 1989, p. 38).

And IBM lost sight of its customers in other ways. Company decision makers failed to perceive the importance of growing new niches in the field of laptops and technical workstations:

Faster-moving specialist – Compaq and the clone-makers in personal computers, Digital in minicomputers and NEC, Fujitsu and Hitachi in mainframes – have captured niche after niche in the exploding data-processing market (Hamilton, 1989, p. 44).

Ironically, one major attempt by IBM to move into a new niche got into trouble due to organizational culture difficulties. Perceiving the importance of telecommunications to the company's development, IBM decided to enter that niche by way of a buy-out of an existing company, and in 1984 it bought Rolm, a US switch manufacturer. Rolm, however, presented IBM with a very different cultural environment, one that fundamentally clashed with its own:

At Rolm, employees enjoyed a relaxed and spontaneous atmosphere with weekly "beer busts" where they could let themselves go. It was a shock to the strict IBM culture of blue suits and a preference for teetotalism (Hamilton, 1989, p. 46).

This addition to the IBM empire did not work out and in 1988 Rolm was sold to Siemens of Germany.

A major problem that has inhibited IBM from recognizing a need for – let alone instituting – change has been its bureaucratic management structure:

Its corporate management board with 18 senior executives, was handing down decisions from world headquarters in Armonk, New York, on everything from advertising campaigns to R & D allocations for specific products.

IBM was not thinking about the limitations of top-down management when the world began to get more competitive. Convinced that the biggest threat was Japan's awesome manufacturing prowess, the company spent $16.5 billion on new plants and focused upon improving productivity and quality (Dreyfuss, 1989, p. 32).

In 1985, a new CEO – John Akers – took over IBM and set about far-reaching organizational change. One key factor that Akers could not ignore was the company's downwardly spiralling profits. In attempting to address profitability, Akers decided upon a series of measures to make the company more cost-effective and to change its production strategies. Both sets of decisions centred upon radical organizational changes. He began by reducing the 400,000-strong workforce by 20,000, cutting back on the number of managers, closing plants and reassigning 20,000 administrative and manufacturing personnel to programming and sales. Interestingly, Akers achieved the large staff reduction within the confines of existing social regulative rules which inhibit lay-offs – all the reductions being achieved through natural wastage and early retirement. It has been estimated that the 'no lay-off' policy may be contributing to high costs within the company, pulling profits down by 35% (Dreyfuss, 1989). A further 10,000 staff reduction was announced in 1989, and this time the company offered cash incentives to quit – a way of getting around the spirit, if not the letter, of the 'no lay-off' principle (Rowan, 1989).

In order to move into new niches, Akers has made some structural changes of a different order. Addressing the problems of a differentiated market and the need for a more 'open systems' approach, Akers has developed some swingeing changes inside the company. In 1988, he reorganized the core company, IBM USA,

> into seven autonomous business units: PCs, mainframes, minicomputers, communications, microchip manufacturing, programming, and software, with an eighth unit that handles marketing for all the others (Dreyfuss, 1989, p. 33):

He has also forged several business partnerships and was instrumental in the establishment of a consortium – the Open Software Foundation – to address the open systems problem. Dealing with the problem of 'a lumbering bureaucracy', Akers decided, despite cuts in levels of management, to encourage entrepreneurship by tapping the spirit from outside through a network of new partnerships. Alongside all of this, IBM is relying on old-style strategic rules to remain competitive:

> In its 76 direct subsidiaries and branches outside the US, IBM's policy to employ mostly nationals, and use mostly local suppliers. It thus wields immense power in many countries. It fought, for example, a Mexican government regulation forbidding wholly foreign-owned companies to set up in the country. (And IBM did not change its policy; the government changed the regulation) (Hamilton, 1989, p. 49).

This company ensures that subsidiaries are placed in competition with one another and this helps to keep them in line. Commenting on the fact that IBM UK won 'the bid' to be Europe's PC manufacturing base for IBM, Tony Cleaver, the managing director, has stated that:

> 'The PC didn't have to be made in the UK'. About 20,000 PCs now roll off the production line each week at the Greenock plant. But Cleaver knows that manufacture could be switched elsewhere at any time if the UK does not keep in shape (Hamilton, 1989, p. 49).

The changes that Akers has introduced have been called culture transforming:

> So sweeping are the changes that Akers could stamp the most enduring mark on the company since Thomas Watson Jr. propelled it to world dominance (Dreyfuss, 1989, p. 31).

The significance of this point is not lost within the company. Len Peach, personnel director of IBM UK, found great differences on his return to the company after three years secondment.

> The vocabulary had changed, he says. No one talked about computer hardware anymore. Instead, 'partnerships and total solutions' were on everyone's lips (Hamilton, 1989, p. 44).

Case II; Equality and the Canadian Public Service

The history of the Federal Public Service in Canada has been one of twists and turns in regard to the issue of sexual equality. The gendered nature of the service and its embeddedness within a bureaucratic structure have greatly influenced the process (N. Morgan, 1988). Nicole Morgan argues that it is important to understand that change is often one of twists and turns:

> The linear models of women's progress are based on the idea that the structure and the mandate of the public service or any other organization are static, that they form part of a passive block from which anyone can come and carve out an equal share thanks to affirmative action programs. But organizations grow, shrink, change their mandate, adapt their product, target different clienteles, restructure their human resources – in short, they are constantly changing to suit their own requirements and those of the environment around them (N. Morgan, 1988, p. 2).

None the less, as Nicole Morgan (1988, p. 2) reminds us: 'the fact is that the public service is a fluctuating organism, its culture is rooted in the past and still unconsciously bears its marks'.

The existence of different sets of rules at different periods of time help to explain the Canadian public service's response to sexual equity. In the period 1908 to the onset of the Second World War, the extra-organizational rules within the public sector reflected a Canadian society in which women were virtually second-class citizens. The public service was designed exclusively for men, constituting 'a sort of appendage to political authority, which at that time was, of course, male' (N. Morgan, 1988, p. 5). The fact that women were even allowed to enter the service in this period seems to have been largely due to the fact that salaries were so low as to not be attractive to sufficient numbers of male candidates. None the less, women's positions were largely temporary and those who married were supposed to resign from the service.

Following the First World War, the public service introduced a policy which placed an emphasis on hiring returning veterans. This had a dual effect on the employment of women – it reduced the number of female employees in the service while creating an even more male 'paramilitary subculture'. Women were almost exclusively employed as stenographers, typists, secretaries and girl Fridays, and were not even dignified in the service's annual reports – being classed under the category of 'Women and Boys', as opposed to men who were either 'Veterans' or 'Civilian Men'. During the Depression in the 1930s, men were retained in preference to women.

Despite the various preferences given to veterans in particular and men in general, females made up around 30% of the service by the outbreak of the Second World War. Nicole Morgan (1988) argues that this was due to the fact that the service increasingly relied on secretarial duties (technical rules), and that these were rigidly defined as female jobs (extra-organizational rules):

> Uneducated or inexperienced males were hired as clerks. The service could turn a blind eye to the presence of a certain number of unproductive male clerks but it could not

afford inefficiency at the typewriter. As a result, educated and productive women retained their positions despite the influx of veterans (N. Morgan, 1988, p. 8).

This may have saved women's jobs, but in the event it created *women's work*. Clerking, for which women could have easily qualified, was denied to women. 'Men became clerks while women became steno-typists. The die was cast for the next four decades' (N. Morgan, 1988, p. 8).

These technical rules influenced the development of whole departments. Between 1940 and 1946, the largest number of female appointments were made by the departments of National Defence and Veterans' Affairs – both of whom relied heavily on typists – while the Post Office – which relied mostly on clerical and operations staff – virtually excluded women.

During the Second World War, with men going off to the armed forces, women were treated as valued workers, the social regulative rules had to change in the face of new realities. While this situation changed briefly following the end of the war and a large influx of new veterans, women still remained in the service in high numbers.

By 1959, those in charge of the Canadian public service were faced with changing attitudes (extra-organizational rules), a large and stable female workforce (around 44% of the service), a period of full-employment (technical rules), and a growing need for female labour (strategic rules). The low wages were no longer attracting or keeping female employees, many of whom were attracted to better paid private sector work. New rules were developed to cope with the situation; restrictions on the employment of married women were dropped, females were now allowed to compete for the position of clerk, salaries were increased and training introduced, and advertising encouraged female applicants.

The recruitment of females to the public service continued at a rapid pace throughout the 1960s. Of the women in the service, some gains were made: a handful of women entered the ranks of senior management; the number of women earning the highest salaries increased; women were included in the Career Assignment Program (1967) designed to train people for high public service. Advances were due to a number of factors: externally, the Canadian educational system 'had flung open the doors of education to young people in general and young women in particular' (N. Morgan, 1988, p. 13); internationally, there were equalitarian moves to change the labour laws in various countries; internally, the public service embarked on a massive recruitment programme that was to double the public service employment between 1964 and 1974, the Public Service Commission had a new, dynamic team that took an interest in employment equality, and an active trade union movement developed and pressed for equality for all employees.

The changes throughout the 1960s, none the less confronted an ageing, male hierarchy that was unprepared for change. The presence of a large number of veterans throughout the service and especially in positions of power (several directors general were indeed former military generals) had strengthened the 'military subculture' and had 'created a working environment which was paternalistic, markedly hierarchical, and, while seemingly benign, unsympathetic to women' career advancement' (N. Morgan 1988, p. 16). The outcome was that women were recruited to fill 'typically female positions', junior level positions and most of the low-paid ranks. The discourse of equality was changing but it was met with an ageing, well-established male hierarchy whose thinking was in a different era. It wasn't so much active resistance as a failure to comprehend. It was also an era in which the government had insisted that the service should greatly increase its recruitment and representation of francophones. At the same time, very little official reference was made to sexual discrimination.

In the 1970s, things began to change in terms of the way males reacted to females and the possibility of female advancement within the service. Things were changing politically. This was the early 1970s, and feminism was a voice that was being heard. In April 1972, the Federal Cabinet sent *Directive* 44 to all deputy ministers, asking them to actively promote the advancement of women to middle and upper positions. This led to some change; gender specificity in job advertising was dropped, the growth rate for female recruits was double that of men, and the number of women in senior management or equivalent posts reached 33. But the fact that change was not more rapid was largely due to the culture of the organization, which was left unaddressed:

> the Cabinet was not taking into account the inertia that reigns in bureaucracies and large organizations. Radical or important changes rarely spring from within such organizations because they go against the territorial interests of those who are supposed to apply them. The Cabinet was also ignoring the thousand and one techniques that an organization as legally complicated as the federal bureaucracy can use to resist change. It was ignoring the informal organization, or 'old boys' club', which is of immense strategic importance . . .
>
> The outcome should not surprise anyone, for it was predictably human: islands of enthusiasm adrift in a sea of indifference, inertia, and resistance. And it provides a remarkable demonstration of the grip of bureaucratic culture and ideology (N. Morgan, 1988, p. 24).

However, rapid external changes were overtaking the slowness of pace within the service:

> In short, the culture of the organization resisted so well that towards the mid-1970s, the political masters could not help but notice. It was obvious that the statistics were not in line with the rhetoric. The near absence of women in the upper echelons looked especially bad in light of the fact that between 1972 and 1975, the number of women in the public service had increased by 30.5% in comparison with only 13.3% for men. Added to this were International Women's Year (1975) and federal elections that were going to be a close race. Women would have to be courted more persuasively. The public service, whether it wanted it or not, would have to do better (N. Morgan, 1988, p. 36).

The late 1970s saw new rule configurations that affected female advancement and male resistance. The new government issued sharper directives on the issue of sexual equality in the public service (state rules). This time departments were expected to develop plans and come back with detailed responses. At the same time, there was an economic downturn (technical rules) which was reflected in cuts in the public service (employment was reduced by 1.3% in 1978, and by a further 4.4% in 1979):

> This abrupt halt in growth had two important consequences: first, it was felt mostly among the male workforce, which decreased by 6.2% between 1975 and 1980 while the female workforce grew by 7.1%. Second, the culture of the organization changed considerably. . . . It was then that the battle for power really started, and the resistance turned into a defensive stance (N. Morgan, 1988, p. 39).

Not only were women present in substantial numbers but they were being taken seriously. Actions taken in regard to females received close attention for fear of charges of discrimination. Many men in positions of authority now became defensive in their approach to women, seeking to find rationalizations rather than platitudes for the slow pace of reform. Now tolerance turned into anger.

The trends of the late 1970s have developed apace through the 1980s. Employment equity policies have been taken to new levels, with affirmative action programmes being introduced in 1980, and the establishment in 1984 of a Royal Commission into the issue of employment equity. Women have made significant advances in the Canadian public service. Only the female population has continued to grow within the service: by 1987 females made up 42.4% of public service staff, between 1985 and 1987 the promotion rate for women exceeded that of men. This has led to fear on the part of some men in the service. Some men have begun to complain about reverse discrimination, and most believe that 'it is impossible to make a career in the federal public service today' (quoted in N. Morgan, 1988, p. 58):

> Men in their forties expressed the most vehement frustration . . . [fearing] that, if the cuts continue and affirmative action programs are stepped up, men will have to be dismissed in order to make room for women. . . .
> While not all the men necessarily felt the fear of losing their jobs, they all nevertheless expressed the fear of no longer being promoted. They were particularly obsessed by the idea that rare openings would go to women (N. Morgan, 1988, p. 58).

In the midst of this angst, the public service has, none the less, settled into something less than a haven of equity. Suitability for high office is still judged according to male-associated criteria; male advancement has also continued – with men gaining a large number of positions on an expanded managerial base; women have swelled the non-management levels, occupying limited, gender-typed occupations; gender-typing is continuing at management levels, with females occupying the lesser-paid, less powerful posts. Within that framework, the tactics of resistance seem to have become 'trivial and childish', targeted at feminists and feminism:

> newspaper articles attempting to prove that feminist arguments are wrong were

systematically posted on staff bulletin boards, newspaper cuttings of lingerie were systematically sent to a woman known for her participation in the women's movement (N. Morgan, 1988, p. 59).

As we move into the 1990s, the discourse on sexual equality in Canada appears to be at an uneven and uneasy crossroads. A number of governmental and judicial actions (state/extra-organizational rules) have challenged women's rights, established over the last two decades; newspaper surveys have indicated that a considerable number of men have a sense of unease over the advancement of women (reproduction/extra-organizational rules); men have begun to challenge in the courts women's rights of abortion; and, most tragic of all and likely symptomatic of the close of the era, 1989 saw two mass killings of women in Canada – one, a series of 'serial' killings in New Brunswick in which three women were battered to death, and the other, the shooting of 14 Montreal University students by a man who blamed 'feminists' for the problems in his life. Women, on the other hand, have continued to organize and to protest; female's have begun to take over the leadership of political parties at provincial (e.g. Manitoba Liberals) and federal level (the NDP), and within the public service a number of women's networks have been established. The new rules and tensions will no doubt shape the public service of the 1990s.

Personalities.
As we have indicated throughout this chapter, the actions of organizational members play a crucial role in the enactment, application and resisting of organizational change. Organizational change can arise from the perception of leaders that change is necessary, e.g. as in the case of Wardair where Max Ward decided to enter the charter business and to relocate to Edmonton. That set of decisions led to a radical altering of the way the company was controlled. Perceptions of external pressures can lead to organizational change, as in the case of say Polish leader General Jarizelski's decision to hand over government to *Solidarity* or John Akers' decision to reduce staffing levels. Organizational change is likely to happen each time a new leader comes to the fore or in the event of a takeover.

But organizational change also comes from another direction – from the middle or from below. Organizational members not only resist change but sometimes initiate change. Pressure in the Canadian public service was not only from the top but from a number of women (and some sympathetic men) throughout the ranks of the service. Rank-and-file pressure within the Hungarian Communist Party led to its transformation into a social democratic style party. Widespread industrial unrest, political strikes and sit-ins in Britain in the early 1970s contributed to legislation aimed at a restructuring of decision making in large UK companies (Mills, 1982). Through conflict over the rules, some structural changes have occurred, and it is to that issue that we turn in Chapter 6.

Conflict: the rules of the game

Introduction

Power in the organization [is] . . . rather like a game of chess. . . . [It] is a function of the relationship of pieces (units) to rules, in that rules invest a certain power in a piece, independently of its position on the board.

Imagine a game more analogous to social reality. In this game the rules are frequently changing and not at all clear. Whoever was able to exploit this uncertainty, and rule in his interest, would in this sense have power. . . . To the extent that all pieces were able to negotiate their positions, more or less, then in a game with a fixed number of pieces, that piece which ended up ruling on the greatest number of pieces, serving its interests in preference to theirs, would be the most powerful. But obviously a piece like the Queen would start in a more privileged position than a pawn, simply because the extant rules, which are now open to interpretation, enable her to begin the sequence with more potential moves to make (Clegg and Dunkerley, 1980, p. 444).

The wicked at heart probably know something (Woody Allen).

One of the most popular games around – far exceeding that of football, fishing, hockey or baseball – is organizational life. It is a game that is played by billions of people each day and the stakes are high. Success can lead to promotion, profitability and increased salaries and benefits. Failure can lead to closure, dismissal, financial losses and salary and benefits reductions. In some games, the stakes can be higher yet – with the survival of a community resting on the outcome.

Organizational life is a deadly serious game. It is played on a board or field of play called an organization and according to a series of formal and informal rules. Organizational rules determine the specific character of the game, who can play, how they are to play, and what particular variation of the game is to be played. As in all good games, organizational life involves a number of players who stand in particular relationship to the rules. These players usually include *enactors*, those who play a key role in the development of rules, *enforcers*, those who play an important role in the process of rule compliance, and *followers*, those who are primarily charged with complying with the rules. It follows that a person's position on the board plays a significant role in their ability to manipulate the pieces successfully.

If all that organizational life boiled down to was the development and carrying out of rules, then organizational analysis would have long since been of little use to anyone. But, as Richard Daft (1989, p. 427) puts it, 'The very nature of organizations invites conflict, because organizations are composed of many groups that have diverse and conflicting interests'. In some ways, these conflicting interests may be a reflection of wider social issues (e.g. class, ethnicity), but in many ways it is the character and construction of organizations themselves that place people in potential conflict positions. In other words, the very fact that people stand in different relationships to organizational rules provides the basis for conflict. Conflict is inherent in the fact that some people get to lay down the rules and others are expected to follow them; that different departments, divisions or groups have to compete for limited resources; that the opportunity structures of organizations are more available to some (e.g. men, whites, the middle class, indigenous) than to other groups (e.g. females, people of colour, the working class, immigrants).

Because of the negative connotations associated with it, organizational conflict is of central interest to management theorists and practitioners alike. Conflict can lead to a rejection of managerial decisions and plans, lowered work morale, higher turnover, increased absenteeism, sabotage and other forms of reduced productivity and/or work commitment. Yet, ironically, as many management theorists have recognized, conflict can also result in positive outcomes – such as reduced tension and hence improved morale, productivity and work commitment and lowered turnover, absenteeism and incidents of sabotage. Whether the eventual outcomes of conflict are viewed as negative or positive will, of course, depend upon the eye of the beholder and the development of a specific set of rules of conflict.

In this chapter we examine some of the ways that rules contribute to organizational conflict and of how conflict rules contribute to the containment of conflict.

Ownership and control

The ownership and control of organizations provides the basis of a series of central conflicts throughout organizations, in particular business organizations. To begin with, there are those who come to establish, own and/or manage the day-to-day activities of the organization and there are those who are employed by those in charge of the organization. The employees are expected to carry out a series of activities designated by those in charge of the organization. This should not be a problem for, as is implicit in much of management theory, there would appear to be a common interest between employer and employee. The employer is able to get a series of tasks completed and, hopefully, to realize a profit in the process, while the employee obtains a job and with it pay and at least a modicum of social status.

However, this 'common interest' is, in fact, a set of ideological rules that have to be constantly kept alive through a series of actions and pronouncements. The notion of a common interest only works in so far as it continues to be accepted. To be accepted, however, it has to be part of a person's felt experience and from time to time that experience breaks down in the face of other contradictory experiences.

PROFITS *vs* COSTS

One area where divergent interests may be felt is in regard to the ability of the organization to remain competitive and the ability of the employee to attain a certain level of remuneration. Both at the level of ideology and of practical outcomes business organizations are expected to make a profit. It is a cardinal rule. Failure to make a profit not only flies in the face of the supposed *raison d'être* of the business organization, but is likely to eventuate in closure. Having entered the game of business, those in charge are faced with a limited number of rules for success. Central among these rules is a requirement that production costs be kept in check. How that rule is enacted will depend upon the particular personnel in charge of the organization and how uncertain the market is perceived to be. For example, costs may be perceived as less of a problem for those in a situation of virtual monopoly as against those facing a highly competitive market situation. In the first case, an understanding that costs can almost certainly be passed on to the customer may allow organizational controllers a fair degree of latitude in responding to internal pressures for higher wages. In the second case, concern about competitiveness may encourage those in charge to either take a highly restrictive approach to demands for improvements in working conditions and payments or actually seek to cut back on existing conditions.

Employees, on the other hand, often find themselves caught in a different logic. At the very least a person will seek employment to gain enough money to be able to survive, i.e. to put a roof over their head, to eat, to be adequately clothed and, in many cases, to maintain dependants. In certain situations (e.g. in underdeveloped nations) and in particular times (e.g. the 1930s) this may be enough, but generally the logic of capitalism has given rise to consumerism and with it the phenomenon of 'rising expectations'. Hence, in capitalist countries in the post-war era, the so-called average worker has come to expect a 'decent standard of living'. The problem with the notion of a 'decent standard of living' is that it is ever changing and will depend, among several other factors, upon the general economic situation that exists at any given time. The attainment of any given standard of living will depend in large part on the level of pay that an individual is able to attain.

Pressures on employees to maintain and advance their levels of wages and salaries conflict with pressures on the employer to stabilize or decrease production costs:

> The wages and conditions sought by the employee as the means to a decent life, both within and outside work, are a *cost* cutting into the employer's profits. In the absence of

specific and untypical countertendencies (the need to recruit and retain scarce categories of labour, or a belief that improved conditions will generate greater worker commitment and productivity), the employer is naturally motivated to resist worker aspirations which are liable to increase labour costs. Moreover, because labour represents a cost to be minimized, it is in the employer's interest to continue a worker's employment only so long as it remains profitable to do so (Hyman, 1980, p. 303).

THE LABOUR CONTRACT

Linked to the question of wages and conditions is the problem of effort. On the surface the labour contract appears fair. The employee undertakes to do a certain job and in return is given a certain remuneration. For example, a bricklayer might undertake to work for a large building company and is given to understand that he or she is expected to work for 40 hours per week at a salary of $600 a week. Both the 40 hours and the $600 appear finite, but that hides the fact that within those 40 hours the company can work the employee as hard or as little as they choose:

> The first thing to note is that the labour contract is not an exchange of equivalents: it is structurally asymmetrical. It is not just that the labourer has to sell his [sic] work in order to live whereas the capitalist is not similarly constrained to buy labour. By the terms of the contract, the worker receives a definite – and usually public – rate for the job whereas the employer receives an impalpable potentiality whose ultimate development it is for him to determine. . . . From the employer's side the labour contract is open-ended. In principle the nature of the exact tasks the worker has undertaken to perform becomes the province of management (Blackburn, 1967, p. 39).

The open-ended nature of the labour contract can assist management in dealing with issues of cost. They may, for instance, be able to reduce costs by speeding up the production process, by increasing the efforts of employees, by the introduction of labour-saving machinery and devices, by simplification of the work through deskilling, reductions in the workforce, and so on. The literature on organizational development is chocked full of examples. Here is a classic one. At the Ford Motor Company in 1913,

> When the waist-level shelving was replaced by a rather more elevated, motorised conveyor belt . . . production time fell still more; and when further analysis refined the division of tasks along the belt, the average assembly time per magneto fell to seven minutes, and then to five. Through the introduction of continuous movement, it had become possible for one man to do the work which had previously occupied three or four – nor was there any longer the need for the worker to be especially skilled. Any manual labourer could do the job (Lacy, 1986, p. 115).

In the period 1913–14, Ford witnessed a doubling of production and a reduction in the labour force from 14 336 workers to 12 880.

The open-ended character of employment contract situations creates a great potential for conflict and will depend in large part upon the way any given set of relationships and understandings is exploited.

DEMOCRATIC SOCIETIES AND AUTHORITARIAN ORGANIZATIONS

It has long been recognized from varying perspectives that the structures of capitalist organizations stand in apparent contrast to the societies within which they are a part. Alan Touraine (1974), for example, long ago cited the contrast between people's experiences of citizenship and of employment as a source of conflict. On the one hand, a series of understandings generate the idea that people are free to determine their own lives and to decide democratically the frameworks under which they will operate. One the other hand, upon entering the world of work, they are confronted by a different set of rules that gives them to understand that their various work activities – including when they may eat, rest, talk and even go to the lavatory – are to be placed under the control of management. Here is one of many examples:

> Churchmans, like any other factory, imposed discipline at several levels. There was the tight hold over the labour process, as described in job evaluation, grading and work study. Then there was personal supervision in the presence of chargehands, foreman and supervisors. And there were rules – the written rules of the rule book, and visual reminders stuck up on notices.
>
> There was rule 7, against moving between departments and 'loitering on the staircases, in the corridors, at the entrance doors or in the lavatories'. There was rule 18, 'No employee is allowed to enter any lavatory or cloakroom except the one provided for his or her use'. And because of the unique value of tobacco to the Exchequer, there were more rules. Like rule 15, the 'right of search': 'Every employee is liable to be searched at any time'. And rule 9: 'SMOKING is NOT allowed on the Factory premises except in the dining rooms at times prescribed by the Management. To enter or leave the Factory with a lighted pipe, cigar or cigarette is prohibited. It was even a crime to *possess* the *wrong* tobacco! (Pollert, 1981, p. 129).

This is not some example from the nineteenth century, but from the 1980s!

People are given little or no choice in the matter as to who is to be in charge of the various aspects of the workplace – managers are not elected from the shop floor:

> workers have little real choice about whether to sell their labour power, or, in practice, even where. And typically, when they pass through the factory gate for the first time, they are confronted by rules and regulations already devised by management. Through struggle, these rules and regulations may be modified but in the absence of effective organization by workers they confront them as a *fait accompli* (Nichols, 1980, p. 287).

The contrast between citizen and employee are in constant tension and how that tension is expressed and kept in check will vary across time and depend upon the particular character of the workplace involved. One major problem relates back to the issue of the labour contract, namely that people are employed not for who they are as persons but primarily what they have to offer in terms of a potential contribution to productivity. In the words of Hyman (1980), labour is sold as a commodity. Employees sell their labour power in return for a wage/salary and often find that their labour is indeed treated as a commodity as witnessed in such phrases as 'we are not paying you to sit around', 'you will do what you are told while you work for me', 'we require you to work at our mid-town office', 'you are being paid to do your work and keep your mouth shut'.

At one level the character of labour as a community may appear fair. A person sells their ability to work in exchange for remuneration. Yet there is a curious and conflictual element to the whole process. The actual commodity being sold is not separable from the seller and this can lead to numerous problems. For example, if a person build's and then sells a machine, that person gives up the commodity and need not care how it is treated. The person who buys the machine may run it day and night, they may shout at it, and they may even physically abuse it at no cost to the seller. But if a person's labour power is used day and night, shouted at and physically abused, it is the seller him/herself who is the object of abuse and misuse. One of the authors once had occasion to work in a butcher's shop. On one particular occasion, he fell down a flight of stairs carrying a tray of meat. As he lay injured at the bottom of the stairs, all he could hear was the voice of the manager demanding 'how is the meat'. He had been reduced in the eyes of the manager to little more than a carrier of meat. In the early 1980s, a local coal miner's strike received critical media attention because miners had walked off the job because a supervisor had sworn at one of their colleagues. The press seemed to feel that grown men – particularly miners – should be used to swearing as part of their daily lives. The miners argument, on the other hand, was why should they have to put up with being sworn at by a supervisor when they would not accept being sworn at by anyone else, i.e. why should organizational status be used as legitimation of unacceptable social behaviour?

Another aspect of conflict is built into the fact that growing numbers of people expect not only to be treated reasonably at work, but to be treated to reasonable working conditions. Increasing employee demands and expectations for improved working conditions have been reflected in various management practices and theories. From Douglas McGregor (1960) onwards, it has been recognized that employees want to be treated with some respect, that they want to be allowed to function as mature adults (Argyris, 1964). Occupational health and safety has also become very much an issue, with employees being less willing to work in unsafe workplaces.

This has led to the development of a number of programmes – job rotation, job redesign, quality circles, Quality of Working Life schemes, health and safety schemes, etc. – designed to placate if not fully address employee expectations. The problem is that such programmes add to the unit costs of production and, as such, raise conflict issues, with management and employees arguing over what determines a 'reasonable' working environment and what counts as 'safe' working conditions. According to Gareth Morgan (1986, p. 289):

> Many employers take account of work hazards only when legislation requires them to do so, and . . . in the developed Western countries, accidents and occupational diseases continue to take an alarming toll on human life.

Morgan goes on to estimate that around 14 000 people are killed and about 2.2

million disabled in the USA each year in industrial accidents, and that a further 100 000 Americans die each year from work-related illnesses.

Following the introduction of the Occupational Health and Safety Act in the UK in the mid-1970s, an increasing number of workers became actively concerned with health and safety issues. The new law empowered the election, by employees, of health and safety stewards whose job it was to oversee the workplace and report 'unsafe' conditions. Tens of thousands of such stewards received training through TUC (Trades Union Congress) approved courses, and for a time there was increasing militancy throughout the country as workers formed plant-wide, city-wide and national health and safety organizations. Conflict easily arose out of competing employee–employer definitions of safe conditions.

While the issue of health and safety has become more of a routine, yet live issue in many companies across Europe and North America, new concerns with broad environmental issues have awoken employees to a renewed interest in the relationship between work and the internal/external environment.

ALIENATION

The key problem of many jobs is their routine, often boring character. Many jobs involve little authority status or recognition, autonomy or advancement opportunities (Wright et al., 1982; Blauner, 1964). And a process of *deskilling* characterizes a number of workplace situations in the modern world (Braverman, 1974):

> One recent estimate suggests that in some modern organizations 87 per cent of manual workers exercise less skill in their jobs than they use in driving to work, and that most jobs could easily be performed by most workers (Morgan, 1986, p. 283).

For many employees, their experience of work is one of powerlessness, self-estrangement, meaninglessness and isolation:

> A typical assembly-line worker can learn his job in thirty minutes. He gains no skill that might qualify him for a better job. He has little incentive . . . to acquire the 'instincts of workmanship,' to take pride in his job, or to feel a sense of purpose. Not only is the worker confronted with a sense of meaninglessness; he cannot engage in reveries because the work requires close attention and resists the kind of detachment that permits the mind to wander (Nash, 1976, p. 71).

Such features of work are not confined to industrial labour. There are many accounts of the alienating features of office work. Kanter's (1977) account of organizational life introduced the notion of 'the stuck', those many people within organizations whose opportunities for advancement are limited. Studying a large corporation, which she calls Indsco, Kanter discovered that:

> The largest category of people among the stuck were those who never had much opportunity to begin with. Low promotion rates, or short ladders and low ceilings in

their job category, meant that few expectations were ever created for such jobs to involve movement. Most women clericals, supervisors of office workers, and some exempt staff, especially in personnel functions, were in this situation. The biggest group was certainly the clerical workers. At most, people could hope for a few steps towards more independence and slightly higher pay during a lifetime, as in a move from Secretary I to Executive Secretary (Kanter, 1977, p. 136).

Various other accounts can be found of deskilling (West, 1982), powerlessness and boredom (Crompton *et al.*, 1982) in office work.

Feelings of alienation result in a number of outcomes, all of which provide the bases for conflict. Employers may adopt an instrumental approach to work, becoming only concerned with what they can get out of it (Goldthorpe, 1966). Instrumentalism can lead to the establishment of a set of informal rules which, if breached, can end up in conflict. Goldthorpe's study of UK car workers in the mid-1960s indicated that the relatively high wages drew workers to the industry and compensated them for the unpleasantness of the tasks involved. Surveying worker attitudes, Goldthorpe concluded that 'given a prior orientation to their work of a largely instrumental nature, car assemblers may well see their relationships with their firm in a generally positive way'. However, what Goldthorpe had missed was that this 'calculative' relationship was not fixed but rested upon a set of shifting understandings and rules. Those rules were put to the test shortly after Goldthorpe had completed his study. Pressured to maintain profit margins and to comply with a government pay freeze, the company initiated a four-day working week, reducing wages by 20%. The result was explosive:

> Near riot conditions developed. . . . Two thousand workers streamed out of the factory gates and tried to storm the main offices. Dozens of police were brought in and an inspector threatened mass arrests when the crowd halted traffic for half an hour. . . . [O]utside the main offices . . . men [sang] 'The Red Flag' and call[ed] 'String him up' whenever a director's name was mentioned. . . . Across the road hundreds of men linked arms and prevented a heavy Bedford truck from entering the factory (report from the London *Times*, quoted in Blackburn, 1967, p. 49).

This group of workers, who days earlier had been described as having 'little tendency to [see] employer–worker relations in fundamentally 'oppositional terms'' (Goldthorpe, 1966), became angry when their single-most rule understanding had been broken.

Feelings of alienation can result in such things as depressed aspirations, low morale, non-responsibility and low commitment (Kanter, 1977), leading to a variety of personal (absenteeism, resignation, restricted work activities, sabotage) and social (shop-floor culture, informal group formation, trade unionism, strikes) actions. While, as we shall see below, informal groups and shop-floor culture can actually contribute to organizational stability, they may be viewed by some managements as undesirable. The Hawthorne Studies, for example, pinpointed the presence of informal groups as a problem. The bank wiring room group, for instance, were viewed by researchers and management alike as acting contrary to company needs through the informal restriction of productivity. Likewise, Pollert's account of the development of a shop-floor culture in a cigarette factory indicates managerial and supervisory displeasure:

> It was in the context of their *general* powerlessness over the labour process . . . that the women created their own shop-floor culture. . . . So women replaced the rule book, as far as possible, without conscious, deliberate organization, with an informal code of resistance to being turned into machines, to boredom, to the humiliation of being ordered around (Pollert, 1981, p. 130).

The developing shop-floor culture in this case involved a struggle between the female employees and the male supervisors over rules. The attitudes of the supervisors to this development can be glimpsed through the words of one of their number:

> the environment of these girls has changed. The permissive society – now these girls are changing with it. Well I'm afraid they're not so mature, not so reliable as they used to be. That makes our job harder (quoted in Pollert, 1981, p. 141).

Burawoy (1979) describes how, at the factory he studied, senior management would balk from time to time at what they saw as the restrictive activities of the shop-floor culture. And Alvin Gouldner (1965) has vividly described how a change in the informal working arrangements of workers at a gypsum mine led to a wildcat strike, the company's first strike in at least 20 years.

CLASS

Historically, the character of capitalist organization has led to the establishment of trade unions and to various forms of socialist parties. Various factors (discussed above) have combined to create the appearance and experience of a 'them' and 'us' feeling throughout organizations. The hierarchical division of organizations into controllers and controlled has served to stress an identity of interest between employees occupying similar relationships to the rules. Many, if not all, of those who are expected to simply obey the rules may well find that they have a common interest in resisting those whose organizational career depends upon rule enforcement. The notion of a common interest will likely be reinforced where organizational stratification is mirrored in social stratification, with the life opportunities of different levels of organizational members varying markedly.

The development of trade unionism has led to new sets of organizational rules. At one level, as we discuss below, those rules can serve to limit conflict, but at another level they provide the basis for new levels and forms of conflict. Trade unions draw together the experiences of the many and, whereas an individual might be reluctant to come into conflict with management, unions may be more likely to. In a prominent study of the British car industry in the 1960s, it was found that when the Ford Motor Company fired a group of militant shop stewards, trade union activity fell but absenteeism and labour turnover sharply increased (Turner *et al.*, 1967); in the absence of trade union activity discontent had not decreased but had found expression in non-conflictual, but none the less dysfunctional, personal resolve. This may well be generally true across a range of industries, i.e. that trade unions channel discontent that might otherwise have taken personal forms (Hyman, 1972). With the advent of trade unionism within organizations, the laying-off or disciplining of individuals was more likely to become a union matter. Management decisions are now monitored and resisted where it is felt they conflict with real or presumed employee interests.

The development of trade unionism at a place of work leads to negotiated rules. The character of the process, however, makes those rules fragile and subject to conflict. At any given time a set of outcomes are arrived at through a process that involves a struggle between the relative strengths of the parties involved. What may be acceptable to one party during a period of weakness may cease to be acceptable if that party perceives that their position has strengthened. Conflict may also arise out of the fact that the character of the negotiated understanding can give rise to varying interpretations, especially when tested by different scenarios. On a national level, trade union activity in the UK in the late-1960s through to the mid-1970s helped to defeat the efforts of two governments (Labour in 1969–70 and Conservative in 1972–4) in their attempts to introduce 'anti-trade union' laws. During the same period, two national coal miners' strikes (1972, 1974) wrung significant concessions out of the employer, the National Coal Board. In less than a decade, with the strength of British trade unions greatly weakened, the Conservative government not only introduced laws designed to curtail trade union activity but took on the miners and won – reversing many of the previous gains that the miners had won in the 1970s. In terms of rule reinterpretation, at a large college in the UK during the 1970s, the unions managed to negotiate a 'no redundancies' rule. This seemed reasonably acceptable to management at the time. There was no apparent need to lay anyone off. However, a few short years later the management did have a need for lay-offs and were successfully able to interpret the rule as meaning 'no compulsory lay-offs'. A number of voluntary redundancy and early retirement schemes were introduced to reduce staffing levels. While these actions ensured that no-one was fired, it contravened the spirit of the union's original intention – the protection of job *positions* and the people occupying those positions. The actions had in fact greatly reduced the number of available positions while *increasing* the workloads of all involved.

Trade unions are not simply reactive to ongoing demands. They involve, to differing degrees, various ideological characteristics; characteristics that generate different sets of rules that help to shape the way members view workplace (and broader) issues. Trade union members, for example, are usually socialized into believing that worker solidarity is a principle rule that should be upheld at all times – that 'workers should always stand together', that one should 'never cross a picket line', that the 'bosses are just out to make money on the backs of the workers', and so on. These are conflict rules designed to ensure that trade union members act in concert. Such rules and their potency can be seen more visibly in situations where they are broken. Here is an example from a welder:

> I was a welder at Vandorn Rubber & Plastics from '78 to '80. We made injection molding machines. I welded the frames.
>
> Japan was making them for about half of what ours cost. The union would say, 'Let's take X hours to do a specific job,' and the company would give us 16 for the frames. I could weld one of those things up in about four hours. But the union started clamping down on my back about doing the job too fast. I don't want to blame them, but they didn't have to say a job would take extra hours and drive the cost of our products up (quoted in Magnet, 1988, p. 47).

For reasons that are likely to be related to protecting union jobs and/or ensuring that the workers were not overworked, that welder's union worked to restrict output. Even among the higher paid, the principle of solidarity is expected to hold up. When Mark Gastineau, defensive end with the New York Jets, crossed the picket line during a National Football League Players Association strike in 1987, he invoked the same type of emotions, slogans and denouncements that any other worker engaged in anti-solidarity action would have received: termed a 'scab' his team-mates refused to have anything to do with him (Saportio, 1987).

Trade unionism contributes to the development of class consciousness in the workplace, providing an ideological framework in which numbers of working people come to view themselves and the world in terms of *class.*, Class consciousness, a phenomena with a long and controversial history (Bloomfield, 1978; Hunt, 1973; Larraine, 1979; Wolpe, 1970), owes its existence to a combination of lived experiences and various trade union and socialist interpretations of reality. It takes many forms, but at its most basic refers to common interests of people based upon their different relationship to the ownership and control of industry, with the main classes being seen as the working class (those non-owners who need to work to live) and the capitalist class (those who own and employ others to produce the wealth). The development of a class consciousness does not simply develop within the confines of an organization – various people enter organizations with a developed sense of class. In effect, they approach the workplace with a developed or developing set of understandings for interpreting their organizational experiences. As a result, the ability of certain people to get their class views of reality accepted within the workplace can provide the basis for conflict or heightened conflict situations. If an employer, for example, manages to convince a number of fellow employers and managers that all trade union activity is 'cummunist agitation', the result may be unnecessary conflict. In the US movie industry in the 1940s, the labelling, blacklisting and arrest of writers, directors and actors for supposed communist activities led to a number of protests and widespread disruption throughout the industry (the movies *The Way We Were* and *The Front* give some feel to those events). On the other hand, socialist leadership of industrial disputes have sometimes managed to win employees to the view that more dramatic actions need to be taken in pursuit of a claim. In 1971, the workers of the Upper Clyde Shipbuilding yards in Scotland were faced with large-scale redundancies.

They may well have embarked upon a more traditional token strike action, but under the leadership of a number of their socialist and communist colleagues they staged the now famous 'work-in', announcing that they were 'taking over the yards'. Communists and other radical socialists were to the fore in the leadership of a series of sit ins, political and industrial strikes throughout the early 1970s but, to be clear, they did not *create* conflict situations – the basis of the conflict existed in the experiences of the workers involved. What the radicals did was to provide leadership in the interpretation and direction of those developing conflict situations.

RULES AND THE CONTAINMENT OF INDUSTRIAL CONFLICT

Over the history of capitalist development there have been a large number of highly significant examples of industrial conflict. Strikes have formed part of broader movements for social change as in the Russian Revolutions of 1905 and 1917, and the Winnipeg and San Francisco Soviets of 1919; there have been general strikes such as the British General Strike of 1926 and the May strikes that swept France in 1968; there have been waves of sit-downs (in the USA in the 1930s), sit-ins (in the UK in the 1970s), strikes and factory occupations (Italy, 1919–20); and there have been national strikes that have gained notoriety (the UK miners' strikes in 1972 and 1974; the US air traffic controllers strike in 1981).

Clearly, from time to time, industrial conflict can and does lead to or form part of far-reaching social unrest and change, and it is this fact that has encouraged Marxists in the belief that there are deep-rooted, structural contradictions within capitalism which will ultimately lead to its demise. Equally clear is the fact that, whatever value we place on capitalism, it has none the less survived through nearly three centuries of strikes and social unrest. This has led Marxists, and others, to seek explanations for the phenomena of capitalist survival in the face of in-built conflict situations.

Hegemony
The most far-reaching explanation of the containment of conflict is Gramsci's (1978) concept of *hegemony*. Gramsci very much refined the argument of Marx that the ideas of the ruling class are the ruling ideas of society. If rulers simply imposed their ideas on society, they would only be carried out, at best, by rote or by fear. Recent events in Romania, with the overthrow of the Ceausescu government, show how imposed views are eventually and often forcefully rejected. Gramsci argues that capitalism needs to be viewed as a cultural system in which the capitalists and those who work for them inject moral and intellectual leadership. People are located within the context of a culture that in various ways integrates a number of ideas, values and activities that help to sustain capitalism. Let us take the example of organizations. Organizations confront us as 'normal', 'objective' entities constructed for the achievement of certain ends. We rarely contest the *idea* of organization, only what goes on *within* their boundaries. Yet organizations are a cultural form which

embody many of the central values of capitalism – a need for efficiency and control in the achievement of profitability. *Inside* the organization, the organization of capitalism is disguised in a number of ways, through particular divisions of labour, specialism, professionalism and managerialism. Hierarchical divisions may lead to conflicts, but it is usually the outcomes rather than the existence of a hierarchy that is challenged, e.g. we might not like the orders given but accept the legitimacy of the person's position to give orders. Through specialisms and professionalization, the occupant of the position operates through a complex of rules in which they are compelled to undertake specific tasks but which also give the appearance of self-interest and autonomy. For example, the person who trains as a chemist may receive some satisfaction from the fact that they are able to pursue their chosen profession despite the fact that they are employed on a restricted number of projects for a deodorant company. Likewise, the modern manager is not simply someone who sees his or her task in terms of naked control of the work process. Management has become a profession in itself, a career to be followed, and the modern manager is aware – aided and abetted by management theory – that he or she needs to develop a range of organizational skills in order to be successful. The various managers, technicians, specialists and professionals act in many ways, according to Gramsci, like organizational 'intellectuals', providing cultural leadership to those within the system.

A recognition of the significance of hegemonic rules can be witnessed in the current interest in theories of organizational culture. Here managerial theorists and practitioners have become concerned with finding ways to win employee commitment and mitigate against organizational conflict. The type and form of hegemonic rules will differ across organizations (Clegg, 1981) and will help to determine the forms that conflict will take. In a study of worker sit-in strikes across Britain in the 1970s, Mills (1982) found the handling of specific situations by management to be poor, as well as poor industrial relations in general to be common features of a large number of strikes. In many of the companies that experienced sit-in strikes, management had made no pretence at decency; mass lay-offs and closures were often introduced in the most callous fashion. Here is an example from the UK:

On July 1 1969 [a] Leicester based company began operations . . . in North West Durham. For operating in this 'development area' the company received thirty thousand pounds in regional employment grants and forty-four thousand in operational grants over the next three years. The company was thriving and by 1972 was rated in *The Times Top 1000 British Companies*. Using government aided grants new machinery worth three thousand pounds was installed . . . and the company publicly announced that its development was a success story. One week later . . . [the] factory was closed.

The workforce responded by staging a sit-in . . . [driven by] the fact that no consultations what-so-ever took place over the redundancies, no advanced warning of the closure was given – the workers were given a day's notice and the full-time union official was not even informed, the factory was being closed after barely meeting the minimum operating period after which grants need not be paid back, and on top of everything else new machinery was bought only . . . to be shifted to the company's Leicester factory a few days later (Mills, 1982, pp. 353–4).

Here the management barely concealed the fact that they had opened a factory in a 'development area' to obtain operating grants and acquire new machinery, and in the process gave little thought to the lives of discarded employees.

This kind of approach can be contrasted with the more hegemonic rule approach of the IBM company. IBM mitigate conflict through a number of rules such as the no-compulsory lay-off rule described in Chapter 5. The approach appears to work. Here is an example from one of its workplaces:

> The system of industrial relations operated by IBM at its main British manufacturing plant in the west of Scotland is designed to individualise workplace relationships whilst, at the same time, generating employee loyalty to a well-defined corporate culture. . . .
>
> [As a result] the last attempt to secure [union] recognition . . . resulted in an ACAS-organized referendum of the plant's employees and a vote *of over 90%* against the proposal. . . .
>
> [Employees hold] positive attitudes . . . towards the company and its industrial relations system. IBM's claim that it never sacks anybody was widely believed and contributed to the strong emphasis placed by most workers on job *security*. The implications of this for attitudes to trade unions was spelt out by the employee who said of his colleagues: 'They feel their job is secure. The company has never made anyone redundant. They have a good standard of working conditions and reasonable expectations, and reasonable rewards if they work. They don't really need a union to fight for them' (Dickson *et al.*, 1988, pp. 506–510).

The internal labour market

Companies such as IBM have instituted a number of rules which are designed to encourage long-term employment within the organization. Collectively, the rules act as an *internal labour market*:

> The emergence of an internal labor market requires, on the one hand, that workers, once recruited, generally choose to remain with the company than seek employment elsewhere, and, on the other hand, that the company tries to fill job opening by selecting from among its own workers before it recruits workers from an external labor market (Burawoy, 1979, p. 97).

Various rules combine to encourage in employees a sense of security – rules of seniority and length of service that are linked to such things as company pensions, improved job opportunities within the company, higher pay and longer holidays. In the factory studied by Burawoy (1979), this had a 'significant impact on the patterns of conflict on the shop floor'.

> The opportunity to move between jobs has the effect of diminishing conflict between workers and the lower levels of management. . . . As long as operators are locked into a single job, they have to fight with the time-study man for better rates (Burawoy, 1979, p. 104).

By expanding the range of job choices that an employee can take on, the company may well expand the commitment of the worker to the company:

> Thus, the internal labor market bases itself in a complex of rules, on the one hand,

while expanding the *number* of choices on the other. Nor should these choices be belittled by saying that one boring, meaningful job is much the same as any other. The choice gains its significance from the material power it gives to workers in their attempts to resist or protect themselves from managerial domination (Burawoy, 1979, pp. 107–108).

In other words, the internal labour market affords the employee some ability to escape the petty tyrannies that can result from being located in a specific job. Burawoy (1979, p. 108) goes on to argue that:

> Workers have a very definite interest in the preservation and expansion of the internal labor market. . . . Moreover, it is precisely that interest that draws workers into the bidding system and generates consent to its rules and the conditions they represent, namely, a labor process that is being emptied of skill.

Trade unionism and the institutionalization of conflict
Many people have commented on the ironic impact of trade unionism on industrial conflict. At a structural level, the development of trade unionism had led to the development of systems of industrial relations. *Industrial relations* involve a complex system of rules for the containment and/or resolution of conflict. In many cases, an individual grievance may have to go from an individual to his or her local union official, then on to higher union officials, and then on to union–management meetings and back down the line before anything is resolved. One of the authors experienced this process. Several years ago, he was fired from his job as an electrician. He took the case to his shop steward. The steward had to wait for a regular meeting of shop stewards before the case could be heard. Once heard it was passed up to a full-time union official. The official then contacted the fired electrician, taking the case back and forward between the wronged employee and management. The case was then passed back down to a meeting of shop stewards for final consideration where it was decided that, 'as four months had elapsed' since the sacking, 'little could be done'! An active trade unionist had been fired and not a single sign of conflict had surfaced. Coupled to industrial relations rules there are the union rules themselves which, in many cases, deem it illegitimate for individuals or groups of workers to engage in conflict action other than 'through channels'. The labels attached to such actions tell the story: 'wildcat strike', 'unconstitutional action', 'unofficial strike'. This may not prevent the outbreak of non-authorized conflict, as the British *Royal Commission on Trade Unions and Employers' Associations* (1968) was to note, but it does inhibit them. The process has been aptly described as the *institutionalization of industrial conflict*. As Dubin wrote way back in 1954:

> That there are conflicts of interest in industry today seems scarcely questionable. That we have institutionalized the mode of conflict through collective bargaining is also clear. We have thus built, in the institutional practice of collective bargaining, a social device for bringing conflict to a successful resolution (quoted in Hyman, 1972, p. 75).

In the process of collective bargaining, trade unionism has contributed to the growing bureaucratization of organizational life (Lockwood, 1966). As Robert Michels (1949) noted, trade unions once established become ends in themselves. Organizers become less and less concerned with principles and more and more concerned with the maintenance and growth of the organization itself. Organizational hierarchies become reflected in trade union organization, with their head offices, office staff, full-time officers, and various ranks of official, from national *down* to shop floor.

Thus, at another level, trade unionism provides a vehicle for the *incorporation* of trade unionists into the mainstream of social and organizational life (Crouch, 1979). The pay, life-styles and social activity of certain trade union leaders and officials come to resemble the employers that they bargain with. Many union leaders are elected or appointed to a life-time position, many become included in a range of government bodies, and many lead prominent social lives. During the 1970s, one prominent UK trade union leader is reputed to have had not only a six-figure salary, but a private jet at his disposal!

The informal rules of consent

The very boredom of work has led some workers to turn the processes of production into a game. In the Hawthorne Studies, it was discovered that groups of workers – in particular those in the bank wiring room – developed informal rules for controlling the work process. Employees were expected to avoid exceeding not only a certain upper limit of production but also a certain lower limit of production. Elton Mayo and his colleagues (Mayo, 1933; Roethlisberger and Dickson, 1939) characterized this activity as negative, seeing it only in terms of 'output restriction'; but, as Bendix (1974) has pointed out, such activity can have positive outcomes from the management's perspective:

> What is feared of integration within a small group is that it may organize itself in opposition to the larger whole – and this it certainly will do if its existence be threatened; but equally, a protected group will endeavour to satisfy its wider interests by collaborating with the organization of which it is a logical part. In this way, its loyalty will extend to the firm as a whole (T.N. Whitehead, 1936, quoted in Bendix, 1974, p. 317).

Michael Burawoy (1979) has provided a fuller explanation of how informal shop-floor practices can in effect serve to integrate the work group into the production process, mitigating worker–management conflict in the bargain. Burawoy describes the process as 'making out', the term developed by the workers themselves. In the plant studied by Burawoy, a piecework system was in operation:

> For each production operation the methods department establishes a level of effort, expressed in so many pieces per hour, which represents the '100 percent' benchmark. Below this benchmark, operators receive a base rate for the job, irrespective of the actual number of pieces they produce. Above this standard, workers receive not only the base rate for the job but, in addition, a bonus or incentive, corresponding to the number of pieces in excess of '100 percent'. Thus output at a rate of 125 percent is defined as the

'anticipated rate,' which – according to the contract – is the amount 'a normal experienced operator working at incentive gait' is expected to produce.

While situations varied from machine to machine, most workers attempted to achieve the 125% level but not to exceed 140%. Variance in machines and other work factors provided levels of uncertainty over the production process which, according to Burawoy, provided the tension required of a game – you could never be quite sure that you would 'make out' on any particular day.

A number of factors combined to draw workers into the game of making out as can be seen from this description of Burawoy's own involvement:

> Once I knew I had a chance to make out, the rewards of participating in a game in which the outcomes were uncertain absorbed my attention, and I found myself spontaneously cooperating with management in the production of greater surplus value. Moreover, it was only in this way that I could establish relationships with others on the shop floor. Until I was able to strut around the floor like a skilled operator . . . few but the greenest would condescend to engage me in conversation. Thus, it was in terms of the culture of making out that individuals evaluated one another and themselves. It provided the basis of status hierarchies on the shop floor (Burawoy, 1979, p. 64).

The game of making out had been developed as a defence to managerial control over the work process and the determination of wages but, as a game, it was also to turn into a means of, what Burawoy calls, 'consent' to ultimate management control:

> The significance of creating a game out of the labour process . . . extends beyond the peculiarities of making out. The very activity of playing a game generates consent with respect to its rules . . . [i.e.] consent rests upon – is constructed through – playing the game. The game does not reflect an underlying harmony of interests; on the contrary, it is responsible for and generates that harmony. The source of the game itself lies not in a preordained value consensus but in historically specific struggles to adapt to the deprivation inherent in work and in struggles with management to define rules (Burawoy, 1979, pp. 81–2).

CONFLICT AND CONSENT IN TENSION

The processes of conflict and consent are in constant tension. Organizations are located within and are part of wider contexts in which rules are constantly changing. A number of factors will help to determine to what extent an organization will experience conflict: stiff market competition, sharply increasing costs and decreasing profitability, the possibility of mass lay-offs and closure, economic crises, sharply increasing wage rates associated with economic booms, a blatant lack of management concern with the needs of employees, dramatic changes in the organizational rules, widespread class struggle within society, and so on.

Likewise, conditions will vary across organizations: in some organizations (e.g. car manufacturers), management may be more or less content to exercise control through the technological processes; in other organizations (e.g. research and development firms), professionalization may substitute for direct control; and yet other organizations (e.g. the large office of a major company), management may feel that more hegemonic control is required (Clegg, 1981). In Mills' (1982) study of British sit-in strikes in the 1970s, strike-prone companies were among the largest (in terms of employment – employing over 2000 workers – and financial standing) in the country, with the strikes usually occurring in the branch plant of a national or multinational company. This suggests that certain factors (size, local control) may inhibit the ability of certain managements to introduce conflict curtailing measures. In Burawoy's study, it was indicated that from time to time the rules of production and of determining piece rates changed and in the process the game of making out was suspended, causing increased conflict. And in Dickson *et al.*'s (1988, p. 520) study of IBM, it was concluded that:

> IBM workers, despite the highly individualized non-union industrial relations system, are not generally opposed to the *principle* of trade unionism or collective action. . . . In the short term, the attempt to unionise IBM may be a futile struggle. . . . In the longer term, the attitudes of IBM employees may indicate some of the challenges facing British trade unionism.

Organizational co-ordination and power

Not all organizational conflict is vertically constructed; the character of organizations also give rise to horizontal conflict. Organizations come into being for the achievement of certain ends and in the process often require the co-ordination of a number of different people and activities in the achievement of those ends. Ironically, the moment an organization comes into being its problems begin. Ends have to be interpreted and carried out and disputes can arise as to whether the ends have been correctly interpreted and as to who should carry out what. Formal goals give way to operative goals and disputes arise as to whether one really contributes to the other. Activities become departmentalized and specialized, and disputes arise as to who is/should be responsible for what. Scarce resources are distributed throughout the organization and disputes arise as to who/what department should get what. Activities stand in different relationships to the production process and disputes arise as to who should decide what and who has more standing than who. Rewards are distributed throughout the organization and disputes arise as to who should get what. Power and control is distributed within the organization and disputes arise as to who should have what power and over various attempts to exercise power.

TROUBLE AT THE TOP

Organizations provide frameworks of power (Clegg, 1989), and as such are arenas of struggle. The occupants of key positions may wish to exercise some say over a situation, but in so doing inhibit the ability of others to have their say. Power struggles are endemic within organizations.

Steve Jobs was a 'brilliant, charismatic folk hero and visionary' with a dream of building a computer company (Sculley with Byrne, 1987, p. 268); Max Ward was a 'knight among free enterprisers' who wanted to build an airline (Newman, 1982, p. 298); and Henry Ford was the 'grass roots hero' with a burning desire to produce automobiles (Lacey, 1986). Yet none of these fledgling entrepreneurs could bring their dreams to fruition without involving other people, without building organizations, and without engaging in power struggles.

Jobs, who founded Apple Computers, had to share his dream with another – his friend and co-founder, Steve Wozniak. Soon they felt the need for someone to manage the company and A.C. Markkula was brought in. Markkula then sought venture capital and recruited outside members to the Board of Directors. Apple's first president, Michael Scott, was appointed; a position that was eventually to be filled by John Sculley. As the company matured to a formalization stage, problems began to grow, problems that were hightened by a crisis within the industry as a whole and within Apple in particular. In 1984–5, Jobs and Sculley, who had previously been described as the 'dynamic duo', clashed repeatedly over the direction of the company. In early 1985, a dispute over which new products to launch arose between Jobs (who favoured a multi-product launch) and Sculley (who favoured a single product-line focus). The conflict was not simply one about goals, but as to who would ultimately stand in supreme relationship to the rules. Sculley won and Jobs left the company.

Max Ward began his career with a single foxmoth plane and operated as a bush pilot in the North West Territories of Canada, but government regulations soon forced him into partnership with George Pigeon. New regulations required that pilots be licensed and this temporarily grounded Ward until he teamed up with Pigeon, a licensed pilot operating out of Yellowknife. The partnership did not last more than a short time, with both men disagreeing as to the aim of the company and its direction. For a while Ward left the industry and entered the building trade. He returned to Yellowknife and the airline industry 4 years later, and this time with four aeroplanes.

Ward had ambitions to grow. He wanted to break into the charter business but needed to draw on the experience of others. He recruited the help of Jim McGuire. McGuire, a pilot with Canadian Pacific Airlines, helped Ward to build the charter operation and went on to become the company's vice president at its new location in Edmonton, Alberta. But soon McGuire and Ward, who had been close friends, clashed over the running of the company, and McGuire was summarily fired, an action that was to end up in a bitter court case that McGuire won. McGuire was not the last Wardair executive to leave in bitter circumstances – Brian Stanley also clashed with Ward and eventually left to found his own charter operation.

Henry Ford took on many partners – both figuratively and financially – on his road to the founding of an empire. His lack of skill in mechanical drawing led him to work with C. Harold Wills. In need of capital, Ford took on a partner Alex

Malcomson – a coal merchant – and in 1902 Ford and Malcomson Ltd came into being. It was not long, however, before the new company needed new capital, because costs had risen higher than Ford predicted. Now a banker, John S. Gray was brought into the business. Gray, who insisted on being the company president, was the first of a number of new investors – including the Dodge brothers – to join the company.

Fairly soon into 1905, sharp conflict took hold in the developing company over its direction. Ford was ever anxious to develop a moderately priced car that 'almost anyone could afford', while Malcomson was interested in aiming at the higher end of the market. An eventual showdown occurred which split the main backers but ended in victory for Ford. He now decided to rid himself of Malcomson, but in so doing he was to reduce the power of two of his backers, the Dodge brothers. At this time the production process was in the hands of the Dodge brothers, whose factory produced Ford cars for *assembly* at the Ford works. Henry had decided that he could affect a more efficient form of production if the production process was in his hands. To do this he set up a new company to work in conjunction with the existing one:

> On November 22, 1905, the Ford Manufacturing Company was incorporated with a capital of $100,000 and the stated object of producing engines, running gears, and other types of automobile parts and appliances – the very manufacturing which the Dodge Brothers had hitherto executed for the Ford Motor Company. Ford Motor and Ford Manufacturing now stood side by side, but with a significantly different pattern of shareholding. Alex Malcomson had no interest whatever in the new manufacturing company, and John Gray explained to Vernon Fry how this bicorporate juggling was essentially a device to squeeze out the coal merchant (Lacey, 1986, p. 85).

In order to make his dream happen, Ford had felt that he needed to lay down not only the development rules but the technical and production rules as well.

In the case of Apple, Wardair and Ford, the companies were developed in a way that placed different people in competing relationships to the emerging and extant rules of the company. In the end – and companies have many end-points – someone pressed their stamp on the company's direction, and someone else was either forced to take a back seat or quit altogether.

Moral mazes
Organizational power creates what Jackall (1988) calls moral mazes – the creation of a series of organizational rules-in-use which determine moral issues:

> the moral rules-in-use that managers construct to guide their behaviour at work . . . are shaped directly by authority relationships or by other kinds of experiences typical of big organizations.
>
>   In fact, bureaucratic contexts typically bring together men and women who initially have little in common with each other except the impersonal frameworks of their organizations [and], the enduring genius of the organizational form is that it allows individuals to retain bewilderingly diverse private motives and meanings for action as long as they adhere publicly to agreed-upon rules. . . . As a former vice-president of a

large firm says: "What is right in the corporation is not what is right in a man's home or in his church. *What is right . . . is what the guy above you wants from you.* That's what morality is in the corporation' (Jackall, 1988, pp. 4–6).

Power brokers, those at the top of the organization, lay down the moral rules of the organization and in so doing open the way to a series of conflict situations. First, this leads – particularly in the USA – to the development of a *patrimonial* form of organization:

> Patrimonial bureaucracy was the organizational form of the courts of kings and princes. There, personal loyalty was the norm, not loyalty to an office. In a patrimonial bureaucracy, one survives and flourishes by currying favours with powerful officials up the line who stand close to the ruler. It is a system marked by patronage and by intrigues and conspiracies among various factions to gain the favor of the ruler and the prerequisites that accompany his good grace. Of course, in America, kings and princes were unavailable as objects of personal attachment. But the hierarchies of bureaucratic milieux allow the hankerings for attachment generated by the intense personalism of our own historical experience to be focused on chief executive officers of corporations, as well as on certain high elected and appointed officials (Jackall, 1988, pp. 11–12).

One has only to look through the major business magazines to see the impact of CEOs upon a company – its thinking, its values, its image. But the person at the top can retire or be replaced; therefore, within the organization there will be a number of powerful cliques waiting to place their people in greater positions of power. Jackall shows how the change of a CEO in a major company can lead to changes in office holders all the way down the line. Those who 'made the right choice' of who to follow early on will stand to prosper while those who didn't are liable to be chopped. An atmosphere of uncertainty and conflict is thus created and people attempt to side with powerful leaders within an organizational struggle for dominance.

Secondly, the *pyramidal structure* of organizations encourages competitiveness and conflict as small players vie to be larger ones. Employees are led to believe that movement up the ladder is an essential sign of organizational importance. Those who fail to rise up the ladder or who move too slowly are doomed to be seen as 'the stuck' (Kanter, 1977) or the 'drones' (Jackall, 1988). This encourages aspiring leaders to compete for limited positions of power.

Thirdly, the whole system generates fear and uncertainty. On the one hand, there is the necessity to conform to the dominant moral theme of the moment as directed by the person in charge. But that view may be contested from time to time by challengers and ultimately by the arrival of a new CEO. The greater the uncertainty, the greater the opportunity for conflict.

Structural antecedents

In the plain fact of organizing, of attempting to co-ordinate activities, a number of rules may come into play which encourage horizontal conflict: the way an organization differentiates its activities; the way it couples its activities into dependent relationships; the way it distributes rewards; the way it distributes tasks and assigns status; and the way it communicates its activities.

Differentiation

As organizations grow, they usually divide off tasks, functions or areas of specialisms into different departments, sections or divisions and this can lead to unintended conflicts. Apple Computers provides a useful example. Under severe competition from IBM, Steve Jobs decided to pull together a team within Apple to design a new generation of personal computers – the result was the Macintosh. In developing the Macintosh, Jobs raided Apple for anyone and anything he needed to build up his team. Things seemed to go well. The new team proved to be energetic and the result was a successful new development. Organizationally, however, things began to fall apart. Conflict began to occur between the Apple II and Macintosh groups within the company:

> The organizational factors that led to the conflict were physical separation of the two groups and different goals. The trigger for the conflict was an annual meeting in which senior executives devoted most of the program to Macintosh products and ignored Apple II's innovations, which were the backbone of the company at that time. The consequence for Apple was poor morale and decreased performance in the Apple II division (Daft, 1989, pp. 449–50).

Differences between organizational groups can be accentuated where they are also organized along different lines. For example, one group of workers might be organized along strict bureaucratic lines (e.g. a finance department), whereas another group in the same organization may be organized along looser, organic lines (e.g. a group of academics). Here conflict may be encourged in a number of ways. First, the academic faculty and the finance department may at times compete for much needed resources. Secondly, their different structures may make communication between them awkward and tense with, for example, the finance department expecting clear, documented and speedy responses and the academics responding in a less than formal more or less casual and paced fashion. Thirdly, there is some evidence (Morgan, 1986; Jackall, 1988) that organizational structures and rules-in-use affect the thinking of people and how they view the world. Thus, it is likely that the finance employee will come to view certain ambiguous organizational situations in a different way from that of the academic. High differentiation makes for increased conflict potential.

Interdependency

The work of James Thompson (1967) has indicated that certain forms of interdependencies are more likely to lead to conflict. Thompson suggests that *pooled interdependence* is least likely to cause conflict. In this situation, work units contribute to the overall performance of the organization but with very little need for interaction. The different sections of a department store is an example. The running of the toy department will depend little on the activities carried out at the cosmetics counter. If, however, an organization relies upon *sequential interdependence*, then the conflict potential is increased. In this case, the output of one section becomes the input of the next section. Hence, the second department relies on the first to speed its output along. Automobile plants provide examples of this kind of interdependency. Departmental tensions can be caused where a group's wages or bonuses are linked to output and that output is held up by an interrelated department. Michael Burawoy (1979) describes the various conflicts that occurred within a particular factory between interdependent sections of the workforce. Machine operators had to rely upon employees who worked in 'the crib', a section responsible for the distribution of strategic parts, and upon truck drivers who brought the raw materials to be processed:

> After receiving their first task, operators have to find the blueprint and tooling for the operation. These are usually in the crib. . . . The crib attendant is therefore a strategic person whose cooperation an operator must secure. If the crib attendant chooses to be uncooperative in dispensing towels, blueprints, fixtures, etc., and, particularly, in the grinding of tools, operators can be held up for considerable lengths of time (Burawoy, 1979, p. 52).

Likewise, the cooperation of truck drivers – who were 'responsible for bringing the stock from the aisles . . . to the machines' – was essential.

The character of the interdependent relationships between departments at Athabasca University has also led to conflicts from time to time. The development of academic courses for distance learning have become embedded in a process that begins with the cooperation of an academic (professor) and an editor and, sometimes, an instructional designer, all working out of the same department. The completed course will then go to the media services department, along with all other print production requirements of the university. In the meantime, three other departments will be involved in the process – the registry (busy signing up students), tutorial services (helping to recruit and orient tutors to teach the course) and student services (fielding questions about the availability of the course and its relevance to certain courses of study). If the course has been advertized and these three departments activated to meet the deadline, pressure is on the academic department and media. Media services can get flack if they are assumed to have had the course for a considerable time and it has not yet been produced. The academic department may get flack if it got the course to media services with little time to spare.

Perhaps the greatest tension comes in situations where there is *reciprocal interdependence*. In such situations, a number of sections, groups or divisions needs to interchange activities in order to achieve a successful result, e.g. the emergency room of a hospital, sections of a nuclear power station. We indicated earlier how interdependency in the nuclear power industry can lead to disasters. Tragically, highly interdependent systems often reveal situations of conflict following a major accident, with various sections blaming each other, e.g. pilot error, driver error, maintenance breakdown, insufficient safety checks, traffic controller error, etc.

Daft (1989, p. 444) provides an example of how the interdependencies of a group, coupled with a considerable degree of expected interdependency, led to conflict among scientists working on a key project. In the USA in the 1980s, the Centers for Disease Control set up an AIDS laboratory. However, despite the importance of the project and the fact that several prominent scientists had been employed by the lab, the project ended in failure due to serious organizational conflict. Problems occurred on different fronts. Most of the administrators were epidemiologists – trained in the use of statistical surveys in the investigation of diseases – while most of the researchers were laboratory researchers. This led to confrontation over the type of data that was to be collected. A further conflict developed between those with PhDs (specialized in a given area of research) and those with MDs (knowledgeable across a number of areas); conflict centred upon the type of research that should be undertaken. The rivalries led to the resignations of five of the six senior scientists.

Reward systems

The rules about who is rewarded in an organization can very much influence the generation of conflict. For example, it is not unusual for organizational appraisal systems to take account of a person's contribution to their department or section rather than to the organization as a whole. This can further encourage the development of 'departmental thinking' and associated rivalries.

Jurisdictional ambiguities

Rules about who does what in an organization help to define areas of work. Ambiguities that arise within the system can generate conflict as different people, sections or departments claim the work. At Athabasca University, the potential for departmental conflict arose with the development of a proposal for a Masters Degree in Distance Education. The degree was proposed by the university's research centre and received universal approval. What was less than unanimously agreed upon was the question of where to locate the degree if it received government approval. Some in the research centre felt that it should be located with them – they had developed the proposal. Some in the Administrative Studies Faculty and in the Arts and Sciences Faculty felt that it should be housed with them – each group claiming a relevance to the programme. Although the matter was resolved amicably, the initial greyness of the area – a masters programme was new to the university – led to conflicting viewpoints.

Status ambiguities

The distribution of power throughout an organization is uneven. While some relationships – particularly hierarchical ones – are relatively clear and stable, some are less clear due to the shifting patterns of fortunes and understandings within organizations. In the Apple case quoted above, the Apple II division had been used to a certain status position within the company. The Macintosh division was newer and might have been expected to take a back seat to the Apple II people. However, as things developed, the attention given to Macintosh suggested that its status had overtaken that of Apple II, and the ambiguity of the situation gave rise to conflict. Management responded by reducing the ambiguity through paying increased attention to the Apple II division and by changing conditions so that the division was no longer physically removed from the rest of the organization (Daft, 1989).

Communication systems

A number of communication obstacles are actually built into the system of some organizations. In the Apple case, for example, the separation of two divisions into different physical locations added to a breakdown in communication. In some organizations, an insistence on the use of memos can hinder communication and lead to misunderstandings; electronic-mail, the modern equivalent of the memo, can have the same effect – people seem to come across more terse when producing a message than when they have to communicate it face-to-face. Face-to-face interaction can itself be a problem where it is mediated through hierarchical rules or technical jargon. One of the authors once interviewed a person who worked out of a federal government office in Edmonton, Alberta. In order to communicate certain things to her boss in the next office she had to first go through Ottawa, 2000 miles away! Technical jargon can hinder the ability of one group to effectively understand what it is that another group is communicating to it. In one organization known to us, professional staff are loath to call in computer staff to assist them in understanding hardware/software problems. Computing staff in the building find it hard to deal with minor problems without lapsing into long, technical explanations of what the system does, much to the exasperation of the professional staff who are just interested in getting on with their word processing tasks.

Structural antecedents will vary from organization to organization depending upon the specific rules of the organization and the context of uncertainty and resourcing.

Gender-based conflict

As we have argued throughout this book, organizations are largely composed of rules that favour men over women. The gender bias of much of organizational life provides the bases for a series of conflict situations; conflicts which cut across vertical and horizontal dimensions but which also add new dimensions of conflict to the organization.

SEXUALITY AND POWER

The development of human sexuality has involved an ever-changing process of definition and change involving power relations (Foucault, 1979). Organizations have inevitably been party to the process in which sexual identities are formed and reformed, clarified and struggled over. In a number of ways, organizations have become arenas of struggle over dominant definitions of sexuality (Hearn and Parkin, 1987).

From top to bottom images of organizational power and position have become entwined with images of sexuality. Power and maleness are interconnected. Jackall (1988, p. 97) provides a graphic example from the mouth of an upper-middle manager explaining the 'cardinal rule' of management circles:

> The code is this: you milk the plants; rape the businesses; use other people and discard them; fuck any woman that is available, in sight, and under your control; and exercise authoritative prerogatives at will with subordinates and other lesser mortals who are completely out of your league in money and status. *But you also don't play holier than thou.* This last point is as important as all the others.

Here the manager's main concern is that other managers do not attempt to act hypocritically. Similar sexual metaphors and power associations find expression in the movie *Wall Street*'s depiction of life at the top.

Sexuality is also linked to *hetero*sexuality within organizations. The successful manager is not only male but is a *man*. Lee Iacocca (1984) recounts a story of how Henry Ford II had a manager fired for not appearing 'man enough':

> One day Henry ordered me to fire a certain executive who was, in his judgement, 'a fag'.
> 'Don't be silly,' I said. 'The guy's a good pal of mine. He's married and has a kid. We have dinner together.'
> 'Get rid of him,' Henry repeated. 'He's a fag.'
> 'What are you talking about?' I said.
> 'Look at him. His pants are too tight.'
> 'Henry,' I said calmly, 'what the hell do the guy's pants have to do with anything?'
> 'He's queer,' said Henry. 'He's got an effeminate bearing. Get rid of him' (Iacocca, 1984, pp. 98–9).

In the end, Iacocca had the man demoted rather than fired, but it should be noted that even Iacocca's main concern was to convince Ford that the man was indeed heterosexual and, therefore, a reliable manager.

On the shop floor the language of sexuality is often used as a means of control, particularly in cases where male supervisors are dealing with female subordinates (Davies, 1989), but also between males and females generally. Pollert (1981, pp. 142–3) describes the situation faced by female employees in a tobacco factory:

> Not only were they subjected to the discipline of work and of factory rules, on top of this, as women, they were exposed to constant sexist patronisation, not just from the chargehands and foremen, but from any men that worked around them: 'Hey gorgeous', 'Do us a favour, love', 'Come here, sexy' – all are familiar addresses for most women. Supervision was sexually oppressive, the manner usually cajoling, laced with intimate innuendo, and provocative jokes, hands placed on girls' shoulders as they worked, imposition mixed with flattery.

And females were also expected to be *women*. Lesbian women or those 'suspected' of being lesbian can suffer a number of negative consequences within organizations (Hall, 1989).

Sexuality is fought out in many organizational terrains and is associated with struggles for pay and employment equity, organizational power and position, and sexual harassment. Since the 1960s, and the renewed development of the women's movement, a number of feminist struggles have occurred within organizations, and on many fronts. Female trade unionists, along with a number of their male colleagues, have fought to commit trade union organization to include in the collective bargaining process a range of issues of specific benefit to women (Hunt, 1982; Heery and Kelly, 1988). There have been numerous strikes and sit-ins for improved conditions for women (Mills, 1982). In a number of places, women have established counter cultures in opposition to the sexual oppression they have felt on the shop floor (Pollert, 1981; Leonardo, 1985; Lamphere, 1985; Zavella, 1985). Groups of women have organized in the local community and within organizations themselves with the specific aim of effecting changes in hiring and other discriminatory practices. In the employ of the Federal Government of Canada, for example, there are a number of 'women's networks' that hold education sessions, exchange ideas and work collectively to ensure organizational change. At the time of writing, a women's group (NOW) has been established in the town of Athabasca to ensure that specific organizations begin to recruit female candidates. Conflict has also ended in court cases, e.g. the cases of sexual harassment.

In their efforts to effect improvements women encounter various resistance and conflict from male colleagues. In Canada, for instance, efforts to achieve employment equity have met with considerable resistance (Tancred-Sheriff, 1988). Universities, where one might have expected more enlightened times, are no exception (Tancred-Sheriff, 1987) and inequities of pay have altered little over the last two decades (Guppy, 1989). Female managers find it a constant struggle to balance between images of management and of women. If they effect too 'strong' an image they may find themselves accused of not being a *real woman* and thus suspect anyway, but as far as they conform to stereotypical images of being female they stand to be accused of being 'too soft to be a manager'. The association of masculinity and manager are so closely related that it is hard not to imagine the impact of a female manager upon the psyche of some males. Mary Cunningham's elevation to corporate vice president of the Bendix company, for example, led to sharp conflict within the organization in a manner that has been charged with being sexist in motivation (Cunningham and Schumer, 1984).

The most emotionally charged area of gender-based conflict revolves around issues of sexual harassment. The widespread nature of this phenomenon, its invidious character and the uncertainty that surrounds it, make sexual harassment an organizational minefield. Research over the last decade has revealed the depth to which sexual harassment has occurred throughout organizations (MacKinnon, 1979; Gutek, 1985; DiTomaso, 1989). And laws have been passed to address the issue. The problem, however, remains, and does not appear to be getting any better. For example, a 1988 US report on *Sexual Harassment in the Federal Government* indicated that the harassment rate of 42% in 1980 remained unchanged in 1987. The situation is not helped by the fact that the laws on sexual harassment are unclear (Khan and Mills, 1990) and that there are constant examples of sexual harassment among the law makers themselves, i.e. the sexual harassment of women by lawyers (Rutter, 1989), police officers (Mills, 1988b) and politicians (Kramer, 1989).

Despite the fact that sexual harassment has been a reality in the workplace for a long time, phenomenon of *sexual harassment* (i.e. attempts to develop rules, codes and laws about sexual behaviour) is relatively new. There is a new discourse in operation, the rules of which are only just being worked out, fought over and clarified in a multitude of organizations. For women, many are as yet unclear as to what they can justifiably claim as 'unwanted attention of a sexual nature'. Organizations often do not assist people to address the problem, and women are not encouraged to complain. A complaint of sexual harassment by several female secretaries against a former employer in Edmonton, Alberta ended up with three managers being moved to other work but with golden handshakes. The females, all of whom had previously resigned to escape the harassment, were left with the firm impression that they should not have bothered making a case of it (Mills, 1988b). On the other side, excluding most of the worst and clearest offenders, there are a number of men who now have to be careful about their behaviour in a context where the rules are less clear than the potential penalties. It is a much needed, albeit fraught, process and will not end in reduced conflict until the rules become more clear and officially sanctioned.

Organizations give rise to a number of rules which serve to guide and make sense of its various activities. In many ways, the rules serve to socialize members, provide a cultural framework for organizational being and control the actions of organizational members. But rules are not one-sided – they invite players. The players are people with minds of their own trapped in organizational uncertainties, hopes, aspirations and confusions. As a result, rules are contested as the players attempt to move up the board, resist unfair treatment, reduce uncertainty and fear. Conflict is as much a part of the game of organizational life as is institutionalization and stability.

7

Markets, environments, boundaries and the process of adaptation

Introduction

Burns and Flam (1987) draw a distinction between two kinds of market-places and the rules that apply within them. The first form of market-place is that which has strong ideological or moral commitments. In such a market-place, strong religious beliefs, political decisions or laws are enacted and both implicit and explicit social-action rules act to shape and determine buyer and seller behaviour. One such community at this time would be Iran in relation to goods and services provided by US suppliers. In contrast, the second form of market-place is one in which such rule-sets are weak. While there are a variety of forms of this second category of market, the common characteristic of such markets is that they are unstable, both in terms of the reliability of transactions and in terms of the extent to which the explicit and implicit rules of the market are obeyed. An example of such an unstable market at this time would be Lebanon, and most especially Beirut. The key point provided by Burns and Flam's analysis is that markets are functions of social rule systems and as such reflect the predominant sense of rule and order in a given society or community.

Whether the market for a product or service is strongly guided by moral, political, religious or legal codes or not, that market will have its own rule-related characteristics. For example, some markets are seasonal, others are not. Some markets are price-sensitive, others not. Some markets are quality-sensitive, others are not. Some markets are growing, others are stable or declining – and some of these features are cyclical in some industry segments and others are not. Some markets are in highly competitive arenas, others are not. Even 'black markets' generally have rules about territory and service. Markets thus reflect what might be referred to as market-situational rules.

The third set of rules which help shape the market for a particular good or service are the rules associated with competition. These rules could relate to:

1 *Suppliers*: rules concerning the timing of supplies for manufacture or the quality

of these goods or services can be imposed by the producer and affect the competitive position of the company (for an example, see Tse, 1985).

2 *Buyers*: buyers impose rules through actions and expectations on companies and these consumer behaviour rules help shape the competitive environment in which a company operates within a given market.

3 *New entrants*: as a market develops, so does the interest in entering the market, and as the number of providers increases so the competitive environment becomes more complex and both formal and informal rules develop to self-regulate that environment.

4 *Threat of substitutes*: as a market becomes profitable others look to that market as an arena for the introduction of substitute products or new technologies which help to improve the service to the market and the evolution of the product.

5 *Regulatory change*: in both embryonic and established markets, governments seek to establish standards and norms by means of health regulations, anti-trust laws, import quotas and national content rules, and laws concerning employment relationships, etc., and by so doing delineate a framework for competition.

6 *Firm rivalry*: when there is more than one company working in a particular market, the nature of the rivalry between them shapes the competition and often this competition is regulated by industry-wide self-rules.

This framework for the study of the competitive environment, which is based on the work of Michael Porter (1980), applies equally to certain not-for-profit organizations and for government activities in certain segments. For example, in education it is possible to apply this analysis to the competition between public and private schools and other alternatives (e.g. home schooling) and examine the way in which the deregulation of schooling in some societies is shaped by competitive forces (Murgatroyd, 1989). For this analysis, the key point to note is that the competitive environment generates rules by which competition is conducted. Some of these rules are explicit – anti-trust legislation, rules and laws concerning mergers and acquisitions, and advertising standards are all good examples of formal rules – whereas others are implicit, such as the fact that the name 'Pepsi' was not to be used in the Coca Cola Company by a Coca Cola employee (at least when in the presence of an executive) until the mid-1970s (Louis and Yazijian, 1980; Oliver, 1986).

A final set of rules which shape responses to market conditions can be referred to as the rules of global competition. Porter (1986) identifies certain impediments to the globalization of markets. These are:

1 Heterogeneous local conditions and needs in relation to particular products, services or goods.

2 Lead times for market entry and penetration.

3 The costs of transacting business in more than one market.

4 The differing policies and laws of differrent governments.

5 The complexity of the organizational design needed to deliver products, goods and services to more than one market and the costs of this design.

These impediments lead organizations seeking global markets for their products to 'exploit the similarities across countries while country centred producers tend to be more responsive to differences among them' (Ghemawat and Spence, 1986). They can also lead companies to the formation of coalitions and alliances which in turn become important in 'home' or country-specific markets. These global competition rules developed by organizations change the boundaries between one organization and another and can alter the social position of an organization within a given market or community. By doing so, both internal rules concerning adaptability and relationships and external rules concerning boundaries are affected.

By beginning this chapter with the identification of these four rule sets – community, market, competitor and globalization – we wish to examine the way in which organizations frame their actions in and are themselves framed by both market and competitor-environment factors. Our analysis here will focus upon the meanings given to these factors in terms of establishing conditions for change within the organization and the maintenance of boundaries between the organization and its competitors and the community of which it is a part. Specific cases will be used to illustrate key points throughout this chapter.

Inside-out and outside-in thinking

Before exploring the key themes of this chapter, it is worth drawing attention to a distinction between two ways in which the environment and competition can be viewed. In one way of thinking, the market environment for a product or service is internalized. For example, some universities in developing courses and programmes will frequently make assumptions about what their students need and what those who will seek to use their services will want once a programme of studies has been completed. They do so by internal processes – by reference to experience and insights – and will modify their programmes in the light of experience and self-reflection. While sensitive to the concerns of their consumers, universities often pursue their own routes and concerns despite social pressures to do otherwise (Bloom, 1987). This kind of thinking is referred to here as inward-out thinking. For it begins and ends with the view of the world which the organization *wishes to* see and hear.

In contrast, other organizations (and some universities) spend a great deal of time, energy and money seeking to better understand the environment and market in which they find themselves, so that they can adapt and modify their thinking accordingly. In this outside-in thinking, organizations are systematically trying to listen and understand the markets in which they operate in the terms which those in that market wish to use.

The difference between inward-out and outward-in is not one of semantics; rather, it is in the extent to which organizational members wish to genuinely hear what the market wishes to say so that it may become more adaptable and responsive. In one form (inward-out) market research is conducted on terms acceptable to the organizations beginning frame of reference; in the other (outward-in), market research begins from the consumers' experience and moves into the company so that the language and experience of consumers shapes the actions and behaviours of the organization.

In terms of rules, inward-out companies assume that their rule-set is adequate for success and sustainable advantage, whereas in outward-in companies their rule-set is one in which customers systematically shape company development. Pettigrew (1985), in his account of the changes and developments within ICI, highlights this distinction and refers to it as the 'inclusive' *vs* 'exclusive' stance. The *exclusive stance* involves an organization having a strong sense of its own values, a tight boundary, unilateral exchanges with its environment, a limited set of networks and linkages to its environment and with its competitors, and limited transactions with its market environment. In contrast, the *inclusive stance* involves an organization having highly permeable boundaries, diffuse values, mutual exchanges with the environment, well-developed networks and linkages and a broad range of organizational–environment transactions. This distinction builds on the work of Olson (1965), Curtis and Zurcher (1974) and others. It can also be seen to be closely related to the distinction made in general systems theory between open systems and closed systems, as described by Beer (1972).

To understand the difference between these two rule-sets, consider the contrasting histories in the 1970s of Apple Computers and other computer manufacturers in terms of their entry into the personal and desk-top computer markets. Steve Jobs and Steve Wozniak were both working for others in the computer business – Atari and Hewlett-Packard, respectively – and could not convince them that their thinking about a new market territory was anything more than a hobby idea. They founded Apple in 1977 with an initial working capital of US$1300 and began developing what became known as the Apple II. By 1987, the company had worldwide sales of US$1.9 billion and made a net profit in that year of US$154 million. The estimated market value of the 'hobby' [*sic*] company for 1987 was US$7 billion (*Business Week*, 27 October 1987, p. 14). According to its CEO, John Sculley (Sculley with Byrne, 1987), the success of this venture depended crucially on customer empathy and futures thinking.

IBM took some time to enter the personal computer market, considering it for a while to be a temporary phenomenon. When it decided to enter the market fully, it established an independent business unit under the direction of Don Estridge in Boca Raton, Florida, and asked him to develop a unique product as quickly as possible, bypassing the normal IBM routes for product development and approval. To gain market share as quickly as possible, Estridge decided to create a product that depended upon a larger number of suppliers than was the norm for IBM systems: the IBM *pc* monitor came from Matsushita, its floppy disks from Tandon, its microprocessor from Intel, its printer from Epson and its operating system from Microsoft (Foster, 1986). The *pc* project was completed in 9 months and under budget. Using unorthodox marketing methods (at least for IBM) – selling through third-party retailers – Estridge was able to secure 12% market share within 18 months and a 23.4% share within $2\frac{1}{2}$ years. Despite some dramatic failures – notably the IBM *pc/jnr*, rated as the Ford Edsel of the computer industry (Mayer, 1985) – IBM managed to enter and quickly succeed in this market.

Looking at the Apple and IBM histories, it is possible to suggest that:

1 Apple began and remains an outside-in company, securing its sustained leadership in the *pc* and desk-top market by means of customer empathy and futures thinking.
2 IBM initially resisted the *pc* market on the grounds of its traditions and inside-out assumptions about the nature of the computer industry.
3 In the light of being shown to be wrong about their inside-out assumptions, IBM learned to be adaptive (i.e. it switched from being exclusive to inclusive) and to respond to the market in a new way using a new structure (one which could be inclusive) and by doing so created a new product line and a new business unit.
4 The success of the IBM *pc* venture led to other major changes within IBM which have had a dramatic affect upon the organizational structure and culture of the company.

Indeed, the size of IBM as an organization makes this latter point a dramatic one. In 1988, total IBM sales across all product lines exceeded US$54 billion and its profit was estimated at US$5.258 billion. The company operated in some 60 countries (Mittelstaedt, 1989, p. 79). In the UK alone, IBM-UK declared a profit of some £510 million on sales of £3.863 billion (*Business*, October 1989, p. 69) – success being mainly due to mainframe sales – giving this company a relatively high profit-sales margin rating (13.2% as compared to ITT's 5.4% and DEC's 10.9%). Changing the orientation of such a leviathan organization from inside-in to outside-in has been no mean task and has been accomplished at some cost and the process of change is still 'in train'. The change has involved changing the rules about adaptability and blurring the boundaries between the customer and the organization and between different business units within the organization. This in turn has had an affect on the culture of the organization. Recent changes within IBM have been seen as a 'cultural revolution' by some observers (De Lamarter, 1986), a revolution that is very problematic for the company (Hamilton, 1989).

This inside-out/outside-in distinction also parallels the distinction made by Alvin Toffler (1985) between the adaptive and maladaptive corporation. Noting some rapid changes in the nature of certain markets – globalization, deregulation, privatization, quality sensitivity and the rapid development of subsitute products – Toffler suggests that companies who build a strategy on the basis of past success and seek to retain their operating structures and practices over a long period of time are likely to fail and become dinosaurs. Success will come to those who show adaptive responses to nuance and change in the market and who invest in customer empathy and futures thinking.

Toffler's analysis of the problems facing the AT&T (Bell) organization in the late 1960s and early 1970s is incisive. He draws distinctions between inside-out and outside-in thinking in management (without using these precise terms) as follows:

- Between thinking in straight lines (year-to-year incrementalism) and discontinuous thinking (also known as generational thinking).
- Between one-off problem solving and integrated and relational problem solving.

- Between stable solutions (ones which do not affect the operating environment of the organization) and destabilizing solutions (ones which deliberately seek to solve the problem by changing the operating environment of the organization).

These distinctions are used to highlight some of the organizational consequences of these two rule-sets. They make clear that the distinction is primarily concerned with the adaptability dimension introduced in Chapter 2: with the responsiveness of the organization to threat, challenge or change. Outside-in organizations are responsive to change and are flexible. Inside-out organizations are less responsive to change and are more likely to be rigid.

Two further examples of inside-out thinking within organizations will also make this clear. In the 1970s Coca Cola was a company in trouble. In 1979, the average age of the board of the company was 70, and only one of its 14 directors was under 50. Robert Woodruff became President of Coca Cola in 1923 and was still at the helm throughout the 1970s. He did not see much reason to change the company. This stoicism was as classic example of success breeding failure, or at least the ingredients of failure. In the latter half of the 1970s, compound return on shareholder investment was less than 1%. The capital-intensive soda-fountain business within the organization was producing a return of some 13% on investment, but the interest costs of the capital investments themselves were 14%. Growth rates of sales of its flagship products dropped from 13% in 1976 to a meagre 2% in 1979. Profits between 1978 and 1981 grew at a compound annual rate of just 7% and net income rarely exceeded 1% (Oliver, 1986). By seeking to maintain traditions, culture and stability, this company was in a crisis. Oliver (1986), commenting on this state of affairs, notes:

> Coca-Cola remained a leviathan with atrophied muscles, and myopia, a company more comfortable in dreaming about the days when it ruled the world of soft drinks than in adapting to new times and a new market place . . . it certainly spent those years faltering . . .

making clear that the key dimension here was adaptability.

A second and more recent example of inside-out thinking is the case of the German steel-making and arms manufacturer company of Friedrich Krupp GmbH. From being a mainstay of German industry from the early 1870s and having continued to operate successfully throughout two world wars, Krupp posted 1987 profits of Dm42 million (approximately £130.8 million) as compared to Dm126 million the year before. Attempts by the company to diversify have failed. Management turnover has been high and corruption charges have been laid against some. In 1986, it announced the closure of a loss-making steel plant in Rheinhausen at a cost of 5300 jobs. Rationalization that would have been forced on a public company (Krupp is controlled by a philanthropic foundation, controlled largely by one man, Berthold Breitz) has been systematically avoided. At the end of the 1980s, this major German company is just beginning to adapt to new market circumstances, but in the view of some it may be too late (Muller, 1988). By persisting in the old and previously successful way of working, the company has become what Toffler would call a candidate for the dinosaur hall of fame.

Outside-in organizations use a variety of devices to blur the boundary between the organization and its environment. These can include some or all of:

1 Communication councils between the organization, its regulators, suppliers and major customers.
2 Future user committees comprised of identified potential users of products or services in development.
3 Focus groups of customers meeting regularly to examine products and services in a critical and informative way.
4 Systematic surveys by means of billing systems of consumers.
5 Suggestion programmes for customers and employees aimed at securing continuous improvements in products and services and at rewarding talk-back and innovation.
6 Community advising programmes in which specific communities or user groups provide advice and feedback to the organization.
7 An ombudsman to ensure that complaints and concerns are properly dealt with and that the generic issues raised are included in planning and development work.
8 Referendum programmes in which controversial issues between user groups or between the organization and its customers are dealt with.

Each of these measures or devices seeks to connect the organization to the value system(s) of its customers while at the same time making porous the boundary between the organization and its environment.

Inside-out organizations tend not to use these devices but commission market studies which are closed-questioned or rely on senior staff for planning and improvement suggestions. Indeed, some of the features of failures to change companies from within or by means of consultants (see Pettigrew, 1985) are often a consequence of the firms' lack of awareness of the nature of their own market for their own product or service.

The contrast between these two ways of thinking has been presented primarily in terms of adaptability and boundaries. In one form (outside-in), adaptability within the organization is high and the boundaries between the organization and the environment in which it is placed are weak. In the other form (inside-out), adaptability is low and the boundary between the organization and the environment is strong. Some case vignettes have been presented of organizations in which these characteristics can be detected.

Adaptability is, however, also strongly related to the interpersonal features of an organization. In the Apple Corporation, all who have ideas are listened to and consumers with ideas are listened to frequently. In the Coca Cola of the 1960s and 1970s, ideas from employees were not welcomed. When an organization develops implicit or explicit rules about adaptability they also affect the nature of relationships within the organization and between one organization and another, as we shall see.

Boundaries, coalitions and alliances

It is often assumed that a fact of competition is that competitors jealously guard their secrets and their 'turf': that market rivals are engaged in battle and as such maintain rigid boundaries around their organizations. In this section we wish to look at the boundaries between companies and examine some of the implicit and explicit rules which govern these boundaries. Our reason for doing so is to examine the extent to which inter-organizational relations affect the adaptability of the organization. Our hypothesis is that organizations who are connected to others in the same market will be more adaptable than those who are disengaged.

One trigger for our exploration of this issue is the case of JVC and the introduction of home video systems in the 1970s. In 1970, three companies – Matsushita, Sony and JVC – met in Osaka, Japan to discuss the technical problems each were having with their development of video-cassettes. While each was fiercely competitive in sales, they were also frequent collaborators in the field of research and development (R&D). At this meeting, Sony introduced their competitors to the U-Matic video-cassette and shared with them their technical problems. The other two companies agreed to cooperate. Indeed, the three participants signed a cross-licensing agreement that gave Sony, Matsushita and JVC free access to all the technical innovations each of them created in their research on the development of video-tape recorders: none would have to pay for the use of the others' VTR-related patents. While the agreement lasted only a short time, it was enough for each company to secure major if unequal benefits (Nayak and Ketteringham, 1986).

Such arrangements are not uncommon. Ghemawat et al., (1986) have studied the nature of coalitions and alliances between companies between 1970 and 1982 as reported in the *Wall Street Journal*. In all, 1144 coalitions and alliances were formed during this period. Only 57% of the coalitions studied were joint-venture or licence arrangements – the two forms most extensively studied in the past and most commonly regarded as normative between competitors in the same industry. Almost a third of the coalitions and alliances were focused around R&D and sharing of operational and logistical information, with only 12% being concerned with supply arrangements. While the coalitions and alliances span a variety of industry types, the largest number are concentrated in the following industries: (1) crude petroleum and natural gas; (2) motor vehicles and passenger cars; (3) electronic computing equipment; (4) biological products and biotechnology; (5) semiconductors and related products; (6) motor vehicle parts and accessories; and (7) industrial organic chemicals.

The existence of these kind of coalitions and alliances can lead to oligopolies and this development is protected against nationally through various forms of anti-trust and monopoly legislation and internationally through the policing of trade practices by means of GATT and other sector-wide trading arrangements. More particularly in recent years, rules concerning local content (the proportion of a manufactured good or service that can be imported) have forced companies to localize some aspects of production (though assembly arrangements are often used to reduce the impact of such legislation). Despite these precautions, the globalization of companies and markets is creating some complex business coalitions and mergers. The United Nations Centre of Transnational Corporations has recently shown that a group of 600 companies, each with sales of more than US$1 billion, produces over one-quarter of everything made in the world. These same companies between them account for between 80 and 90% of all exports between countries in the developed world. All told, these companies employ some 3% of the worlds' workforce – 65 million persons (Mittelstaedt, 1989, pp. 72–81). Many of these 600 companies are engaged in coalitions and alliances.

Coalitions and alliances formed between organizations can be one of three primary kinds:

1 A *coalition* or *alliance for* some purpose, such as for sharing research and development as in the case of the Sony-JVC-Matsushita licensing arrangement.
2 A *coalition* or *alliance against* something, such as the alliance formed between airlines in seeking to inhibit the growth of Freddie Laker's air-charter services in the 1970s.
3 A *coalition* or *alliance of convenience* which, while having no specific purpose, is in the general interests of those involved – an example of this being the 'special relationship' for economic, political and military purposes between Britain and the United States (see Horne, 1988–9, for a detailed account).

Coalitions and alliances can be either *exclusive* in terms of membership (i.e. membership is fixed and determined and not open to others) or *inclusive* (i.e. open to others sharing a common cause or wishing to engage in the same purpose). They may also be time-limited or purpose-limited. For example, the pact between the British Labour Party and the Liberal Party (the Lib-Lab pact) was both time-limited (to a specific period of government) and purpose-limited (to a set of governance and policy-related issues). Once the Labour Prime Minister, Jim Callaghan, called an election, this form of alliance was ended. The Sony-JVC–Matsushita licence arrangement was also time-limited and purpose-limited.

One difference between the three primary types of coalition and alliance concerns the nature of boundary and entrance rules. In the first type of coalition, those with skills and commitment are encouraged to cooperate and join, and the boundary between the group and others with vested interests may be porous or strong, depending upon the purpose. For example, a coalition between different research units concerned with the search for a cure for AIDS or diabetes will initially involve weak boundaries, whereas a coalition formed for the purpose of securing increased access to Japanese markets of British or Canadian goods may be seen to have slightly stronger boundaries, at least when looked at from a global point of view. Thus it is possible to suggest that some coalitions and alliances which are for something may have inclusion or exclusion rules which shape the nature of the boundary around them.

Coalitions tend to arise in response to events – changes in markets, new technical developments, the emergence of substitute products or services, changes in supply arrangements or in government regulations – rather than as a part of an organizational design (Johnson *et al.*, 1989). Thus, coalitions may not always be evident from an analysis of organizational charts or specific in-organization actions. In the Sony–JVC–Matsushita example, only the R&D units were engaged in the direct aspects of the coalition: the marketing departments of all three organizations continued to compete with each other and the respective manufacturing units were not directly involved at all.

Coalitions and alliances involve many potential benefits and some potential costs. On the benefit side, Porter and Fuller (1986) suggest that coalitions and alliances between firms involve one or more of four strategic advantages: (1) economics of scale; (2) access to knowledge and skills where these are asymmetrical between coalition members; (3) reducing risk; and (4) shaping the nature of the competitive forces by the power of the coalition itself. When one or more of these advantages appears greater than the alternatives (and the alternatives are essentially these: internal development, merger or arms-length transaction) then a coalition or alliance would seem to be advantageous. The costs of coalitions are potentially three-fold: (1) the direct costs of co-ordination, communication and collaboration, i.e. *transaction costs*; (2) the costs associated with any erosion of competition that might ensue from the coalition, i.e. *the costs of industry change*; and (3) the creation of an adverse bargaining position – one or more partners in a coalition may benefit disproportionately from the coalition, i.e. *unequal outcome costs*. These costs often act as inhibitors to the conclusion of coalition agreements, despite good intentions.

These features of coalitions and alliances can be related directly (with some elaboration) to Karl Weick's observations that:

1 Organizations are segmented rather than monolithic – coalitions can be formed within organizations or between one segment of an organization and other segments in other organizations.
2 Stable segments in organizations are often small units, usually ones which are problem-focused rather than time-constrained.
3 Connections between segments within and between organizations are of variable strength – strong coalitions have strong rule-sets governing membership, public statements, transactions and consequences for rule violation, whereas weak coalitions have much weaker rule-sets in relation to these items and often have disagreements about these rules.
4 Ambiguity is a function of the strength of coalition rules – the weaker the rule-set, the greater the ambiguity (Weick, 1985).

Coalitions and alliances between organizations represent a statement about organizational boundaries. Where such coalitions and alliances exist, they represent an attempt by an organization to be connected to others while at the same time maintaining a degree of separateness (the degree of connectedness and separateness is a function of the strength of the rule-set governing the alliance or coalition). This indicates a degree of boundary-openness. Where organizations resist coalitions or alliances they can be seen to be disengaged and rigidly maintaining their boundary. Where the coalition and alliance dominates all thinking and activity within the organizations concerned – where the coalition is one of enmeshment – then the organization has lost its boundary and has been consumed.

As markets for certain products become more global, the number and nature of coalitions and alliances appears to be increasing, especially in capital-intensive industries or industries which involve high R&D costs. For example, such coalitions are now commonplace in the aircraft (GE-Semca, Air Bus Industrie), automobiles (Chrysler-Mitsubishi, Volvo-Renault) and electrical products (Siemens-Allis-Chalmers, Gould-Brown-Boveri) industries. Often these coalitions will be between unequal partners with different interests in the same industry segment or between partners with different skills in different countries.

As such coalitions become more evident in certain industries, they can lead to an increase in ambiguity *within* an organization. In part, this results from uncertainty about the new rules of the organization as affected by the coalition and in part because of questions about where power does and does not lie (Ott, 1989). An example will illustrate this point. The Milk Marketing Board was formed in the UK as a means for rationalizing the production and operating systems for milk producers and ensuring product quality and market stability. While the market for milk grew, participating farmers (who had to sell their milk through the board) had only minor concerns about the board's working – ambiguity within the coalition was low. When Britain joined the EEC, the board itself became part of a supra-coalition and, as a result of over-production and the guarantee of access for French milk producers to the UK market (for UHT milk), the board was required to significantly reduce milk production in the UK. This led angry milk farmers to protest about both the EEC commission (which had established the milk production quotas) and the board (which had to act to implement the EEC quotas) – ambiguity within the UK coalition was high. The key issue facing UK farmers was: 'Where does the power lie?' A related issue for these farmers has been: 'Under what rules can they challenge the workings of the board and the EEC?' – to their distress, they found that the rule-set binding the coalition within the UK and between the UK and the EEC were exceptionally strong. Power was seen to reside not just in the institutions which reflected the coalition, but in the rules which established them.

There are essentially three alternatives to coalitions and alliances of the type identified here in a market sphere in which competition takes place:

1 Letting the market shape the nature of the competition between organizations while at the same time relying on the internal development of the organization to remain adaptable to market conditions.
2 Bargaining between organizations about territory, pricing, supply and service – arms-length agreements.
3 Takeovers and mergers leading to a reduction in the competitive elements within the market (Thompson and McEwan, 1958).

As has been suggested, the choice made by an organization will reflect its futures thinking and its understanding of its strengths and weaknesses. For many organizations, coalitions and alliances represent an important stragegic choice and provide a framework for rule assumptions about inter-organizational relationships.

Competition rules

To this point we have been concerned with the way in which an organization relates to the environment in which it is placed – with the nature of boundary between one organization and another and to the way in which an organization is adaptive in its response to other organizations engaged in the same social activity. We now wish to examine the nature of organizational adaptability and inter-organizational relationships when the organization has chosen direct competition as its response to its business environment.

In 1983, soft drink companies in the USA were seeking permission from the Federal Drug Administration (FDA) to use aspartame (a sugar substitute) in their products. All of the soft drink companies acted collectively in an alliance known as the National Soft Drink Association to pressure the FDA to ensure that the testing process was thorough and complete and that approval, once given, would not be removed (as it was with cyclamates some years before). While all the companies were acting collectively (Coca Cola chaired the association in that year) in seeking to secure permission, two companies – Coca Cola and Pepsi – were also major rivals in seeking to secure access to the product once it was approved, for it was clear to these companies that the supply of aspartame would not be sufficient to satisfy likely demand, and that this would be the case for some months after FDA approval was given. The account given by the President and CEO of Pepsi (Enrico and Kornbluth, 1986) of the attempt to secure this contract reveals two interesting assumptions concerning the rules of such a competition. First, he suggests that it may be improper for the company acting as chair of the alliance to also be bidding for the product. Secondly, he suggests that the company who won this competition may have had unfair advantage in the marketplace. What he does not give emphasis to is that Pepsi had a first chance at securing this product and failed to take it.

The notion of fair competition is a dominant one in several countries and market sectors. The underlying assumption is that all of those competing in a market should have an equal opportunity to succeed. Indeed, there are regulatory requirements in certain countries and markets that seek to enforce 'fair competition' rules and advertising standards can be seen as another rule-set that relate to this notion.

What is 'fair' and 'equal', however, is open to some interpretation. For example, the USA has sought import quota restrictions and surcharges on certain Canadian goods entering the USA on the grounds that they are subsidized products and as such compete unfairly with unsubsidized products manufactured in the USA. The nature of some subsidy claims (dismissed at this time by the US regulators) revolves around the idea that countries with unemployment insurance and social medical systems (e.g. Canada and the UK) are subsidizing employers and employees through social programmes and that this is unfair to those countries which do not have such social welfare systems (e.g. the USA). Other subsidy claims compare Canadian subsidy programmes (e.g. government stabilization programmes for agricultural prices, especially grain) with the US policy position of no subsidies to farmers, when in fact farmers on both sides of the border are subsidized, but in different ways.

To explore the question of fair trade in terms of its utility in revealing market rules which organizations have to adapt to, let us look in some detail at one industry – informatics. This growth industry – which brings together telecommunications, data technologies, expert systems and information systems – is a rapidly growing area in which several organizations have major interests. For example, the following is a listing of the top four telecommunication/informatics companies in the UK showing their pre-tax profits for 1988, the number of employees and their return on capital. Also shown is their rank in the corporate 1000 for 1988 in the UK as defined by *Business* magazine (November 1989). As can be seen, these companies have a substantial place in the UK economy.

Rank	Company	Profit (£000s)	Employees	Return on capital
4	British Telecom	2 437 003	242 723	17.7
27	IBM (UK)	510 102	20 146	49.3
56	STC	229 372	33 848	24.7
88	Cable & Wireless	420 500	29 320	18.3

Each of these companies operates on either a multinational basis (as in the case of IBM, Standard Telephone and Cable & Wireless) or on a more than one country market basis (as in the case of British Telecom, who own companies in Canada and in EEC countries). As can be seen, as they operate in the UK these companies are large and powerful. They are also extremely profitable.

On a worldwide basis, this industry is dominated by IBM. Despite the reassurances of its president and CEO, John Akers, that IBM does not have a stranglehold on the market, IBM dominates eight out of the ten market segments in which it operates and has such significant profits that it can out-invest and out-purchase others in the marketplace. In some of these segments – especially mainframe computers and the mass storage of data – its market lead is so great that those who are second and third in these markets are operating in less than half of the available market.

According to one analyst (De Lamarter, 1986), IBM is simply too big and powerful and acts as a monopolistic force in the informatics market not only in the USA but in the majority of markets in which it is active:

IBM is in fact a major problem for practically every country in which it does business, even the United States. By maintaining everywhere a self-perpetuating, lopsided market structure in which it towers over all competitors, IBM has amassed entirely too much power to be considered 'good' for any nation as a whole. . . . Without effective structural change and a reduction of IBM's power, the problem will only get worse as the company pursues its goal of dominating the expanding information procesing market (De Lamarter, 1983, p. 326).

What De Lamarter proposes is that IBM should be broken down into several equal-sized, vertically integrated companies in much the same way that the AT&T system was in 1984 following a successful anti-trust action in the USA.

Accepting this analysis for one moment, what are the barriers to changing the rules under which IBM is permitted to operate – the barriers to be fair competition in the informatics industry? There are essentially three. These are: (1) the vested interests of the current stakeholders, most notably IBM and those who favour the status quo; (2) a feeling within the USA that only mega-corporations can stave off the market onslaught feared from Japan in the informatics industry; and (3) the ineffectiveness of the available anti-trust legislation, as evidenced by the fact that the most recent attempt to break up IBM in 1982 was dismissed on the decision of an Assistant Attorney General who decided to abandon the case rather than bring it through the due processes of the anti-trust laws then in force in the USA. In fact, several earlier anti-trust suits against IBM have failed.

These three reasons for the failure of legislative rules to control the power and influence of a large corporation take us to the heart of theoretical questions about the place of an organization in society. What is at issue is the nature of power and control and the politics associated with the exercise of power and control in society – a key theme in organizational analysis since Marx and Durkheim (Clegg, 1977; Burrell and Morgan, 1979; Silverman, 1970). IBM's market domination in the informatics industry can be seen as an examplar of the domination of one class (those who already have power, wealth and influence) over others (those who seek entry into this class). It is interesting to note that the continued power of IBM is a consequence of contradictions (Hydebrand, 1977) between conflicting rule-sets. For example, the formal rules state that monopoly practices are to be constrained, yet informally there is a feeling among the politicians and rule-enforcers that breaking up a monopoly could, in the long term, be damaging to the competitive position of the USA. A second contradiction is between the basis on which anti-trust assessments are normally conducted (in which price competitiveness and market share *together* are used as a basis for assessment, together with other factors) and the reality of the experience of other producers. These contradictions reflect the transition from an industrial form of capitalistic monopoly to a technological form of capitalistic monopoly (Karpik, 1977, 1978).

This example, and there are others, suggests that the organization is not simply a product of its environment, as some have supposed (Radice, 1973; Tugenhadt, 1973). Rather, in the case of IBM, the organization seeks to so shape its environment that it remains in control and able to ensure that the perceptions held within its environment of the organization are favourable to its purposes. Only when the organization loses its ability to control environmental perceptions will it be possible for social control to be exercised. In the absence of the exercise of social authority through legislative rules, the organization's relationship to the environment can be regarded as one of structural immobility (Burns, 1966).

That this is so is reflected in some of the internal rules within IBM about what can and cannot be said in documents written for the organization, especially documents relating to markets, forecasting, new products or new services. All such documents have to be 'cleared' through IBM's anti-trust unit within IBM Corporate Legal Services (De Lamarter, 1986, pp. 367–8) – a unit which has issued a 27-point guide to the writing of such documents.

In this industry, it does not look likely that explicit legal rules designed to ensure fair competition will succeed in so changing the workings of IBM as to make fair competition possible. However, some other explicit rules are making for fairer competition, at least in some segments. For example, nine key competitors in the *pc* industry (AST Research, Compaq, Epson, Hewlett-Packard, NEC, Olivetti, Tandy, Wise and Zenith) have agreed on a basic set of standards with respect to personal computers and this extended industry standard architecture (EISA) provided a platform for fairer competition between rivals. The original nine have been joined by a further 200 companies who have announced that they will continue to provide service to EISA equipment, whatever technological developments occur in the industry. By the voluntary creation of an open standard – involving the sharing of key technical information and developments between companies which otherwise compete – will affect this segment of the informatics market. (Interestingly, the EISA is an extension of, and develops from, the former industry standard architecture ISA developed by IBM in 1981 with the introduction of the IBM *pc* AT and the Intel 286 CPU). The EISA can itself be regarded as a prescriptive rule-set for *pc* technology architecture to be followed by a large number of market competitors, but not IBM or Apple (Frank, 1989).

Not all competition rules are formal, such as those associated with anti-trust or monopoly control or the formal rules agreed by an alliance of computer manufacturers, software developers and distributors. Some are informal. For example, software manufacturers who have developed dictionaries and grammar-checking software for use with word-processors have an informal rule about which thesaurus they will use as a basis for these packages – all use the same. This is not an industry standard in the same way that EISA is – there are no written agreements, it was simply easier to do it this way.

There are also etiquette rules associated with competition, at least in the private sector.* These involve decency rules for advertising, product benefit claims and the use of promotional devices (give-aways, discounted prices, etc.). Writing about this in the 1970s, Leavitt *et al.*, (1973, pp. 222–3), suggested that:

---

* Recent election strategies in the USA have made considerable use of personal attacks as a basis for campaigning, including attacks on the moral, financial and personal standards of opposing candidates. Hence the distinction drawn between public and private organizations.

Perhaps the best way to answer the morality question is by the same means we use in many other situations: by letting the pressure build up around specific situations. Where advertising or other marketing tactics get out of line, we protest to the marketers, newspaper reporters, or government officials who can put pressure on the offending companies. The wise company expects pressure from customers. . . . The wise customer, in turn, recognizes the importance of thinking through what he wants and of taking time to make his voice heard.

This suggests the existence of some social contract between the organization and its customers. Since this was written there has been a significant growth of consumer organizations and agencies (some backed with government funds) to act as watchdogs over the actions of organizations. The existence of these organizations has in turn led companies to develop self-regulatory standards both on an industry-wide basis and on a company basis. Further, the growth of an ethical focus for business practice following several major financial, environmental and corruption cases in the USA, Japan, Canada and Britain are creating environments in which ethical questions are factors which influence competitive strategy.

The external–internal link

The activities of an organization in the public domain – its ethical practices, marketing strategies, collaboration with market rivals – have a direct effect on the internal workings of the organization. In particular, when an organization seeks to adapt to changes in its market condition this has an effect on the internal relationship qualities of the organization: dealing with adaptability has an impact on relationship rules.

A number of examples will make this point clear. Kodak (Canada) manufactures a range of photographics products, including microfilm, motion picture film and colour print film. While their primary market rivals are other companies (especially Japanese companies, such as Fuji), they also have to compete in some of these market segments with other Eastman-Kodak companies: it is a conglomerate which believes that internal competition is likely to remove ineffective business operations from the conglomerate. So as to maintain its integrity as a business and stave off competition from others and from within, Kodak (Canada) has had to cut operating costs, improve quality and satisfy increasingly demanding customer specifications for products, especially in the fields of health care and informatics. In describing the company response to this market situation, Corbett (1989) gives emphasis to:

1 Changes in the extent to which workers can participate through quality teams and a Quality Management Process (QMP) of decision making.
2 The search for constant improvement is itself an improvement on 'top-down' change strategies which were the hallmark of the company some years ago.
3 By sharing problems and concerns throughout the organization, management has been surprised at the extent and quality of worker adaptability.

All three of these features represent internal changes that are a consequence of changes in the market conditions. They are also changes which affect the nature and meaning of relationships within the organization.

A second example, which also concerns quality improvement, is provided by Velcro USA. General Motors (GM) uses Velcro products in their car interiors. While Velcro is not the only provider of its products in the market (its patents expired in 1978), it has held a sustained leadership position in the market, especially for some of its lines. In 1985, GM told Velcro that it was changing its quality rating from the highest level to the one below. They were given 90 days to establish a total quality programme or else face further changes to the relationship between GM and Velcro. According to the account provided by the president of Velcro (Krantz, 1989), the implications of this decision by a company with whom they were both supplying and collaborating were these:

1 Consultants had to be hired to push the company and staff to understand the imperatives of their situation.
2 The introduction of new methods and tools (notably, statistical process control) required a company-wide education and training programme.
3 Workers had to be involved in the task of identifying potential sources for improvement and change, which in turn meant a change of relationship between staff at different levels within the organization.
4 There was a need to see teamwork rather than line control as the basis for all worker activity in the organization.
5 Improvement had to be measurable.

The consequences of the changes made at Velcro (USA) were dramatic, and they surprised many managers and workers. In the first year, waste reduction as a percentage of total manufacturing was reduced by 50% and in the second year by a further 45%. Interestingly, this was achieved while reducing the number of people designated as quality controllers and ensuring that everyone felt that this was a function they held too.

A third example here is that of the ethical issues faced by Boeing, the US aircraft and defence contractor. Boeing pleaded guilty to criminal charges relating to the illegal and illicit use of government planning documents in its attempts to secure major defence contracts in November 1989. In addition to paying a fine of more than US$5 million to the government of the USA, Boeing (or some of its divisions) may also be debarred from bidding for a fixed time for some or all defence contracts. These criminal acts occurred despite the fact that there are 4000 separate legal rules governing defence contracting, 30 000 pages of related regulatory control rules, 26 000 individuals whose sole government work is to regulate and control defence contracting, and that there are 29 congressional committees (and 55 sub-committees) who have, as part of their mandate, the task of overseeing the US$150 billion annual expenditures on defence (Augustine, 1988).

According to the account provided by Pasztor and Wartzman (1989), Boeing has taken a number of steps to prevent this happening again. These include:

1 Trebling the number of people whose sole job it is to act as security supervisors and document administrators in relation to government documents within the company.
2 Revising ethics policies throughout the organization and engaging in a major employee training programme dedicated to ethical education.
3 Changing the tracking and reporting systems for document use and access within the organization.

These measures will have consequences for some relationships in the organization and will also lead to some new questioning of a general ethical nature within the organization (Cornog, 1962; Silk and Vogel, 1976; Werhane, 1985).

The Boeing case carries implications for other organizations too. The Defense Criminal Investigation Service in the USA is also investigating the activities of several others in this arena, including the Martin Marietta Corp., Lockheed Corp. and General Dynamics Corp. Changes in one organization can lead to changes in others, especially when the first organization through a process sets some response criteria for that process.

Conclusion

In seeking to understand the points raised in this chapter from a rules perspective, it is possible to suggest some basic principles. These are:

1 *As an organization responds to its social condition (its environment), it does so in terms of its adaptability and relationship to others.* In the examples given, Kodak is responding to perceived market conditions, Velcro is responding to an actual change in its status relationship with GM and Boeing is responding to potentially damaging and difficult charges in law.
2 *Adaptive responses to environmental conditions may have consequences for relationships within the organization. In any case, implicit rules of how internal relationships affect adaptability are thrown into relief.* In the case of both Kodak and Velcro, changes in the nature of internal relationships were a key part of the adaptability strategy adopted to deal with perceived or actual environmental changes. In the case of Boeing, the need to demonstrate control and ethical monitoring may create more top-down management than is currently the case in that organization. In the case of IBM, the organization has issued guidelines as to what can and cannot be said in documents relating to markets, future developments and other issues as a means of avoiding anti-trust challenges – such rules for writing can affect the way in which issues are understood within an organization. The creation of coalitions and alliances can also lead to an increase in ambiguity within each of the organizations which form part of the coalition.
3 *The organization is not simply a mirror of the social rule system of which it is part – it may also be a controlling element in that rule system.* The study of IBM examined earlier suggests that this is the case. While some organizations may simply be

products of the social rule systems, others are formers of social rules. It is clearly an iterative process. What is important, according to Burns and Flam (1987), is the strength of the social rule system in which the organization functions.

4 *Organizations do not always act independently in their environment; they may form relationships with others (coalitions and alliances). When they do, these may be examined in terms of the relationship and adaptability dimensions introduced in Chapter 2.* When a strategic choice is made to enter a coalition or alliance, the organizations engaged in this choice are making a statement about both their own status and their relationship to the market in which they are placed. These coalitions and alliances are also new ways of ordering power and seeking control.

5 *The underlying purpose of adaptive responses is to maintain or increase power in terms of both the power of the organization in the environment and in terms of the power of key organizational members to influence the actions of the organization in terms of the environment.* As with the case of IBM described earlier in this chapter, IBM seeks to use its resources to maintain its market leadership within the industry segments in which it competes, but does so in such a way as to sustain its power relationships with the socio-political structures within which it has to operate. Boeing's failure to manage these power relationships, as evidenced by its recent criminal admissions, empowers the political system to act against this organization; indeed, the political system is forced to act against Boeing in response to the social dimensions of Boeing's criminal actions. In the case of Boeing, the company can be seen to have broken a truce between itself and others about what is and is not permissible in the maintenance of structural power relations; in the case of IBM, the truce remains intact at this time. Indeed, for communicative and symbolic purposes, the Boeing case is likely to be used repeatedly by those elected to ensure social order as a means for reinstigating the truce in the defence procurement industry. This is not to say that the kind of document exchange that led to the Boeing case will not continue, but that their use will be restrained so as to reinforce the truce rules which hitherto were in force.

Some of the constructs introduced in this chapter will be re-examined in a broader framework in Chapter 8. What is important to note here is that the relationship between an organization and the environment in which it is placed is shaped by explicit and implicit rule assumptions about relationships and adaptability.

__ 8 __

Using rules

Introduction

The previous chapters have set the construct 'rules' in the context of a developed body of organizational theory. It has been suggested that the use of rules as a basis for the study of organizational action permits a dialectic between theoretical paradigms hitherto seen as insulated from each other by the very nature of their own epistemological rules. In addition, a specific interactionist model of rules concerning cohesion (or relationship quality) and adaptability has been introduced and explored. This model seeks to embody rules concerning individual action and rules concerning structure and, by doing so, provides a comprehensive framework for understanding organizational action.

More specifically, we have examined the processes of socialization (especially – but not exclusively – in terms of gender), organizational change, organizational conflict and environmental positioning through the use of rules as an organizing frame.

In these explorations, we have essentially developed a framework for studying 'organizational practice' in the sense suggested by Harris (1980) and developed by Reed (1985). We have done so through utilizing the ideas of ecological adaptivity and rule-matrix development (described in Chapters 2 and 3) and applying them to a variety of situations and issues which face organizational members. It is important to note here that the development of a rule-matrix by the individual is a source of tension within that individual and that his or her decision to act on the basis of the rule-matrix they are developing can create tension between that individual and others in the organization. Furthermore, by suggesting that groups of individuals with like-minded rule-sets collaborate through alliances and coalitions within the organization, we are suggesting that organizations are generally 'many world' in type, i.e. they are essentially comprised of subgroups holding to different rules. By proposing that organizational action is mediated by truce assumptions (see Chapter 3) of varying strengths, we are suggesting that an ongoing dialectic takes place within organizations between the formal and informal rules and between different subgroups. Finally, we are suggesting that the process of rule-matrix formation and 'trucing' we outline is constant and dynamic – it is a journey rather than a destination: a process of becoming, both for individuals and organizations.

The practice framework

Critical to the practice framework developed by Harris (1980, p. 29) is the development of constructs and concepts 'which will carry back reference to the constituent categories of action, but at the same time be of such a nature as to constitute an element of structure'. Structure here refers to the ongoing processes of institutionalization which are in force at a particular time and which exhibit a degree of structural continuity and cultural continuity.

The construct 'rules', as introduced and developed in this text, provides just such a device which links a variety of forms of action back to structural features, especially when these features are expressed directly. Indeed, whether at the level of seeking to understand the social mechanisms of control over the power and influence of organizations (as in the case of IBM) or the action of an individual in being negativistic towards some subgroup within an organization, rules have utility and value.

A second key feature of Harris's conception concerns the need to understand the relationship between individual action and 'imperative co-ordination', Harris's term for the management of processes which produce the goods and services which characterize the organization. Again, rules provide a valuable starting point for just such an analysis. When an individual acts, he or she does so in terms of a rule-matrix which is *in part* informed by the rules of the organization as formally established and informally communicated – this is their understanding of the imperatives of coordination. However, their actions are also in part informed by their own judgements, experiences and rules (especially at moments of truth) and it is through an understanding of these two sets of rules working and acting concurrently (and sometimes in opposition) that we can develop an understanding of organizational action.

The third feature of Harris's conception concerns the process of change and transformation. By seeing organizations as processes rather than entities (a point stressed throughout our analysis), Harris suggests that the sources of social change must be examined in terms of the endogenous transformation of practices. We interpret this (see Chapter 5) in terms of changes in the rules for action within the organization and the meaning given to these rule changes by organizational members. By shifting attention from the specifics of the practice changes and from the sources of the change to the processes by which change occurs (the transformation, transubstantiation or alchemy of rules) and the way this process is experienced within the organization, we are able to look more directly at the relationship between structure and action.

Indeed, it is precisely because the attempt to understand the different levels of the rule operation within an organization (especially in terms of cohesion and adaptability, subgroup conflicts, change and the process of 'trucing') and its impact upon the rule-matrix continually being constructed in an ecological-adaptive way by the individuals who comprise the organization, that rule analysis forms the basis of a practice sociology and a psychology of organizational action. This is the central concern of this text.

Some observations about methodology

The primary methodology used in this text has been sociological organizational analysis and the minor use of case vignettes. However, our primary purpose was exposition. The following comments are meant to indicate some of the methodological possibilities a focus on rules permits.

First, and perhaps most important, the study of rules as a basis for understanding practice in organizations permits a multi-method, multidimensional approach to the study of organizational action – an approach long advocated by sociologists (Brewer and Hunter, 1989; Cicourel, 1973) and psychologists (Reason and Rowan, 1981) alike. For example, in studying an action it would be possible to use a combination of participant observation, interview and secondary source analysis to study some aspects of rules. In several cases, it may also be possible to design practice case experiments which also make use of participant observation and interview methods as a basis for study. In short, some combination of ethnography and survey/interview methods would directly benefit the study of rules for practice.

A particular proposal for multi-method research which focuses upon rules and their impact on cultural action has been made by Maruyama (1969, 1981). He proposes that organizational studies conducted by insiders using their own epistemology and their own structure of relevance can provide valuable insights into rule operation and formation, especially in terms of the rules of communication, the rules associated with relevance and dissonance and the rules of critical dissonance. The research form, which Maruyama refers to as 'endogenous research' by individuals who are not trained in research methods or 'academic' research designs, is often, according to Worth and Adair (1972), superior in terms of insight than parallel studies conducted by trained researchers who are external to the organization.

Secondly, so as to examine rules and their interpretation at moments of truth – moments at which rules are thrown into relief and action is essential – critical incident analysis is seen as a valuable methodological tool. In particular, such an analysis of critical incidents which treats players in such a moment as interdependent actors in a scene which is framed by both structural and process rules and which seeks to unmask the rule-matrix used by the individual actors and their assumptions about each other, would be a powerful form of critical incident examination. Some psychological methods are also available for looking at cognitive-emotive components of such moments of truth (see the work by von Cranach and Harré, 1980 and Brenner 1978 for illustrations).

Thirdly, there are a variety of tools from both sociology and psychology which could (with some reworking) prove of considerable value in unmasking the rule-matrix held by individuals, groups and subgroups, especially in terms of cohesion (or relationships quality) and adaptability. For example, sociographs of the organization coupled with repertory grids about the adaptability of subgroups would be revealing about the psychosocial assumptions being made by individuals about their own place in the organization. Individual pursuit studies, such as used by Hargreaves (1986) in his studies of the experience of schooling, in which an individual worker is followed and traced for a period of time and interviewed at key points in each day about their experience, may also begin to unravel the rule-matrix which informs their actions and engages their interests. Q-sorts (McKeown and Thomas, 1987; Scott and Cowley, 1988) and focus groups (Morgan, 1988) could be used as a basis for examining the assumptions which individuals make about cohesion and adaptability when they engage in certain actions and practices within the organization. The intent behind these methods (and others like them) is to provide insight and some comparative basis for looking at the rule-matrix at a particular stage in an individual's development or an organization's history.

Perhaps the most powerful studies are those in which narratives and conversations are used as a basis for reviewing implicit and explicit rule and truce assumptions. Some general methods are suggested in Antaki (1988) and Fielding (1988). An especially insightful paper concerning these methods and their utility is provided by Abel (1988). These methods are powerful because they involve naturalistic field work and inquiry (Lincoln and Guba, 1985) focused upon real-event conversations concerning normative and typical processes which take place in an organization, a point we shall return to below.

These observations about the potential use of a variety of methods for the study of rules, moments of truth and trucing within the organization are in themselves illuminative of the hermeneutic properties of a rule-based practice sociology and action psychology of organizations. The fact that a diversity of methods can be used to unmask and reveal the frame of the rule-matrix used by an individual, group or subgroup as testimony to the value of this approach.

Some cautions

When studying the rule-matrix and truce behaviour which informs actions in the setting of an organization, there is a need to be reminded of certain cautions. In particular, the work of Giddens (1976, 1979) provides some constant reminders to enthusiastic sociologists of the need for interpretive honesty and caution. For example, contemporary accounts of organizational action appear to suggest that action is largely rational and purposive. It appears that many researchers and writers have equated action with purposive action (or intended action) and meaningful act with intended outcome (Giddens, 1976, p. 156). Yet experience of organizations makes clear that not all actions are intentional or rational: some actions are unintentional (but consequential) and others are driven more by emotion than cognition (Ortony *et al.*, 1988), e.g. actions that display anger, excitement, guilt or humour may not be 'purposive' or 'intentional' (Apter, 1988a, de Rivera, 1977). Furthermore, not all actions are preceded by conscious awareness of intention, even though the act itself may display some features of apparent intentionality (Dennett, 1981). This is a massive subject which has preoccupied many, especially in philosophy (Aquila, 1977), information processing and cognitive psychology (Kosslyn, 1980) and law (see especially Cross, 1974, pp. 502–518). Our point in making these observations is that there is a need for care when examining the rule-matrix and framing of action in an organization. Our own rule-sets as investigators should be seen as necessary precursors and potential impediments to the study of action.

Using Giddens' (1976) new 'rules' (a term he uses with irony) of sociological method as summarized in his text of this name, we wish to draw the reader's attention to a number of other cautions and links between different sections of this text.

1 Giddens states that '*sociology is not concerned with a "pre-given" universe of objects, but with one which is constituted or produced by the active doings of subjects*'. This is the central feature of our analysis of the nature of cohesion and adaptability rules and the process of socialization, gender enculturation, change, conflict and environmental positioning. We have argued that the genesis and reproduction of action within an organization is the product of a continuous dialectic between individuals, groups and subgroups operating from different rule-sets mediated by trucing processes. Thus, organizations are a human agency constantly in the process of becoming. This is why we see the study of organizational rules in this pluralistic sense as a form of practice sociology.

The danger is that rule analysis and research might always seek to generate scientific rules of predictability and causality. Rule formation is not biologically programmed in complex organizations. While organizations have a high level of structure which permits predictability at a certain level, human agency can render such structures unpredictable by a single act or a sequence of actions. As we have made clear, rules of structure (expressed through imposed relationships and adaptability) and agency (expressed through the experience of relationships and adaptability) are part of a constant process of trucing and development in which uncertainty and inconsistency are just as likely outcomes as predictability at certain levels of analysis.

2 Giddens observes that '*the realm of human agency is bounded. Men produce society, but they do so as historically located actors and not under conditions of their own choosing.*' This too is emphasized in our treatment of rules with organizations and the process of socialization. We would add that our exploration of rule-matrix formation and the processes of enculturation, socialization and gender-enculturation all demonstrate the adoption of this assumption.

The caution here is that action which reproduces the history of either the person's own rule-matrix or that embodied in the culture of the organization is subject to ecological adaptability: cultures can change, as our exploration of this question in Chapter 5 demonstrates, as can individuals. It is a key tenet of contemporary cognitive psychology that historiographic features of action do not necessarily inhibit new actions, but do provide a frame from within which individuals, groups or organizations view such a new action (Watzlawick, 1983). This is why Giddens' comment that 'structures must not be conceptualized as simply placing constraints upon human agency, but as enabling' is of importance. Stability and security can be one of the platforms from which innovation and change can occur, a point stressed several times by W. Edwards Deming (1982).

3 Central to the ideas in *New Rules of Sociological Method* is the assertion that '*processes of structuration involve an interplay of meanings, norms and power*' and that all intentional acts and all structural processes involve these three components.

The caution we wish to suggest here is that the interpretation of 'power' is too often associated with position in organizational analysis and in studies of leadership and authority. Murgatroyd and Reynolds (1984) review situational leadership using constructs derived from rational-emotive and cognitive psychotherapy to make the case that leadership can be seen to be just as much about the dominance of one rule-matrix and trucing process over another at any one particular time as it is about positioning or granted authority: ideas and experience have power just as do persons. We suggested in Chapter 3 that a third view of power which encompasses these broader assumptions needs to be examined when the rules which exist within the organization are used as a basis for the study of action.

Giddens offers a number of other observations which are pertinent, but which have already been examined directly in this chapter. In particular, the need to see immersion in a form of life as 'the necessary and only means' (1976, p. 161) by which the observer is able to come to understand the implicit and explicit rules of an organization and the process of socialization and trucing which characterize it and make it unique is commensurate with many of the suggestions we made about methodology earlier in this chapter.

Conclusion

Our intention was to introduce the reader to the richness of rules as a basis for thinking about organizational life. Furthermore, we wished to ensure that the reader was aware of the complexity and subtlety of the analysis we offer, as well as some of its shortcomings. For us, this text is an indication of the value of rule analysis for understanding practice in organizations. Such an analysis is always 'in progress'; our own rule-matrix is still becoming – a journey not a destination.

References

Abel, E. (1966). *The Cuban Missile Crisis*. New York: J.B. Lippincott.

Abel, P. (1988). The structuration of action – inference and comparative narratives. *In* Fielding, N.G. (ed.), *Actions and Structure – Research Methods and Social Theory*. Beverly Hills, Calif.: Sage.

Abella, R.S. (1984). *Equity in Employment – Report of the Royal Commission (Canada)*. Ottawa: Ministry of Supply and Services Canada.

Abelson, R.P. (1976). Script processing in attitude formation and decision making. *In* Carroll, J.S. and Payne, J.W. (eds), *Cognition and Social Behaviour*. Hillsdale, N.J.: Lawrence Erlbaum Associates Ltd.

Abrams, P. (1982). *Historical Sociology*. London: Open Books.

Ackoff, R. (1974). *Redesigning the Future*. New York: John Wiley.

Agocs, C. (1989). Walking on the glass ceiling: Tokenism in senior management. Paper presented to the 24th Annual Meeting of the Canadian Sociology and Anthropology Association, Lavel, Quebec, June.

Aird, A.R., Nowak, P. and Westcott, J. (1988). *Road to the Top – The Chief Executive Officer in Canada*. Toronto: Doubleday.

Albano, C. (1974). *TA On the Job*. New York: Harper and Row.

Albrecht, K. (1988). *At America's Service – How Corporations can Revolutionize the way they Treat their Customers*. Homewood, Ill.: Dow Jones-Irwin.

Albrecht, K. and Zemke, R. (1985). *Service America! Doing Business in the New Economy*. Homewood, Ill.: Dow Jones-Irwin.

Aldrich, H. (1979). *Organizations and Environments*. Englewood Cliffs, N.J.: Prentice-Hall.

Allen, V.L. (1975) *Social Analysis – A Marxist Critique and Alternative*. London: Longman.

Anderson, P. (1980). *Arguments within English Marxism*. London: NLB/Verso.

Antaki, C. (ed.) (1988). *Analysing Everyday Explanation – A Casebook of Methods*. London: Sage.

Apter, M.J. (1982). *The Experience of Motivation – The Theory of Psychological Reversals*. London: Academic Press.

Apter, M.J. (1988a). *Reversal Theory: Motivation, Emotion and Personality*. London: Routledge.

Apter, M.J. (1988b). Reversal theory as a theory of the emotions. *In* Apter, M.J., Kerr, J.H. and Cowles, M.P. (eds.), *Progress in Reversal Theory*. Amsterdam: North-Holland.

Aquila, R. (1977). *Intentionally – A Study of Mental Acts*. Philadelphia, Penn: Pennsylvania State University Press.

Argyle, M. (1975). *Bodily Communication*. New York: International Universities Press.

Argyris, C. (1957). *Personality and Organization*. London: Harper and Row.

Argyris, C. (1964). *Integrating the Individual and the Organization*. New York: John Wiley.

Argyris, C. (1977). *Personality and Organization*. London: Harper and Row.

Argyris, C. and Schon, D. (1978). *Organizational Learning – A Theory of Action Perspective*. Reading, Mass.: Addison-Wessley.

Asch, S.E. (1958). Effects of group pressure upon modification and distortion of judgement. *In* Maccoby, E.E., Newcomb, T.M. and Hartley, J.E. (eds.), *Readings in Social Psychology*, 3rd edn. pp. 174–83, New York: Holt.

Astley, W.G. and Van de Ven, A.H. (1983). Central perspectives and debates in organizational theory. *Administrative Science Quarterly*, **28**, 245–73.

Augustine, N.R. (1988). Defense – A case of too many cooks. *Fortune*, 5 December, 219–20.

Bacharach, S. and Lawler, E. (1980). *Power and Politics in Organizations*. San Fransisco: Jossey-Bass.

Bandura, A. (1986). *Social Foundations of Thought and Action*. London: Allen and Unwin.

Bartlett, C. (1989). Let's talk. *Alberta Business*, April.

Beer, S. (1972). *Brain of the Firm: The Managerial Cybernetics of Organization*. London: Allen Lane/Harmondsworth: Penguin.

Bell, E. (1989). The mammy and the snow queen. Paper presented at the National Centre for Management Research and Development Conference on Research on Women and Management, Kingston, Ontario, September.

Bendix, R. (1974). *Work and Authority in Industry*. Berkeley, Calif.: University of California Press.

Bennis, W. (1966). *Changing Organizations*. New York: McGraw-Hill.

Benson, J.K. (1977). Organizations – A dialectical view. *Administrative Science Quarterly*, **22**, 1–21.

Berger, P.L. and Luckman, T. (1984). *The Social Construction of Reality*. Harmondsworth: Penguin.

Berger, P.L., Berger, B. and Kellner, H. (1974). *The Homeless Mind*. Harmondsworth: Penguin.

Berne, E. (1961). *Transactional Analysis in Psychotherapy*. New York: Grove Press.

Berne, E. (1964). *Games People Play: The Psychology of Human Relationships*. New York: Grove Press.

Beynon, H. (1973). *Working for Ford*. Harmondsworth: Penguin.

Bilton, T., Bonnett, K., Jones, P., Stanworth, M., Sheard, K. and Webster, A. (1983). *Introductory Sociology*. London: Macmillan.

Bittner, E. (1974). The concept of an organization. *In* Turner, R. (ed.), *Ethnomethodology*, pp. 69–82. Harmondsworth: Penguin. Also in Salaman, G. and Thompson, K. (eds), *People and Organizations*. Buckingham: Open University Press.

Blackburn, R. (1967). The unequal society. *In* Blackburn, R. and Cockburn, A. (eds), *The Incompatibles*. Harmondsworth: Penguin.

Blauner, R. (1967). *Alienation and Freedom*. Chicago: University of Chicago Press.

Block, J.H. (1984). *Sex Role Identity and Ego Development*. San Francisco: Jossey-Bass.

Bloom, A. (1987). *The Closing of the American Mind*. New York: Simon and Schuster.

Bloomfield, J. (1978). A discussion of Marxist writing on class. *Marxism Today*. October, 328–32.

Bogomolova, N. (1973). *'Human Relations' Doctrine: Ideological Weapon of the Monopolies*. Moscow: Progress Publishers.

Boland, R.J. and Hoffman, R. (1982). Humour in a machine shop – An interpretation of symbolic action. *In* Frost, P.J., Mitchell, V.F. and Nord, W.R. (eds), *Organizational Reality – Reports from the Firing Line*. Glenview, Ill.: Scott, Foresman.

Bonarius, J.C.J. (1965). Research in the personal construct theory of George A. Kelly: Role construct repertory test and basic theory. *Progress in Experimental Personality Research*, **2**, 2–46.

Brady, F.N. (1987). Rules for making exceptions to rules. *Academy of Management Review*, **12**(3), 436–44.

Braverman, H. (1974). *Labour and Monopoly Capital*. New York: Monthly Review Press.

Brenner, M. (1978). Interviewing – The social phenomenology of a research instrument. *In* Brenner, M., Marsh, P. and Brenner, M. (eds), *The Social Contexts of Method*. London: Croom Helm.

Brenner, O.C., Tomkiewicz, J. and Schein, V.E. (1989). The relationship between sex role stereotypes and requisite management characteristics revisited. *The Academy of Management Journal*, **32** (3), 662–9.

Brewer, J. and Hunter, A. (1989). *Multimethod Research – A Synthesis of Styles*. Beverly Hills, Calif.: Sage.

Bronfenbrenner, U. (1979). *The Ecology of Human Development – Experiments by Nature and Design*. Cambridge, Mass.: Harvard University Press.

Buchanan, D.A. and Huczynski, A. (1985). *Organizational Behaviour*. London: Prentice Hall.

Burawoy, M. (1979). *Manufacturing Consent*. Chicago: University of Chicago Press.

Burck, C. (1981). How General Motors stays ahead. *Fortune*, 9 March, 100.

Burns, T. (1966). Introduction. *In* Burns, T. and Stalker, G.M., *The Management of Innovation*, 2nd edn. London: Tavistock.

Burns, T. (1981). *A Comparative Study of Administrative Structure and Organizational Processes in Selected Areas of the National Health Service*. London: Social Science Research Council Report HRP.6725.

Burns, T. and Flam, H. (1987). *The Shaping of Social Organizations – Social Rule System Theory with Applications*. London: Sage.

Burns, T. and Stalker, G.M. (1961). *The Management of Innovation*. London: Tavistock.

Burrell, G. (1984). Sex and organizational analysis. *Organizational Studies*, **5**(2), 97–118.

Burrell, G. and Morgan, G. (1979). *Sociological Paradigms and Organizational Analysis*. London: Heinemann.

Busfield, J. (1989). Sexism and psychiatry. *Sociology*, **23**(3), 343–54.

Cameron, K. and Whetten, D. (1981). Perceptions of organizational effectiveness across organizational life cycles. *Administrative Science Quarterly*, **26**, 525–44.

Chandler, A. (1962). *Strategy and Structure*. Cambridge, Mass.: MIT Press.

Chandler, A. (1977). *The Visible Hand*. Cambridge, Mass.: Harvard University Press.

Child, J. (1972). Organization structure, environment and performance – the role of strategic choice. *Sociology*, **6**(1), 1–22.

Chua, W.F., Laughlin, R.C., Lowe, A. and Puxty, A.G. (1982). An integrated epistemology of theory and practical action for management science. *In Proceedings of the Workshop on the Epistemology of Management Research*, Part II. Brussels: European Institute for Advanced Studies in Management.

Cicourel, A. (1973). *Cognitive Sociology*. Baltimore, Md.: Penguin.

Clegg, S. (1975). *Power, Rule and Domination*. London: Routledge and Kegan Paul.

Clegg, S. (1977). Power, organization theory, Marx and critique. *In* Clegg, S. and Dunkerley, D. (eds), *Critical Issues in Organizations*. London: Routledge and Kegan Paul.

Clegg, S. (1981). Organization and control. *Administrative Science Quarterly*, **26**, 532–45.

Clegg, S. (1983). Phenomenology and formal organizations: a realist critique. In S.B. Bacharach (ed.), *Research in the Sociology of Organizations*, Volume 2, pp. 109–52. Greenwich, Conn: JAI Press.

Clegg, S. (1989). *Frameworks of Power*. London: Sage.

Clegg, S. and Dunkerley, D. (1980). *Organization, Class and Control*. London: Routledge and Kegan Paul.

Cockburn, C. (1985). *Machinery of Dominance*. London: Pluto Press.

Cohen, S. and Taylor, L. (1976). *Escape Attempts – The Theory and Practice of Resistance to Everyday Life*. London: Allen Lane.

Collins, R. (1981). On the microfoundation of macrosociology. *American Journal of Sociology*, **86**, 984–1014.

Collinson, D.L. (1988). Engineering humour: Masculinity, joking and conflict in shop-floor relations. *Organizational Studies*, **9**(2), 181–99.

Cook, M. (1971). *Interpersonal Perception*. Harmondsworth: Penguin.

Cooley, C.H. (1902). *Human Nature and the Social Order*. New York: Scribner's.

Cooper, C. and Davidson, M. (1982). *High Pressure, Working Lives of Women Managers*. Glasgow: Fontana.

Corbett, B. (1989). Kodak Canada focuses upon employees. *Canadian*, November, 62–8.

Cornog, G.Y. (1962). Creating moral conditions in organizations: The challenge of executive responsibility. *Public Administration Review*, Spring, 98–103.

Crean, S. (1987). *Newsworthy – The Lives of Media Women*. Halifax, N.S.: Formac.

Crompton, R., Jones, G. and Reid, S. (1982). Contemporary clerical work – A case study of local government. *In* West, J. (ed.), *Work, Women and the Labour Market*. London: Routledge and Kegan Paul.

Cross, R. (1974). *On Evidence*. London: Butterworths.

Crouch, C. (1979). *The Politics of Industrial Relations*. Glasgow: Fontana.

Cunningham, M. and Schumer, F. (1984). *Powerplay*. Toronto: Random House.

Curtis, R.L. and Zurcher, L.A. (1974). Social movements: an analytical exploration of organizational forms. *Social Problems*, **21**(3), 356–70.

Cyert, R.M. and March, J.G. (1963). *A Behavioural Theory of the Firm*. Englewood Cliffs, N.J.: Prentice-Hall.

Daft, R. (1986). *Organizational Theory and Design*, 2nd edn. St Paul, Minn.: West.

Daft, R. (1989). *Organizational Theory and Design*, 3rd edn. St Paul, Minn.: West.

Dandridge, T.C. (1985). The life stages of a symbol: When symbols work and when they can't. *In* Frost, P.J., Moore, L.F., Louis, M.R., Lundberg, C.C. and Martin, J. (eds), *Organizational Culture*. Beverley Hills, Calif.: Sage.

Davies, S. (1984). *Managing Corporate Culture*. Cambridge, Mass.: Ballinger.

Davies, S. (1989). Inserting gender into Burawoy's theory of the labour process. Paper presented at the Annual Conference of the Canadian Sociology and Anthropology Association, Laval University, Quebec, June.

Dawe, A. (1979). Theories of social action. *In* Bottomore, T. and Nisbett, R. (eds) *A History of Sociological Analysis*. London: Heinemann.

Deal, T.E. and Kennedy, A.A. (1982). *Corporate Cultures*. Reading, Mass.: Addison-Wesley.

de Lamarter, R.T. (1986). *Big Blue – IBM's Use and Abuse of Power*. New York: Dodd, Mead.

Deming, W.E. (1982). *Out of the Crisis*. Cambridge, Mass.: MIT Press.

Denhardt, R.B. (1981). *In The Shadow of the Organization*. Lawrence, Kansas: Regents Press.

Dennett, D.C. (1981). *Brainstorms – Philosophic Essays on Mind and Psychology*. Cambridge Mass.: MIT Press/Bradford Books.

de Rivera, J. (1977). A *Structural Theory of Emotions*. New York: International Universities Press.

Dermer, J. (1988). Control and organizational order. *Accounting, Organization and Society*, **13**(1), 25–36.

Dermer, J. and Lucas, R. (1986). The illusion of managerial control. *Accounting, Organization and Society*, **11**(6), 471–82.

de Vries, M.F.R.K. and Miller, D. (1986). Personality, culture and organization. *Academy of Management Review*, **11**(2), 266–79.

Dickson, D. (1974). *Alternative Technology and the Politics of Technical Change*. London: Fontana.

Dickson, T., McLachlan, H., Swales, K. and Prior, P. (1988). Big Blue and the unions – IBM, individualism and trade union strategy. *Work, Employment and Soceity*, **2**(4), 506–520.

Diesing, P. (1962). *Reason in Society*. Urbana, Ill.: University of Illinois Press.

DiTomaso, N. (1989). Sexuality in the workplace – Discrimination and harassment. *In* Hearn, J., Sheppard, D.L., Tancred-Sheriff, P. and Burrell, G. (eds), *The Sexuality of Organizations*. London: Sage.

Donzelot, J. (1981). Pleasure in work. *Ideology and Consciousness*, **9**, 3–28.

Douglas, K. (1988). *The Ragman's Son*. New York: Pocket Books.

Douglas, M. (1986). *How Institutions Think*. Syracuse, N.Y.: Syracuse University Press.

Doyle, J.A. (1985). *Sex and Gender: The Human Experience*. Dubuque, Iowa: William C. Brown.

Dreyfuss, J. (1989). Reinventing IBM. *Fortune Magazine*, 14 August.

Dubeck, P. (1979). Sexism in recruiting management personnel for a manufacturing firm. *In* Alvarez, R. (ed.), *Discrimination in Organizations*. London: Jossey-Bass.

Durkheim, E. (1966). *The Division of Labour in Society*. New York: Free Press.

Durkheim, E. (1968). *Suicide*. London: Routledge and Kegan Paul.

Dusky, L. and Zeitz, B. (1988). The best companies for women. *Savvy Magazine*, May, 48–9.

Duveen, G. and Lloyd, B. (1986). The significance of social identities. *British Journal of Social Psychology*, **25**, 219–30.

Dyer, W.G. (1984). *Strategies for Managing Change*. Reading, Mass.: Addison-Wesley.

Edelman, M. (1964). *The Symbolic Use of Politics*. Urbana, Ill.: University of Illinois Press.

Eemeren, E., Grootendorst, R. and Kruiger, T. (1987). *Handbook of Argumentation Theory*. Dordrecht: Foris.

Ehrenreich, B. and English, D. (1973). *Witches, Midwives, and Nurses: A History of Women Healers*. New York: The Feminist Press.

Eldridge, J.E.T. and Crombie, A.D. (1974). *A Sociology of Organizations*. London: Allen and Unwin.

Ellis, A. (1962). *Reason and Emotion in Psychotherapy*. Secaucus, N.J.: Citadel Press.

Emerson, J. (1970). Behaviour in private places: Sustaining definitions of reality in gynaecological examinations. *In* Salaman, G. and Thompson, K. (eds), *People and Organizations*. Milton Keynes: Open University Press.

Emery, F.E. and Trist, E.L. (1973). *Towards a Social Ecology – Contextual Applications of the Future in the Present*. New York: Plenum Press.

Enrico, R. and Kornbluth, J. (1986). *The Other Guy Blinked – How Pepsi Won the Cola Wars*. New York: Bantam Books.

Erikson, E. (1959). Identity and the life cycle. *Psychological Issues*, 1, 18–164.

Erikson, E.H. (1975). *Life History and the Historical Moment*. New York: W.W. Norton.

Etzioni, A. (1961). *A Comparative Analysis of Complex Organizations*. New York: Free Press.

Evans, T. (1988). *A Gender Agenda*. Sydney: Allen and Unwin.

Evered, R. (1983). The language of organizations: The case of the Navy. *In* Pondy, L.R., Frost, P.J., Morgan, G. and Dandridge, T.C. (eds), *Organizational Symbolism*. Greenwich, Conn.: JAI Press.

Feldberg, R. and Glenn, E.N. (1979). Male and female – Job versus gender models in the sociology of work. *Social Problems*, 26(5), 525–38.

Ferguson, K.E. (1984). *The Feminist Case Against Bureaucracy*. Philadelphia, Penn.: Temple University Press.

Fiber, B. (1986). Poll find Canadian men losing self confidence. *Globe & Mail* (Toronto), 4 September.

Fielding, N.G. (ed.) (1988). *Actions and Structure – Research Methods and Social Theory*. Beverly Hills, Calif.: Sage.

Fleck, L. (1979). *The Genesis and Development of a Scientific Fact*. Chicago: University of Chicago Press.

Fleishman, E.A. (1953). Leadership, climate, human relations training and supervisory behaviour. *Personnel Psychology*, 6, 205–222.

Flick, R. (1983). The truth about girl scouts. *Harper's Magazine*, March.

Flugel, J.C. (1945). *Man, Morals and Society*. Harmondsworth: Penguin.

Folkman, S. and Lazarus, R.S. (1980). An analysis of coping in a middle aged sample. *Journal of Health and Social Behaviour*, 21, 219–39.

Foster, R. (1986). *Innovation – The Attacker's Advantage*. New York: Summit Books.

Foucault, M. (1979). *Discipline and Punishment*. New York: Vintage Books.

Frank, J. (1989). Gaining competitive advantage in the 1990's. *Wall Street Journal Advertising Supplement*, 14 November, 23.

Franklin, U. (1989). On science and technology. *Ideas*. Radio Broadcast, Canadian Broadcasting Corporation, Tuesday 14 November.

French, M. (1985). *Beyond Power*. New York: Summit.

Garson, B. (1979). Women's work – Some lousy offices to work in and one good one. *In* Moss-Kanter, R. and Stein, B.A. (eds), *Life in Organizations*. New York: Basic Books.

Garvey, C. (1984). *Children's Talk*. London: Fontana.

Gecas, V. (1981). Contexts of socialization. *In* Rosenberg, M. and Turner, R. (eds), *Social Psychology – Psychosocial Perspectives*. New York: Basic Books.

George, A.L. (1976). Adaptation to stress in political decision making: The individual, small group and organizational contexts. *In* Coelho, G.V., Hamburg, D.A. and Adams, J.E. (eds), *Coping and Adaptation*. New York: Basic Books.

Gerth, H.H. and Wright Mills, C. (1974). *From Max Weber*. London: Routledge and Kegan Paul.

Ghemawat, P. and Spence, A.M. (1986). Modeling global competition. *In* Porter, M.E. (ed.), *Competition in Global Industries*. Boston, Mass.: Harvard Business School Press.

Ghemawat, P., Porter, M.E. and Rawlinson, R.A. (1986). Patterns of international coalition activity. *In* Porter, M.E. (ed.), *Competition in Global Industries*. Boston, Mass.: Harvard Business School Press.

Giddens, A. (1976). *New Rules of Sociological Method: A Positive Critique of Interpretive Sociologies*. London: Hutchinson.

Giddens, A. (1979). *Central Problems in Social Theory – Action, Structure and Contradiction in Social Analysis*. Berkeley, Calif.: University of California Press.

Giddens, A. (1982). *New Rules of Sociological Method*. London: Hutchinson.

Gilmore, T.N. (1988). *Making a Leadership Change*. San Francisco: Jossey-Bass.

Glennon, L.M. (1983). Synthesism – A case of feminist methodology. *In* Morgan, G. (ed.), *Beyond Method*. Beverly Hills, Calif.: Sage.

Goffman, E. (1957). On the characteristics of total institutions. *Proceedings of the Symposium on Preventive Social Psychiatry*. Washington: Walter Reed Army Institute of Research.

Goffman, E. (1959). *The Presentation of Self in Everyday Life*. New York: Doubleday.

Goffman, E. (1974). *Frame Analysis*. New York: Harper and Row.

Goffman, E. (1984). *Asylums – Essays on the Social Situation of Mental Patients and Other Inmates*. Harmondsworth: Penguin.

Goldthorpe, J.H. (1966). Attitudes and behaviour of car assembly workers. *British Journal of Sociology*, **17**(3), 227–44.

Goldthorpe, J.H., Lockwood, D., Bechofer, F. and Platt, J. (1968). *The Affluent Worker: Industrial Attitudes*. Cambridge: Cambridge University Press.

Gordon, M.M. (1985). *The Iacocca Management Technique – A Profile of the Chrysler Chairman's Unique Key to Business Success*. New York: Ballantine.

Gouldner, A. (1954). *Patterns of Industrial Democracy*. New York: Free Press.

Gouldner, A.W. (1965). *Wildcat Strike*. New York: Free Press.

Gramsci, A. (1978). *The Modern Prince and Other Writings*. New York: International Publishers.

Gregory, K.L. (1983). Native-view paradigms: Multiple cultures and culture conflicts in organizations. *Administrative Science Quarterly*, **28**, 359–76.

Greiner, L.E. (1972). Evolution and revolution as organizations grow. *Harvard Business Review*, July/August, 37–46.

Griffin, C. (1985). *Typical Girls*. London: Routledge and Kegan Paul.

Guppy, N. (1989). Pay equity in Canadian universities, 1972–73 and 1985–86. *Canadian Review of Sociology and Anthropology*, **26**(5), 743–58.

Gutek, B. (1985). *Sex and the Workplace*. San Francisco: Jossey-Bass.

Haley, J. (1976). *Problem Solving Therapy*. San Francisco: Jossey-Bass.

Hall, M. (1989). Private experiences in the public domain – Lesbians in organization. *In* Hearn, J., Sheppard, D.L., Tancred-Sheriff, P. and Burrell, G. (eds), *The Sexuality of Organizations*, London: Sage.

Hall, R.H. (1978). Professionalisation and bureaucratisation. *In* Salaman, G. and Thompson, K. (eds), *People and Organizations*. Buckingham: Open University Press.

Hamilton, S. (1989). Culture shock hits Big Blue. *Business (UK)*, September, 44–52.

Handy, C. (1983). *Understanding Organizations*. Harmondsworth: Penguin.

Hannan, J. and Freeman, R. (1977). The population ecology of organizations. *American Journal of Sociology*, **82**, 929–64.

Hannan, J. and Freeman, R. (1984). Structural inertia and organizational change. *American Sociological Review*, **49**, 149–64.

Hargreaves, A. (1986). *The Two Cultures of Schooling*. Lewes: Falmer Press.

Harre, R., Clarke, D. and DeCarlo, N. (1985). *Motives and Mechanisms – An Introduction to the Psychology of Action.* London: Methuen.

Harriman, A. (1985). *Women/Men, Management.* New York: Praeger.

Harris, C.C. (1980). *Fundamental Concepts and the Sociological Enterprise.* London: Allen and Unwin.

Hazer, J.T. and Alvarez, K.M. (1981). Police work values during organizational entry and assimilation. *Journal of Applied Psychology,* **66,** 12–18.

Hearn, J. and Parkin, P.W. (1983). Gender and Organizations – A review and critique of a neglected area. *Organization Studies,* **4**(3), 219–42.

Hearn, J. and Parkin, W. (1987). *"Sex" at "Work" – The Power and Paradox of Organizational Sexuality.* Brighton: Wheatsheaf.

Heery, E. and Kelly, J. (1988). Do female representatives make a difference? *Work, Employment and Society,* **2**(4), 487–505.

Heritage, J. (1984). *Garfinkel and Ethnomethodology.* Cambridge, Mass.: Polity Press.

Herzberg, G. (1966). *Work and the Nature of Man.* New York: Staples Press.

Hinings, C.R. and Greenwood, R. (1989). *The Dynamics of Strategic Change.* New York: Blackwell.

Hisrich, R.D. and Brush, C.G. (1986). *The Woman Entrepreneur.* Lexington, MA: Lexington Books.

Hochschild, A.R. (1983). *The Managed Heart.* Berkeley, Calif.: University of California Press.

Horne, A. (1988–9). *Macmillan – The Official Biography,* 2 Vols. London: Macmillan.

Howard, R.W. (1984). *Coping and Adapting.* London: Angus and Robertson.

Hunt, A. (1973). Class structure in Britain today. *Marxism Today – Special Issue on Class.*

Hunt, J. (1982). A woman's place is in her union. *In* West, J. (ed.), *Work, Women and the Labour Market.* London: Routledge and Kegan Paul.

Hurrelman, K. (1988). *Social Structure and Personality Development.* Cambridge: Cambridge University Press.

Hydebrand, W. (1977). Organizational contradictions in public bureaucracies. Toward a Marxian theory of organization. *Sociological Quarterly,* **18,** 83–107.

Hyman, R. (1972). *Strikes.* Glasgow: Fontana.

Hyman, R. (1980). Trade unions: Control and resistance. *In* Esland, G. and Salaman, G. (eds), *The Politics of Work and Occupations.* Buckingham: Open University Press.

Iacocca, L. with Novak, W. (1984). *Iacocca – An Autobiography.* New York: Bantam.

Illes, P. and Auluck, R. (1989). From racism awareness training to strategic human resource management in implementing equal opportunity. *Personnel Review,* **18**(4), 24–32.

Illich, I. (1973). *Tools for Conviviality.* London: Fontana/Collins.

Illich, I. (1981). *Deschooling Society.* London: Calder Boyars.

Imai, M. (1986). *KAIZEN – The Key to Japan's Competitive Success.* New York: Random House.

Isaksson, E. (1988). *Women and the Military System.* New York: St Martin's Press.

Jackall, R. (1988). *Moral Mazes.* Oxford: Oxford University Press.

Jackson, S. (1984). *Yellowknife Homecoming.* Yellowknife, N.W.T.: Type Unlimited.

Jacobson, G. and Hillkirk, J. (1986). *Xerox – American Samurai.* New York: Mcmillan.

James, M. and Savary, L. (1977). *A New Self – Self Therapy with Transactional Analysis.* Reading, Mass.: Addison-Wesley.

Jelinek, M., Smircich, L. and Hirsch, P. (1983). A code of many colours. *Administrative Science Quarterly,* **28,** 331–8.

Johnson, G., Scholes, K. and Sexty, R.W. (1989). *Exploring Strategic Management.* Scarborough, Ont.: Prentice-Hall.

Jones, B.W. (1987). Race, sex and class: Black female tobacco workers in Durham, North Carolina 1920–1940 and the development of female consciousness. *In* Deegan, M.J. and Hill, M. (eds), *Women and Symbolic Interaction.* London: Allen and Unwin.

Jones, E.E. (1964). *Ingratiation.* New York: Appleton-Century-Crofts.

Jourard, S.M. (1971). *The Transparent Self.* New York: Van Nostrand Reinhold.

Juran, J.M. (1988). *Juran on Planning for Quality.* New York: Free Press.

Kanter, R.M. (1977). *Men and Women of the Corporation.* New York: Basic Books.

Kanter, R.M. (1979). Power failure in management circuits. *Harvard Business Review,* **57**(4), 65–75.

Kanter, R.M. (1983). *The Change Masters – Innovation and Entrepreneurship in the American Corporation.* New York: Simon and Schuster.

Kao, R.W.Y. and Knight, R.M. (1987). *Entrepreneurship and New Venture Management.* Scarborough, Ont.: Prentice-Hall.

Karpik, L. (1977). Technological capitalism. *In* Clegg, S. and Dunkerley, D. (eds), *Critical Issues in Organizations.* London: Routledge and Kegan Paul.

Karpik, L. (1978). Organizations, institutions and history. *In* Karpik, K. (ed.), *Organizational Environment: Theory, Issues and Reality.* London: Sage.

Kaufman, H. (1960). *The Forest Ranger.* Baltimore, Md.: Johns Hopkins University Press.

Khan, A. and Mills. A.J. (1988). Retirement and sex discrimination. *Solicitors Journal,* **132**(22), 805–808.

Khan, A. and Mills, A.J. (1989). Discrimination – A decision on damages. *Solicitors Journal,* **133**(31), 986–90.

Khan, A. and Mills, A.J. (1990). Sexual harassment. *Solicitors Journal,* **134**(3), 66–9.

Khan, V.S. (1984). The role of the culture of dominance in structuring the experience of ethnic minorities. *In* Husband, C. (ed.), *Race in Britain.* London: Hutchinson.

Kiesler, C.A. and Kiesler, S.B. (1976). *Conformity.* Reading, Mass.: Addison-Wesley.

Kimberly, J. (1979). Issues in the creation of organizations: Initiation, innovation and institutionalisation. *Academy of Management Journal,* **22**, 437–57.

Kirkland, R.I. (1987). Russia: Where Gorbanomics is leading. *Fortune Magazine,* 28 September.

Kirkpatrick, D. (1988). How the workers run Avis better. *Fortune,* 5 December, 103–114.

Klapp, O. (1962). *Heroes, Villains and Fools: The Changing American Character.* Englewood Cliffs, N.J.: Prentice-Hall.

Knapp, M.L. (1980). *Essentials of Nonverbal Communication.* New York: Holt, Rinehart and Winston.

Kosslyn, S.M. (1980). *Image and Mind.* Cambridge, Mass.: Harvard University Press.

Kraar, L. (1989). Top US companies move to Russia. *Fortune Magazine,* 31 July.

Kramarae, C. (1988). *Technology and Women's Voices.* London: Routledge and Kegan Paul.

Kramer, L. (1989). A guilty plea confirms the dark rumors about Capitol Hill aide Quentin Crommelin. *People Magazine,* 21 August, 49–50.

Krantz, K.T. (1989). How Velcro got hooked on quality. *Harvard Business Review,* **89**(5), 34–40.

Krech, D., Crutchfield, R.S. and Ballachey, E. (1962). *Individual in Society – A Textbook of Social Psychology.* New York: McGraw-Hill.

Krefting, L.A. and Frost, P.J. (1985).Untangling webs, surfing waves and wildcatting – A multiple metapohor perspective on managing organizational culture. *In* Frost, P.J., Moore, L.F., Louis, M.R., Lundberg, C.C. and Martin, J. (eds), *Organizational Culture*. Beverly Hills, Calif.: Sage.

Kunen, J.S. (1989). Queen, pawns, checkmate. *People Magazine*, 11 September, 94–9.

Labich, K. (1987). Boeing battles to stay on top. *Fortune Magazine*, 28 September.

Lacey, R. (1986). *Ford – The Men and the Machine*. New York: Ballantine.

Lamphere, L. (1985). Bringing the family to work – Women's culture on the shop floor. *Feminist Studies*, **11**(3), 519–40.

Langer, E.J. (1978). Rethinking the role of thought in social interaction. *In* Harvey, J.H., Ickes, W. and Kidd, R.F. (eds), *New Directions in Attribution Research*, Vol. 2, Hillsdale, N.J.: Lawrence Erlbaum Associates Inc.

Large, M. (1988). Graphic design and corporate identity. Paper presented at the Canadian Sociology and Anthropology Association annual meeting, Windsor, Ontario, June.

Larraine, J. (1979). *The Concept of Ideology*. London: Hutchinson.

LaSota, M. (1985). *Women and Business Ownership*. Mankato, MN: Minnesota Scholarly Press.

Lawler, E.E. (1976). Control systems in organizations. *In* Dunnette, H.D. (ed.) *Handbook of Industrial and Organizational Psychology*. Chicago: Rand McNally.

Lawrence, B. (1987). The fifth dimension – Gender and general practice. *In* Spencer, A. and Podmore, D. (eds), *In a Man's World*. London: Tavistock.

Lawrence, P.R. and Lorsch, J.W. (1967a). *Organization and Environment*. Cambridge, Mass.: Harvard Graduate School of Business Administration.

Lawrence, P.R. and Lorsch, J.W. (1967b). Differentiation and integration in complex organizations. *Administrative Science Quarterly*, **12**, 1–47.

Leavitt, H., Dill, W.R. and Eyring, H.B. (1973). *The Organizational World*. San Diego, Calif.: Harcourt Brace Jovanovich.

Lebas, M. and Weigenstein, J. (1986). Management control: The roles of rules, markets and culture. *Journal of Management Studies*, **23**(3), 259–72.

Lee, R. and Lawrence, P. (1985). *Organizational Behaviour: Politics at Work*. Harmondsworth: Penguin.

Legge, K. (1984). *Evaluating Planned Organizational Change*. London: Academic Press.

Leinster, C. (1989). We need yuppies in Moscow. *Fortune Magazine*, 20 November.

Leonard, P. (1984). *Personality and Ideology – Towards a Material Understanding of the Individual*. London: Methuen.

Leonardo, M. di (1985). Women's work, work culture and consciousness. *Feminist Studies*, **11**(3), 491–5.

Lester, J. (1976). Being a boy. *In* David, D.S. and Brannon, R. (eds), *The Forty Nine Percent Majority – The Male Sex Role*. Reading, Mass.: Addison-Wesley.

Lewin, K., Lippit, R. and White, R.K. (1939). Patterns of aggressive behaviour in experimentally created social climates. *Journal of Social Psychology*, **10**, 271–99.

Lincoln, Y.S. and Guba, G.E. (1985). *Naturalistic Inquiry*. Beverly Hills, Calif.: Sage.

Lippitt, G.L., Langseth, P. and Mossop, J. (1985). *Implementing Organizational Change*. San Francisco: Jossey-Bass.

Livingstone, D.W. and Luxton, M. (1989). Gender consciousness at work: modification of the male breadwinner norm among steelworkers and their spouses. *The Canadian Review of Sociology and Anthropology*, **26**(2), 240–75.

Lockwood, D. (1966). The *Blackcoated Worker*. London: George Allen and Unwin.

Louis, J.C. and Yazijian, H. (1980). *The Cola Wars*. New York: Everest House.

McGregor, D. (1960). *The Human Side of Enterprise.* New York: McGraw-Hill.

McGuire, S. (1988). In new clothing – Academics in distance education. Athabasca University (mimeo).

McKeown, B. and Thomas, D. (1987). *Q Methodology.* Beverly Hills, Calif.: Sage.

McLennan, R. (1989). *Managing Organizational Change.* Englewood Cliffs, N.J.: Prentice-Hall.

Mackie, M. (1984). Socialization: changing views of child rearing and adolescence. *In* M. Baker (ed.), *The Family: Changing Trends in Canada,* pp. 35–62, Toronto: McGraw-Hill Ryerson.

Mackie, M. (1987). *Constructing Women and Men.* Toronto: Holt, Rinehart and Winston of Canada.

MacKinnon, C. (1979). *Sexual Harassment of Working Women.* New Haven, Conn.: Yale University Press.

Maccoby, E.E. and Jacklin, C.N. (1974). *The Psychology of Sex Differences.* Stanford, Calif.: Stanford University Press.

Maccoby, E.E. and Martin, J.A. (1984). Socialization in the context of the family: Parent–child interaction. *In* Hetherington, E.M. (ed.), *Handbook of Child Psychology,* Vol. 4, New York: John Wiley.

Magnet, M. (1987). 1987 Need not become 1929. *Fortune Magazine,* 23 November.

Magnet, M. (1988). How the workers fared. *Fortune Magazine,* 15 August.

Manchester, W. (1988). *The Last Lion – Winston Churchill, Alone 1932-1940.* Boston: Little, Brown (esp. pp. 75–156).

Mandel, E. (1975). *Late Capitalism.* London: New Left Books.

Mandel, E. (1979). *From Stalinism to Eurocommunism.* London: New Left Books.

Manley, M. (1975). *A Voice at the Workplace.* London: Andre Deutsch.

Marsden, D. (1982). *Workless – An Exploration of the Social Contract Between Society and the Worker.* London: Croom Helm.

Marsden, D. and Duff, E. (1975). *Workless – Some Unemployed Men and their Families.* Harmondsworth: Penguin.

Martel, L. (1986). *Mastering Change.* New York: Simon and Schuster.

Martin, J., Feldman, M.S., Hatch, M.J. and Sitkin, S.B. (1983). The uniqueness paradox in organizational stories. *Administrative Science Quarterly,* **28,** 438–53.

Martin, S.E. (1987). Sexual politics in the workplace – The interactional world of policewomen. *In* Deegan, M.J. and Hill, M. (eds), *Women and Symbolic Interaction.* Boston: Allen and Unwin.

Maruyama, M. (1969). Epistemology of social science research: Exploration in culture researchers. *Dialectica,* **23,** 229–80.

Maruyama, M. (1981). Endogenous research: Rationale. *In* Reason, P. and Rowan, J. (eds), *Human Inquiry: A Sourcebook of New Paradigm Research.* London: John Wiley.

Marx, K. (1966). *The Civil War in France.* Peking: Foreign Language Press.

Marx, K. (1973). *Grunrisse – Introduction to the Critique of Political Economy.* Harmondsworth: Penguin.

Marx, K. and Engels, F. (1967). *The Communist Manifesto.* Harmondsworth: Penguin.

Marx, K. and Engels, F. (1969). The Communist Manifesto. *In* Feur, S. (ed.). *Marx and Engels – Basic Writings and Politics and Philosophy.* London: Fontana.

Marx, K. and Engels, F. (1976). *The German Ideology* (Collected Works, Vol. 5). Moscow: Progress.

Maslow, A.H. (1943). A theory of human motivation. *Psychological Review,* **50,** 370–93.

Maturana, H. (1988). Reality – The search for objectivity or the quest for a compelling argument. *Irish Journal of Psychology*, **9**(1), 25–82.

Maturana, H.R. and Varela, F.J. (1972). *Autopoesis and Cognition – The Realization of the Living*. Dordrecht.: Reidel.

Mayer, C.E. (1985). New Coke joins marketing hall of flops. *Washington Post*, 12 July, B1–B2.

Mayo, E. (1933). *The Human Problems of an Industrial Civilisation*. New York: Mcmillan.

Medina, W.A. (1982). *Changing Bureaucracies*. New York: Marcel Dekker.

Mead, G.H. (1934). *Mind, Self and Society*. Chicago: University of Chicago Press.

Meissner, M. (1986). The reproduction of women's domination in organizational communication. *In* Taylor, L. (ed.), *Organization-Communication: Emerging Perspectives*. Norwood, N.J.: Ablex.

Melady, J. (1989). *Pilots*. Toronto: McLelland and Stewart.

Merton, R.K. (1936). The unanticipated consequences of purposive social action. *American Sociological Review*, **1**(1), 894–904.

Merton, R.K. (1940). Bureaucratic structure and personality. *Social Forces*, **18**, 560–68.

Merton, R.K. (1949). *Social Theory and Social Structure*. Glencoe, Ill.: Free Press.

Michels, R. (1949). *Political Parties*. Chicago: Free Press.

Miles, R.H. (1980). *Macro-organizational Behaviour*. Santa Monica, Calif.: Goodyear.

Milgram, S. (1963). Behavioural study of obedience. *Journal of Abnormal and Social Psychology*, **67**, 371–8.

Miller, J. (1986). *Pathways in the Workplace*. Cambridge: Cambridge University Press.

Mills, A.J. (1974). Factory work-ins. *New Society*, **489**, 22 August.

Mills, A.J. (1982). Worker occupations, 1971–1975: A socio-historical analysis of the development and spread of sit-ins, work-ins and worker co-operatives in Britain. Unpublished Ph.D. thesis, University of Durham.

Mills, A.J. (1988a). Organizational acculturation and gender discrimination. *In* Kresl, K. (ed.), *Women and the Workplace*. Ottawa: Association for Canadian Studies.

Mills, A.J. (1988b). Organization, gender and culture. *Organization Studies*, **9**(3), 351–69.

Mills, A.J. (1988c). Gareth Morgan: An interview. *Aurora Magazine* (Athabasca University), **11**(2), 42–6.

Mills, A.J. (1989a). Gender, sexuality and organization theory. *In* Hearn, J., Tancred-Sheriff, P., Burrell, G. and Sheppard, D. (eds), *The Sexuality of Organization*. London: Sage.

Mills, A.J. (1989b). Reversal theory and organizational analysis – A critique. Paper presented at the 4th International Conference on Reversal Theory, Athabasca, June.

Mills, A.J. and Chiaramonte, P. (1990). Organization as gendered communication act. Paper presented at the Annual Conference of the Canadian Sociology and Anthropology Association, Victoria, May.

Mills, A.J. and Tancred-Sheriff, P. (in Press). *Gender and Organizations: Critical Writings in the Field*.

Mintzberg, H. (1978). Patterns in strategy formulation. *Management Science*, **24**(9), 934–48.

Minuchin, S. (1974). *Families and Family Therapy*. London: Tavistock.

Minuchin, S. (1984). *Family Kaleidoscope – Images of Violence and Healing*. Cambridge, Mass.: Harvard University Press.

Minuchin, S. and Fishman, H.C. (1981). *Family Therapy Techniques*. Cambridge, Mass.: Harvard University Press.

Mittelstaedt, M. (1989). Business goes global. *Globe and Mail Report on Business*, February, 72–81.

More, T. (1969). *Utopia*. Harmondsworth: Penguin.

Morgan, D.L. (1988). *Focus Groups as Qualitative Research*. Beverly Hills, Calif.: Sage.

Morgan, G. (1980). Paradigms, metaphors and puzzle solving in organizational theory. *Administrative Science Quarterly*, **25**, 605–622.

Morgan, G. (1986). *Images of Organization*. Beverly Hills, Calif.: Sage.

Morgan, G. (1988). *Riding the Waves of Change*. San Francisco: Jossey-Bass.

Morgan, N. (1988). *The Equality Game: Women in the Federal Public Service (1908–1987)*, Ottawa: Canadian Advisory Council on the Status of Women.

Moss-Kanter, R. (1977). *Men and Women of the Corporation*. New York: Basic Books.

Muller, D. (1988). Krupp fails the family. *Business*, December, 68–72.

Murgatroyd, S. (1984). Relationships, change and the school. *School Organization*, **4**(2), 171–8.

Murgatroyd, S. (1986). Management teams and the promotion of staff well-being. *School Organization*, **6**(1), 114–22.

Murgatroyd, S. (1989). KAIZEN – School wide quality improvement. *School Organization*, **9**(2), 241–60.

Murgatroyd, S. and Reynolds, D. (1984). Leadership and the teacher. *In* Harling, p. (ed.), *New Directions in Educational Leadership*. Lewes: Falmer Press.

Murgatroyd, S. and Woolfe, R. (1982). *Coping with Crisis – Understanding and Helping the Person in Need*. London: Harper and Row.

Murgatroyd, S. and Woolfe, R. (1985). *Helping Families in Distress – An Introduction to Family Focused Helping*. London: Harper and Row.

Murray, E.A. (1978). Strategic choice as negotiated outcome. *Management Science*, **24**(9), 960–72.

Nash, A. (1976). Job satisfaction – A critique. *In* Widick, B.J. (ed.), *Auto Work and its Discontents*. Baltimore, Md.: Johns Hopkins University Press.

Nayak, P.R. and Ketteringham, J.M. (1986). *Breakthroughs!* New York: Rawson Associates.

Newhall, E.F., Kirsch, J., Morris, H. and Borger, G. (1982). Abusing sex at the office. *In* Frost, P.J., Mitchell, V.F. and Nord, W. (eds), *Organizational Reality*. Glenview, Ill.: Scott, Foresman.

Newman, P.C. (1982). *The Acquisitors. Vol. II: The Canadian Establishment*. Toronto: Seal Books.

Nichols, T. (1980). Management, ideology and practice. *In* Esland. G. and Salaman, G. (eds), *The Politics of Work and Occupations*. Buckingham: Open University Press.

Nielson, G.P. (1982). *From Sky Girl to Flight Attendant*. New York: ILR Press.

Oakley, A. (1981). *Subject Women*. New York: Pantheon.

O'Day, R. (1974). Intimidation rituals – Reactions to reform. *Journal of Applied Behavioural Science*, **10**(3), 373–86.

Oliver, T. (1986). *The Real Coke, The Real Thing*. New York: Random House.

Olson, D.H.L., Sprenkle, D.H. and Russell, C. (1979). Circumplex model of marital and family systems I: Cohesion and adaptability dimensions, family types and clinical applications. *Family Process*, **18**, 3–28.

Olson, M. (1965). *The Logic of Collective Action*. Cambridge, Mass.: Harvard University Press.

Ortony, A., Clore, G.L. and Collins, A. (1988). *The Cognitive Structure of Emotions*. Cambridge: Cambridge University Press.

Osborne, A. and Dvorak, J. (1984). *Hypergrowth – The Rise and Fall of Osborne Computer Corporation*. New York: Avon Books.

Ott, J.S. (1989). *The Organizational Culture Perspective*. Pacific Grove, Calif.: Brooks/Cole.

Ouchi, W.G. (1980). Markets, bureaucracies and clans. *Administrative Science Quarterly*, **25**, 129–41.

Ouchi, W. (1981). *Theory Z*. Reading, Mass.: Addison-Wesley.

Padsakoff, P.M., Williams, L.J. and Tudor, W.D. (1986). Effects of organizational formalization on alienation among professionals and nonprofessionals. *Academy of Management Journal*, **29**, 820–31.

Palazzoli, M.S., Boscolo, L., Cecchin, G. and Prata, H. (1978). *Paradox and Counter-Paradox*. New York: Aronson.

Palazzoli, M.S., Anolli, L., DiBlasio, P., Giossi, L., Pisano, L., Ricci, C., Sacchi, M. and Ugazio, V. (1986). *The Hidden Games of Organizations*. New York: Random House/Pantheon Books.

Palmer, D. (1983). Broken ties: Interlocking directorates and intercorporate coordination. *Administrative Science Quarterly*, **28**, 40–55.

Parmer, P. (1984). Gender, race and class: Asian women in resistance. *In* Centre for Contemporary Cultural Studies (ed.), *The Empire Strikes Back*. London: Hutchinson.

Pasztor, A. and Wartzman, R. (1989). Boeing pleads guilty in the use of documents. *Wall Street Journal* (US edn), 14 November, A4.

Pearlin, L.I. and Schooler, C. (1978). The structure of coping. *Journal of Health and Social Behavior*, **19**, 2–21.

Pearson, G. (1975). *The Deviant Imagination - Psychiatry, Social Work and Social Change*. London: Methuen.

Pearson, J.C. (1985). *Gender and Communication*. Dubuque, Iowa: William C. Brown.

Perrow, C. (1984). *Normal Accidents*. New York: Basic Books.

Petchinis, S.G. (1989). *Women and Work*. Toronto: McClelland and Stewart.

Peters, T. (1989). Making constant improvement a way of life. *Inside Guide (Canadian Airlines)*, **3**, 1.

Peters, T. and Waterman, R. (1982). *In Search of Excellence - Lessons from America's Best Run Companies*. New York: Warner Communications.

Pettigrew, A. (1985). *The Awakening Giant - Continuity and Change in ICI*. Oxford: Blackwell.

Pfeffer, J. (1981). *Power in Organizations*. Marshfield, Mass.: Pitman.

Pfeffer, J. (1982). *Organizations and Organization Theory*. Boston: Pitman.

Piaget, J. (1950). *The Psychology of Intelligence*. London: Routledge and Kegan Paul.

Pollert, A. (1981). *Girls, Wives, Factory Lives*. London: Macmillan.

Pondy, L.R. (1978). Leadership is a language game. *In* McCall, M.W. and Lombardo, M.M. (eds). *Leadership - Where Else Can We Go?* Durham, N.C.: Duke University Press.

Porter, M.E. (1980). *Competitive Strategy*. New York: Free Press.

Porter, M.E. (1985). *Competitive Advantage - Creating and Sustaining Superior Performance*. New York: Free Press.

Porter, M.E. (1986). Competition in global industries - A conceptual framework. *In* Porter, M.E. (ed.), *Competition in Global Industries*, pp. 15–60. Boston, Mass.: Harvard Business School Press.

Porter, M.E. and Fuller, M.B. (1986). Coalitions and global strategy. In Porter, M.E. (ed.), *Competition in Global Industries*. Boston, Mass.: Harvard Business School Press.

Potter, J. and Wetherell, M. (1987). *Discourse and Social Psychology - Beyond Attitudes and Behaviour*. London: Sage.

Pugh, D.S. and Hickson, D.J. (1976). *Organizational Structure in its Context: The Aston Programme I*. Farnborough: Saxon House.

Pugh, D.S. and Hinings, C.R. (eds). (1976). *Organizational Structure - Extensions and Replications: The Aston Programme II.* Farnborough: Saxon House.

Pugh, D.S. and Payne, R.L. (eds). (1977). *Organizational Behaviour in its Context: The Aston Programme III.* Farnborough: Saxon House.

Radice, H. (1973). *International Firms and Modern Imperialism.* Harmondsworth: Penguin.

Reason, P. and Rowan, J. (1981). Issues in the validity of new paradigm research. *In* Reason, P. and Rowan J. (eds), *Human Inquiry - A Sourcebook of New Paradigm Research.* Chichester: John Wiley.

Reed, M. (1985). *Redirections in Organizational Analysis.* London: Tavistock.

Reynolds, D. (1976). When pupils and teachers refuse a truce: The secondary school and the creation of a delinquency. *In* Mungham, G. and Pearson, G. (eds), *Working Class Youth Culture.* London: Routledge and Kegan Paul.

Reynolds, D.R., Sullivan, M. and Murgatroyd, S. (1987). *The Comprehensive Experiment.* Lewes: Falmer Press.

Rhys, S. (1988). Mastery and sympathy in nursing. *In* Apter, M.J., Kerr, J.H. and Cowles, M.P. (eds) *Progress in Reversal Theory.* Advances in Psychology No.51. Amsterdam: North-Holland.

Richer, S. (1979). Sex-role socialization and early schooling. *The Canadian Review of Sociology and Anthropology,* **16**, 195–205.

Richer, S. (1984). Sexual inequality and children's play. *The Canadian Review of Sociology and Anthropology,* **21**, 166–80.

Riley, P. (1983). A structurationist account of political culture. *Administrative Science Quarterly,* **28**, 414–37.

Robbins, S.P. (1988). *Essentials of Organizational Behaviour,* 2nd edn. Englewood Cliffs, N.J.: Prentice-Hall.

Roethlisberger, F.J. and Dickson, W.J. (1939). *Management and the Worker - An Account of a Research Program Conducted by the Western Electric Company (Hawthorne Works), Chicago.* Cambridge, Mass.: Harvard University Press.

Rogers, B. (1988). *Men Only.* London: Pandora Press.

Root, J. (1984). *Pictures of Women.* London: Pandora Press.

Rose, M. (1975). *Industrial Behaviour.* Harmondsworth: Penguin.

Ross, I. (1987). Is steel's revival for real? *Fortune Magazine,* 26 October.

Rothstein, A. (1950). A *History of the USSR.* Harmondsworth: Penguin.

Rowan, G. (1989). IBM announced $2.3 billion charge, jobs cut. *Globe and Mail (Toronto),* 6 December (Report on Business).

Rowthorn, B. (1976). Review article: Late capitalism. *New Left Review,* **98**, 59–83.

Rubin, J.Z., Provenzano, F.J. and Laura, Z. (1974). The eye of the beholder - Parent's views on the sex of newborns. *American Journal of Orthopsychiatry,* **44**, 512–19.

Ruesch, J. and Kees, W. (1956). *Nonverbal Communication - Notes on the Visual Perception of Human Relations.* Berkeley, Calif.: University of California Press.

Russell, C. (1979). Circumplex model of family systems: III. Empirical evaluation with families. *Family Process,* **18**, 29–45.

Rutter, P. (1989). Sex in the forbidden zone. *Psychology Today,* October, 34–8.

Ryan, M. (1979). *Womanhood in America.* New York: Viewpoints.

Salaman, G. (1983). Roles and rules. *In* Salaman, G. and Thompson, K. (eds), *Control and Ideology in Organizations.* Cambridge, Mass.: MIT Press.

Sales, A.L. and Mirvis, P.H. (1984). When cultures collide - Issues and acquisition. *In*

Kimberly, J.R. and Quinn, R.E. (eds), *New Futures - The Challenge of Managing Corporate Transitions.* Homewood, Ill.: Dow-Jones Irwin.

Sandler, R.L. (1982). You can sell your body but not your mind: A socio-linguistic examination of the folklore on the automobile factory assembly line. Unpublished Ph.D. thesis, University of Pennsylvania.

Santrock, J. (1984). *Adolescence,* Second edition. Dubuque, 10: Wm.C. Brown.

Saportio, B. (1987). The life of a $725,000 scab. *Fortune,* 26 October.

Sarbin, T.R., Taft, R. and Bailey, D.E. (1960). *Clinical Inferences and Cognitive Theory.* New York: Holt, Rinehart and Winston.

Savage, G.T. (1982). Organizations as conflicting small group cultures. Presented at the Annual Meeting of the Speech Communication Association, Louisville, November.

Savvy Magazine (1988). The best (and worst) cities for women, September.

Schall, M.S. (1983). A communication-rules approach to organizational culture. *Administrative Science Quarterly,* **28,** 557-81.

Schotter, A. (1981). *The Economic Theory of Social Institutions.* Cambridge: Cambridge University Press.

Schon, D. (1971). *Beyond the Stable State.* New York: Basic Books.

Schroedel, J.R. (1985). *Alone in a Crowd.* Philadelphia, Penn.: Temple University Press.

Scott, J. and Cowley, P. (1988). Individual and social connections - A perspective from the Q-Analysis method. *In* Fielding, N.G. (ed.), *Actions and Structure - Research Methods and Social Theory.* Beverly Hills, Calif.: Sage.

Sculley, J. with Byrne, J.A. (1987). *Odyssey: Pepsi to Apple. A Journey of Adventure, Ideas and the Future.* Toronto: Fitzhenry and Whiteside.

Seiler, T.B. (1980). Entwicklungstheorien in der Sozialisationsforschung. *In* Hurrelmann, K. and Ulich, D. (eds), *Hanbuch der Sozializationsforschung.* Weinheim: Beltz.

Selznick, P. (1949). *TVA and the Grass Roots.* Berkeley, Calif.: University of California Press.

Sevé, L. (1978). *Man in Marxist Theory and the Psychology of Personality.* Brighton: Harvester Press.

Sherif, C.W. (1982). Needed concepts in the study of gender identity. *Psychology of Women Quarterly,* **6,** 375-98.

Silk, L. and Vogel, D. (1976). *Ethics and Profits.* New York: Simon and Schuster.

Silverman, D. (1970). *The Theory of Organizations.* New York: Basic Books.

Silverman, D. and Jones, J. (1974). Getting in - The managed accomplishments of "correct" selection outcomes. *In* Child, J. (ed.), *Man and Organization.* London: George Allen and Unwin.

Skinner, B.F. (1938). *The Behavior of Organisms.* New York: Appleton.

Skynner, R. (1987). *Explorations with Families - Group Analysis and Family Therapy.* London: Methuen.

Smircich, L. (1983). Concepts of culture and organizational analysis. *Administrative Science Quarterly,* **28,** 339-58.

Smith, C. and Lloyd, B. (1978). Maternal behaviour and perceived sex of infant. *Child Development,* **49,** 1263-5.

Sorensen, T.C. (1963). *Decision Making in the White House.* New York: Columbia University Press.

Spencer, A. and Podmore, D. (1987a). Women lawyers - Marginal members of a male dominated profession. *In* Spencer, A. and Podmore, D. (eds), *In A Man's World.* London: Tavistock.

Spencer, A. and Podmore, D. (eds), (1987b). *In a Man's World*. London: Tavistock.

Spender, D. and Sarah, E. (eds), (1980). *Learning to Lose – Sexism and Education*. London: Women's Press.

Sprenkle, D. and Olson, D. (1978). Circumplex model of marital systems IV: Empirical studies of clinical and non-clinical couples. *Journal of Marriage and Family Counselling*, **4**, 59–74.

Sproull, L.S. (1981). Beliefs in organizations. *In* Nystrom, P.C. and Starbuck, W.C. (eds), *Handbook of Organizational Design*, Vol. 2, pp. 203–224. Oxford: Oxford University Press.

Stearns, P.N. (1979). *Be a Man! Males in Modern Society*. New York: Hokmes and Meier.

Sterniczuk, H. (1988). Institution strategies for rule formation and social order in business organizations – A comparative analysis of communist and market systems organizations. Paper presented at the Annual Academy of Management Meeting, Anaheim, California, August.

Stewart, T.A. (1989). New ways to exercise power. *Fortune Magazine*, 6 November.

Stouffer, S.A., Schuman, E.A., DeVinnery, L.C., Star, S.A. and Williams, R. (1949). *The American Soldier – Adjustments During Army Life*. Princeton, N.J.: Princeton University Press.

Strauss, A.L. (1959). *Mirrors and Masks*. New York: Free Press.

Strauss, A., Scatzman, L., Erlich, D., Bucher, R. and Sabshin, M. (1978). The hospital and its negotiated order. *In* Salaman, G. and Thompson, K. (eds), *People and Organizations*. Milton Keynes: Open University Press.

Struminger, L.S. (1979). *Women and the Making of the Working Class: Lyon 1830–1870*. Vermont: Eden Press.

Stubbs, M. (1983). *Discourse Analysis – The Sociolinguistics of Natural Language*. Oxford: Blackwell.

Sudnow, D. (1978). Normal crimes – Sociological features of the penal code in a public defenders office. *In* Salaman, G. and Thompson, K. (eds), *People and Organizations*. Milton Keynes: Open University Press.

Tancred-Sheriff, P. (1987). Organizational tendencies of Canadian universities: Nature and implications. *University of Saskatchewan Sorokin Lectures, No. 18*. Sasktoon: University of Saskatchewan.

Tancred-Sheriff, P. (1988). Employment equity: What can we learn from other attempts to disestablish privelege? Paper presented at the CRIAW Conference, Quebec City, November.

Taylor, F.W. (1911). *Principles of Scientific Management*. New York: Harper and Row.

Thompson, J. (1967). *Organizations in Action*. New York: McGraw-Hill.

Thompson, J.D. and McEwan, W.J. (1958). Organization goals and the environment. *American Sociological Review*, **23**, 23–31.

Thomson, D. (1980). *Europe since Napoleon*. Harmondsworth: Pelican.

Toffler, A. (1981). *The Third Wave*. London: Pan Books.

Toffler, A. (1985). *The Adaptive Corporation*. New York: McGraw-Hill.

Touraine, A. (1974). *The Post Industrial Society*. London: Wildwood House.

Trist, E.L. and Bamforth, K.W. (1951). Some social and psychological consequences of the Longwall method of coal getting. *Human Relations*, **4**, 1–38.

Tse, K.K. (1985). *Marks and Spencer: Anatomy of Britain's Most Efficiently Managed Company*. London: Pergamon Press.

Tugenhadt, C. (1973). *The Multinationals*. Harmondsworth, Penguin.

Tully, S. (1989). What the "Greens" mean for business. *Fortune Magazine*, 23 October.

Turner, H.A., Clack, G. and Roberts, G. (1967). *Labour Relations in the Motor Industry*. London: George Allen and Unwin.

Urry, J. (1972). Role performance and social comparison processes. In Jackson, J.A. (ed.), *Role*. Cambridge: Cambridge University Press.

Van Maanen, J. (1975). Police socialization. *Administrative Science Quarterly*, **20**, 207–228.

Van Maanen, J. (1976). Breaking in – Socialization to work. In Dubin, R. (ed.), *Handbook of Work, Organization and Society*. Chicago: Rand-McNally.

Van Maanen, J. (1983). People processing – Strategies or organizational socialization. In Allen, R.W. and Porter, L.W. (eds), *Organizational Influence Processes*. Glenview, Ill.: Scott, Foresman.

von Cranach, M. and Harre, R. (1980). *The Analysis of Action – Recent Theoretical and Empirical Advances*. Cambridge: Cambridge University Press.

Walter, G.A. (1985). Culture collisions in mergers and acquisitions. In Frost, P.J., Moore, L.F., Louis, M.R., Lundberg, C.C. and Martin, J. (eds), *Organizational Culture*, pp. 301–314. Beverly Hills, Calif.: Sage.

Walters, P.A. (1987). Servants of the Crown. In Spencer, A. and Podmore, D. (eds), *In a Man's World*. London: Tavistock.

Warren, R., Rose, S. and Bergunder, A. (1974). *The Structure of Urban Reform*. Lexington, Mass.: D.C. Heath.

Watzlawick, P. (1976). *How Real is Real – Confusion, Disinformation, Communication*. New York: Vintage Books.

Watzlawick, P. (1983). *The Situation is Hopeless, Not Serious*. New York: W.W. Norton.

Watzlawick, P. (1984). *The Invented Reality – How Do We Know What We Believe We Know?*. New York: W.W. Norton.

Weber, M. (1922). Three types of legitimate rule. In Etzioni, A. (ed.), *A Sociological Reader on Complex Organizations*, pp. 6–15. New York: Holt, Rinehart and Winston.

Weber, M. (1947). *The Theory of Social and Economic Organisation*, translated by T. Parsons and A.M. Henderson. New York: Free Press.

Weber, M. (1969). *The Theory of Social and Economic Organization*. New York: Free Press.

Weber, M. (1976). *The Protestant Ethic and the Spirit of Capitalism* (translated by T. Parsons). London: Allen and Unwin.

Weedon, C. (1987). *Feminist Practice and Poststructuralist Theory*. Oxford: Blackwell.

Weick, K. (1977). Enactment processes in organizations. In Straw, B. and Salanick, G. (eds), *New Directions in Organizational Behaviour*. Chicago: St Clair Press.

Weick, K.E. (1979). Cognitive processes in organizations. In Straw, B.M. (ed.). *Research in Organizational Behaviour*, Vol. 1, Greenwich, Conn.: JAI Press.

Weick, K.E. (1985). Sources of order in underorganized systems: Themes in recent organizational theory. In Lincoln, Y.S. (ed.), *Organizational Theory and Inquiry – The Paradigm Revolution*, pp. 106–136. Beverly Hills, Calif.: Sage.

Weir, M. (ed.) (1976). *Job Satisfaction*. Glasgow: Fontana.

Werhane, P. (1985). *Persons, Rights, Corporations*. Englewood Cliffs, N.J.: Prentice-Hall.

West, J. (1982). New technology and women's office work. In West, J. (ed.), *Work, Women and the Labour Market*. London: Routledge and Kegan Paul.

Whyte, W.F. (1956). *The Organization Man*. New York: Simon and Schuster.

Williamson, O.E. (1975). *Markets and Hierarchies*. New York: Free Press.

Willis, P. (1977). *Learning to Labour*. London: Saxon House.

Willis, P. (1979). The shop floor culture, masculinity and the wage form. *In* Clarke, J., Critcher, C. and Johnson, R. (eds), *Working Class Culture*. London: Hutchinson.

Wolpe, H. (1970). Some problems concerning revolutionary consciousness. *In* Miliband, R. and Saville, J. (eds), *The Socialist Register*. London: Merlin Press.

Woodward, J. (1958). *Management and Technology*. London: HMSO.

Worth, S. and Adair, J. (1972). *Through Navajo Eyes: An Exploration in Film Communication and Anthropology*. Bloomington, Ind.: Indiana University Press.

Worthy, F.S. (1987). Accounting bores you? Wake up! *Fortune Magazine*, 12 October.

Wright, E.O., Costello, C., Hachen, D. and Sprague, J. (1982). The American class structure. *American Sociological Review*, **47**(6), 709–726.

York, G. (1989). Judge offers an apology for comment on slapping. *The Globe and Mail*, 23 September.

Zavella, P. (1985). Abnormal intimacy – The varying networks of Chicana cannery workers. *Feminist Studies*, **11**(3), 541–57.

Zimmerman, D. (1978). The practicalities of rule use. *In* Douglas, J. (ed.), *Understanding Everyday Life*. London: Routledge and Kegan Paul.

Author index

Subject index